COOK
IT
LIGHT

OTHER BOOKS BY JEANNE JONES

The Calculating Cook

More Calculated Cooking

Diet for a Happy Heart

Secrets of Salt-Free Cooking

Jeanne Jones' Party Planner and Entertaining
Diary

Jeanne Jones' Food Lover's Diet

Fitness First: A 14-Day Diet and Exercise Program
(with Karma Kientzler)

The Love in the Afternoon Cookbook
(with Donna Swajeski, ABC TV)

The Fabulous Fructose Recipe Book
(with J. Thomas Cooper, M.D.)

Stuffed Spuds: 100 Meals in a Potato

Jet Fuel—The New Food Strategy for the High-Performance
Person

The Fabulous High-Fiber Diet

Canyon Ranch Menus and Recipes

Non-Dairy Cookbook

COOK IT LIGHT

Jeanne Jones

COLLIER BOOKS
Macmillan Publishing Company / New York

COLLIER MACMILLAN CANADA   Toronto

MAXWELL MACMILLAN INTERNATIONAL
New York   Oxford   Singapore   Sydney

To all of the readers of my "Cook It Light" column—
and most specifically to my readers who write to me!

In grateful acknowledgment:
William Hansen / Viola Stroup / Paula Todd

Copyright © 1987 by Jeanne Jones

Illustrations copyright © 1987 by Thelma Gomilas

Photographs: "Bouillabaisse, Salad of young greens with Jeanne Jones' Light Tarragon Dressing, and Gingered Fruit Compote" is copyright © 1987 by Kim Brun Studios, Inc. All others are copyright © 1987 by Kevin Schumacher, Collins and Associates. Grateful acknowledgment is made to Bo Danica and to Diehling, The Kitchen Store, both of La Jolla, for the table settings in the photographs.

Collier Books
Macmillan Publishing Company
866 Third Avenue, New York, N.Y. 10022

Collier Macmillan Canada, Inc.
1200 Eglinton Avenue East, Suite 200
Don Mills, Ontario   M3C 3N1

Library of Congress Cataloging-in-Publication Data
Jones, Jeanne.
    Cook it light / Jeanne Jones. — 1st Collier books ed.
      p. cm.
    Includes bibliographical references and index.
    ISBN 0-02-021781-1
    1. Cookery. I. Title.
  [TX714.J65 1991]   90-28152   CIP
  641.5—dc20

Macmillan books are available at special discounts for bulk purchases for sales promotions, premiums, fund-raising, or educational use. For details, contact:

Special Sales Director
Macmillan Publishing Company
866 Third Avenue
New York, N.Y. 10022

10 9 8 7 6 5 4 3 2 1

Printed in the United States of America

CONTENTS

PREFACE

WRITING my column, "Cook It Light," syndicated by King Features, is truly an exciting weekly event in my life. It gives me the opportunity to stay in touch with hundreds of thousands of my readers all over the United States and Canada. The key is that I write what is called in the trade an interacting column; in other words, my readers write to me, and their letters, along with my answers, are printed every week.

I loved it when I was described recently as the "Dear Abby" of the food section because that's exactly what I do. Only my readers don't write to me about personal problems. They send me their recipes that need help. Sometimes they just write asking me how to make a lighter version of an old high-calorie classic without sending a recipe at all—or describe a menu dilemma and ask me if I have a recipe that will get them out of it, such as a low-cholesterol quiche or a low-calorie birthday cake.

When a reader does send me a favorite recipe to be revised so it has fewer calories and less cholesterol and sodium, I first make it just as it is written. This way I have the taste, texture, and appearance I need to duplicate in the revision.

Sometimes it's easy and I am able to come very close to the original recipe with a much lighter version in one or two tries. Other times I have to make numerous passes at it before I am satisfied that my light recipe is close enough to the original that any one of you would be happy with the results.

I have received hundreds of letters telling me how educational my column is. I want to thank all of you and tell you that my column is also an ongoing education for me. I have learned more ways to substitute fresh and natural ingredients for the processed foods found in cans, bottles, boxes, and envelopes than I ever knew existed.

It has been so much fun for me to write this column that I want to share a collection of the recipes from it with you in this book. I am also including a few of my own favorite recipes that I have developed for famous spas, hotels, and restaurants—and some tips on how you can start creating your own LIGHT recipes.

Enjoy my book—and please keep writing to me. I love your letters and I need your recipes!

Jeanne Jones

COOK IT LIGHT

WHY "COOK IT LIGHT"? *Light* is both an adjective and a noun. *Light,* the adjective, means "less heavy." *Light,* the noun, is something that illuminates, enlightens, or informs. When I say "cook it light," I am saying cook it with less fat for fewer calories; less food of animal origin for lower cholesterol; less salt and high-sodium ingredients to reduce the amount of sodium consumed. But "cook it light" also means make it imaginative and satisfying. Deprivation has no place in my cooking vocabulary.

Cook It Light could also be called *Cook It Smart.* Now, more than ever before, we have been made aware of the importance of proper nutrition. "We are what we eat" will probably be remembered as the slogan of the century, and remember the ancient proverb, "What the fool does in the end, the wise man does in the beginning."

Take a good look at the covers of all our popular magazines for both men and women. It is no longer "in" to be thin. It is "in" to be trim and fit. Healthy is beautiful, and we now know that our health has more to do with what we do for ourselves than what our doctors can do for us. We are being told at every turn to take charge of our lives, to be in control of our own destinies. That's what *Cook It Light* is all about—being in control, taking charge of our nutrition. No one else can control how many calories we eat or how much fat, cholesterol, and sodium we consume.

It isn't enough just to lower the number of calories we eat. It is the quality of the calories consumed that is important. The integrity of any item on any menu is totally dependent upon the quality of the ingredients used. In fact, *Cook It Light* isn't so much about watching calories to lose weight as it is about eating well. To achieve you own full dimension in fitness *and* health, good nutrition is essential.

There are still people who think that food has to be *either* good *or* good for you. Fortunately nothing could be further from the truth, and this new culinary concept is truly for everyone—even the meat and potato lovers! People of all ages are dependent on the fuel they take in for their performance. Therefore, whether you are a man or a woman, a child or an adult, you need the best fuel possible to do the best job.

In *Cook It Light,* I have combined gastronomy—the joy of truly fine food—with nutrition—the study of the proper fueling of the body. In *Cook It Light,* gastronomy and nutrition are combined to create dishes that are both delicious and healthy.

Cook It Light will make you a star in the culinary world. It will help you to achieve and maintain a better-looking and healthier body. It will give you the energy necessary for peak performance. It will also help you avoid heart disease and cancer.

Cooking it light is easy, fast, and fun. It is also less expensive than the heavier, more traditional approach to food preparation. You may be surprised to find that this lighter approach to cooking also produces more delicate, flavorful dishes that are more popular with your family and friends.

By learning to *Cook It Light,* you can produce fabulous gourmet meals, or even "junk" foods, that are as good for you as they are appealing and satisfying. Using the recipes in this book you can enjoy the international cuisines and the American regional cooking you like best. Using my techniques for lowering the fat, calories, cholesterol, and sodium, you can lighten your own recipes without losing any of the taste, texture, or appearance of your favorite dishes.

COOK-IT-LIGHT MEAL PLANNING

Putting together a light meal differs in no way from designing a classic heavy meal as far as balance and taste are concerned.

It is important to balance heavy courses with lighter courses. For example, you would not want to serve a rich, hearty soup with poultry or meat in it before serving pot roast for the entrée. A crisp, fresh garden salad would be a better choice.

Also remember you want variety in taste range, color, and texture in your menus. When possible, avoid using the same ingredients in each course. Serving carrot soup with steamed carrots as the vegetable on your entrée plate and carrot cake for dessert will never win an award for exciting menu planning, no matter how good each course may be by itself, any more than a plate with roast chicken, mashed potatoes, and cauliflower would create visual excitement. New potatoes with their reddish-colored skins intact and broccoli, beets, or carrots would make a much prettier and more colorful plate. The combination of texture or "mouth feel" between the ingredients used in any one dish can also add greatly to its appeal. For example, a salad with crisp greens, soft cheese, and crunchy nuts or seeds is much more exciting than a salad with only one texture.

I like to use a theme for my appetizer, entrée, and dessert courses when I am designing menus for my clients or planning my own dinner parties. For example, a Russian dinner might start with Borscht, followed by Chicken Stroganoff for the entrée and Strawberries Romanoff for dessert. By putting together menus that incorporate a national or ethnic theme, the taste ranges will be compatible and you will have more fun planning and preparing the meals. If you wish to decorate, it is much easier with a theme. It is such fun to decorate appropriately for a party; even a small family dinner is more fun and more exciting when you turn it into a dining event.

I have created the following menu suggestions for you to get started planning your own theme parties. The menus range from a Mexican fiesta to a traditional holiday feast. The recipes for all the dishes suggested in the menus are in this book.

COOK-IT-LIGHT MENUS

MEXICAN FIESTA

Make-believe Margarita (page 257)
Gazpacho (page 31)
Fiesta Salad (without cheese) (page 100)
Quesadilla (page 127)
Flan (page 244)

MIDDLE EASTERN

Eggplant Relish with Pita Bread (page 108)
Moroccan Chicken with Couscous (page 175)
Baklava (page 248)

FRENCH

Celery Root Salad (page 87)
Cassoulet (page 197)
Ratatouille (page 115)
Fantasy in Fruit (page 224)

EAST INDIAN

Citrus Salad with Poppy Seed Dressing (page 92)
Chicken Bombay (page 168) with Apple Chutney (page 62)
Brown Rice
Pea Pods
Pineapple Pie (page 237)

ITALIAN

Parsley Salad (page 84)
Light Lasagna (page 132)
Zucchini al Dente
Fresh Fruit

ORIENTAL

Egg Drop Soup (page 30)
Chinese Chicken Salad (page 97)
Spiced Bananas (page 228)
or
Miso Soup (page 28)
Polynesian Prawns (page 152)
Brown Rice
Oriental Vegetables
Vanilla Ice-Milk Crepe with Papaya-Rum Sauce (page 225)

CONTINENTAL

French Onion Soup (page 35)
Chicken in Pink Peppercorn Sauce (page 173)
Rice Pilaf (page 119)
Creamed Leeks (page 109)
Spinach Salad with Toasted Walnuts (page 85)
Pear Crisp (page 232)

ALL-AMERICAN

Lettuce and Tomato Salad with Bleu Cheese Dressing (page 76)
Pot Roast (page 190)
Scalloped Potatoes (page 121)
Colorful Fresh Vegetables
Raisin-Rice Pudding (page 235)

SUMMER BARBECUE

Coleslaw (page 86)
Grilled Turkey Burger (page 183) with Barbecue Sauce (page 64)
Oven Fries (page 122)
Carob-Yogurt Sundae (page 227)

BRUNCH

Cold Gingered Carrot Soup (page 32)
Broccoli-Cheese Pie (page 139)
Our Famous Sugar-Free Bran Muffins (page 215) with Apple Butter (page 61)

HOLIDAY DINNER

Parsley Salad (page 84)
Roast Turkey with Fennel (page 180)
Italian Oyster Casserole in radicchio cups (page 148)
Italian Green Beans
Italian Cherry Trifle (page 238)

COOK-IT-LIGHT RECIPE REVISION

In my column, "Cook It Light," I revise recipes sent to me by my readers. My goal is to make them healthier without changing the taste or texture of the original recipe.

To do this, I first have to make the recipe exactly as it was sent to me. This gives me a basis for comparison, or what we call in my test kitchen the "benchmark."

The following chart will show you how I marked one recipe to start the testing process. For the revised recipe, see page 144.

RECIPE ANALYSIS

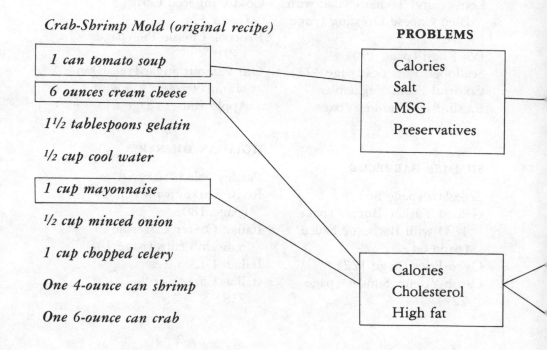

Crab-Shrimp Mold (original recipe)

	PROBLEMS
1 can tomato soup	Calories
6 ounces cream cheese	Salt
1½ tablespoons gelatin	MSG
½ cup cool water	Preservatives
1 cup mayonnaise	
½ cup minced onion	
1 cup chopped celery	Calories
One 4-ounce can shrimp	Cholesterol
One 6-ounce can crab	High fat

The recipe contains three problem ingredients that need to be eliminated, reduced, or replaced.

1. *Problem:* What's wrong with the ingredient? Put the problems in order of importance with your *biggest* concern first.

2. *Function:* What is the purpose of the problem ingredient in the original recipe? Perhaps it can simply be eliminated. List in the order of its perceived importance.

3. *Solution:* What are acceptable ingredients to substitute for the problem ingredients? You may want to try several possibilities, depending on what the desired results are (i.e., tofu *or* reduced-calorie mayonnaise).

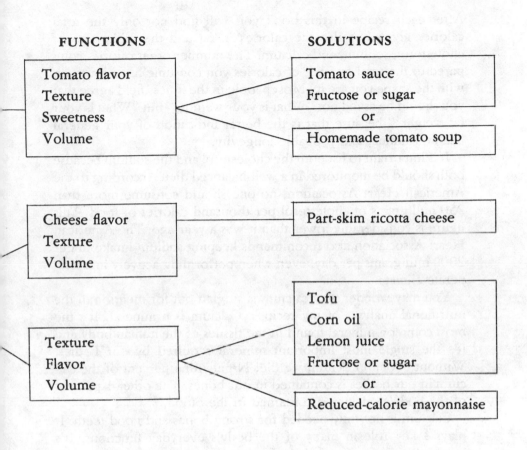

FUNCTIONS | SOLUTIONS

Tomato flavor
Texture
Sweetness
Volume

Tomato sauce
Fructose or sugar
or
Homemade tomato soup

Cheese flavor
Texture
Volume

Part-skim ricotta cheese

Texture
Flavor
Volume

Tofu
Corn oil
Lemon juice
Fructose or sugar
or
Reduced-calorie mayonnaise

4. *Results:* How much did you save? This is the payoff—the rewards are plain to see. You really *can* have it all!

ORIGINAL RECIPE	PER SERVING	REVISED RECIPE
233	Total Calories	74
189	Calories in Fat	27
44 mg	Cholesterol	33 mg
483 mg	Sodium	272 mg

COOK-IT-LIGHT NUTRITION

After each recipe in this book you will find not only the total calories given but also the calories in fat and the milligrams of cholesterol, sodium, and calcium. The number of fat calories compared to the total number of calories you consume has a lot to do with the shape you are in. Most people in the fitness field agree that you should be asked not "What is your weight?" but "What is your fat weight?" because that is the better indication of your general health, stamina, and probable longevity.

It is important to list both the cholesterol and the sodium because both should be monitored in a well-balanced diet. According to the American Heart Association, no one should consume more than 250 milligrams of cholesterol per thousand calories of food. This figure is considerably lower than it was a year ago. The American Heart Association also recommends keeping sodium intake under 2000 milligrams per day, even when performing actively in a temperate climate.

You may wonder why calcium is singled out for mention in the nutritional analyses of my recipes. Calcium is a mineral. It's the most common mineral found in the tissues of the human body and it's the single most important mineral required by our bodies. Without enough calcium, we die! Ninety-nine percent of the calcium in our bodies is contained in our bones. The other 1 percent of the body's calcium is contained in the blood.

Calcium is not only needed for strong bones and good teeth. It plays a key role in many of the body's everyday functions. It's essential for the transmission of nerve impulses, muscular contractions, blood clotting, and functions such as regulation of the heart's rhythm and the chemical activity of all the body's cells.

Most recently, scientists have suggested that calcium may be useful in lowering the blood pressure of those suffering from hypertension. Another report states that there is some evidence to suggest that calcium may be beneficial in preventing cancer of the colon.

Most doctors recommend getting as much calcium as possible from the foods we eat. Without exception, every bit of research and all the reports from the best sources—the La Jolla Cancer Research Foundation, for one—recommend getting your vitamins and minerals from a well-balanced diet rather than through the ingestion of pills. But you don't have to worry about your waistline expanding if you "Cook It Light"!

The nutrition information at the end of each recipe is based upon software designed by Practorcare, Inc. In addition, I have developed a calorie chart to help you compute your own calories quickly and easily.

I routinely round off to the nearest 5 or 0 just as I have on the calorie figures for all servings in this book. The only exception to this is in the calories given for ½ ounce of fish, poultry, or meat, and on this chart I have given an average for each category. For example, ½ ounce of fish at 18 calories is an average or ballpark figure and is actually higher than most fish and seafood; however, all fish in the same category do not have exactly the same number of calories per ounce. It depends upon the fat content of the individual fish.

To further bring calories into perspective, I like to point out that if you take two oranges of exactly the same size and color, and off the same tree, to a laboratory for a calorie count, they will not be the same. In other words, calorie computation cannot be considered an exact science. At best, calories per serving are an educated guess.

AT-A-GLANCE CALORIE CHART

FRUIT	CALORIES	BREADS AND	CALORIES
Fresh		PASTA	
1 cup	50	*Cooked*	
Dried		1 cup	200
1 ounce	70		

VEGETABLES		FISH AND	
Raw Leafy		SEAFOOD	
Vegetables and		½ ounce	18
Herbs	Negligible	1 ounce	36
Root Vegetables		1½ ounces	54
(Carrots, beets,		2 ounces	72
onions)		2½ ounces	90
1 cup	50	3 ounces	108
Starchy Vegetables		3½ ounces	126
(Potatoes,		4 ounces	144
onion, peas,		4½ ounces	162
parsnips,		5 ounces	180
pumpkin)		5½ ounces	198
1 cup	150	6 ounces	216
Dried Beans and			
Legumes (Cooked)			
1 cup	225	POULTRY AND	
Other Vegetables		LEAN MEAT	
(Broccoli, egg-		½ ounce	28
plant, tomatoes,		1 ounce	56
asparagus, pep-		1½ ounces	84
pers, cauliflower,		2 ounces	112
brussels sprouts,		2½ ounces	140
etc.)		3 ounces	168
1 cup	30	3½ ounces	196
		4 ounces	224
		4½ ounces	252
GRAINS		5 ounces	280
Cooked		5½ ounces	308
1 cup	220	6 ounces	336

TOFU	CALORIES	MILK AND CREAM	CALORIES
2 tablespoons (1 ounce)	20	*Cream* 2 tablespoons	90
½ cup (4 ounces)	80	*Half and Half* 2 tablespoons	30
1 cup (8 ounces)	160	*Whole Milk* 2 tablespoons	17
CHEESES		*Low-Fat Milk (2% fat)*	
Low-Fat Cottage Cheese		2 tablespoons	12
1%–2 tablespoons	20	*Buttermilk*	
2%–2 tablespoons	25	2 tablespoons	10
Part-Skim Ricotta		*Skim Milk (Nonfat milk)*	
2 tablespoons	40	2 tablespoons	10
Part-Skim Mozzarella		*Dry Powdered Nonfat Milk*	
4 tablespoons (1 ounce)	70	2 tablespoons (makes ⅓ cup)	25
Parmesan and Romano		*Canned Skimmed Evaporated Milk*	
4 tablespoons (1 ounce)	100	2 tablespoons	23
All Other Cheeses		*Canned Whole Milk*	
4 tablespoons (1 ounce)	100	2 tablespoons	44
FATS			
Butter, Margarine, and Oils		**STOCK** (totally defatted)	Negligible
1 teaspoon	40		
2 teaspoons	80		
1 tablespoon	120		
2 tablespoons	240		
Nuts and Seeds			
1 tablespoon	45		
2 tablespoons	90		
3 tablespoons	135		
¼ cup	180		

THE COOK-IT-LIGHT KITCHEN

I have worked with food professionals in commercial kitchens all over the world. At the same time I have been writing cookbooks, a syndicated column, and teaching cooking classes for nonprofessional cooks. The major difference I find between the professional and the home cook is simply in organization.

Just knowing where everything in your kitchen is that you need to make a recipe and having all the necessary ingredients for it is a great start. There is nothing more frustrating than finding out halfway through a recipe that the next ingredient called for is not in the house, or the bowl you need to mix the ingredients in is full of leftovers from last night's dinner!

Commercial kitchens remedy this problem and speed up the preparation time by establishing what is called the *mise-en-place,* which means literally, "things in place." In a properly run restaurant kitchen a recipe is never started until all the ingredients are assembled and prepped in the correct measured amounts. And all of the utensils required to make the recipe are gathered together *before* they are needed.

In commercial kitchens par stock levels are established and then maintained. *Par* is the amount of something you never go below without reordering it (putting it on your shopping list in the case of staples such as rice, flour, onions, and so on). Or making more of it as necessary (for example, salad dressings and sauces).

Another way commercial kitchens work that can be of great benefit in the home as well is in the assembly of the recipe on a per-serving or as-needed basis. Even though most of the recipes in this book are written for four, many of them are broken down in the method for each serving. For example, the Chinese Chicken Salad recipe on page 97 gives instructions in the method for each serving. So, if your family is like many, with some eating at one time and others at another time, the servings are clearly described by proportions of each ingredient required to assemble the finished product and the *mise-en-place* is in the refrigerator ready to be assembled. Describing how each serving is assembled also makes it easy for you to cook the same recipe for one or two instead of four.

In the Food Measurements & Equivalents table in the back of this book, I have done for you what I do for my commercial clients. I have listed ingredients by weight as well as by common units and volume. This will help you enormously when you are shopping for ingredients. A scale is essential if you are truly interested in portion control. I always use one in spa kitchens, where portions *must* be controlled.

I've already mentioned that knowing the weight of ingredients required will be helpful in shopping, so now let's talk about modernizing your marketing and storing methods to make food preparation faster, more efficient, and less expensive. The buying, storing, and preparation of food can be fun and easy, if you're well organized.

The first step to shopping is the list. Keep it handy all the time. Each time you run low on anything, write it down. Don't wait until you are out of it—it might be the next thing you need. When shopping day arrives, plan your weekly menu and add all the necessary ingredients to your list.

Plan to shop only once a week for all staple items. Schedule your shopping trip just as you would any other appointment. Don't minimize the importance of food—make it part of your routine. Your shopping "appointment" should include the time it takes to make the list, do the shopping, and store your groceries properly when you return home.

For the best use of your time, write your shopping list according to the geographical layout of the market. Practically all supermarkets are designed the same way. Usually the fresh food items—dairy, fruits and vegetables, meats, fish and poultry—are all on the outside walls. The interior aisles most often contain the packaged, processed, and canned foods. Obviously there are some desirable items you need—such as grains, herbs and spices, frozen foods, and cleaning products—in the middle aisles. The shopping list you take with you should list all of the things you need in the middle aisles by category so that they are easy to find. This saves you time and money.

Watch out for clever advertisers and misleading labeling. There are thousands of different food products loaded with fat, sugar, and salt cleverly concealed by misleading labeling. Just as soon as you have everything on your list that's in the middle of the market, run for the walls!

When planning your weekly menu, be flexible in your selection of fruits and vegetables. Choose from the fresh produce at the market and select from the best quality available. Fruits and vegetables that are in-season are not only your best buy, but they look better and taste better.

Always include enough time in your shopping appointment to wash and store all your vegetables properly. This will save time later on and greatly add to their storage life. Wash and dry all your leafy vegetables and then roll them in towels or put them in plastic bags before refrigerating them. Root vegetables should also be washed and dried before storing in the refrigerator. But don't peel or scrape them until just before you are ready to use them.

Fruits, if ripe, should be washed, dried, and refrigerated to slow down the ripening process. If not yet ripe, leave them out at room temperature until they are ready to eat. As I have often said when people tell me they don't have time to wash their vegetables when they return from shopping, "What do you do, eat dirty vegetables?" At some point they will have to be washed before they can be used. Doesn't it make more sense to wash them right away so that they go into the refrigerator clean and ready to cook or eat as is? Remember, you are much more likely to use your healthier foods if they are ready to use. Otherwise you will be tempted to pass up the good stuff for faster convenience foods when you are pressed for time.

Natural foods such as dried fruits, whole-grain breads, pastas and flours, and nuts and seeds, stay fresh longer if refrigerated. Always be sure you have plenty of storage containers, wrap, and plastic bags on hand to house your groceries properly.

Once your pantry is stocked, turn your attention to organizing your kitchen for easy access, maximum efficiency, and minimum preparation time.

Arrange the herbs, spices, and extracts in a cool place where they are never exposed to sunlight. Alphabetize them so that you can find them quickly—this saves time, frustration, and money. How? Have you ever looked for a spice, thought you had none, and replaced it—only to find later that you now have two of the same? When your herbs and spices are arranged neatly in alphabetical order, chances for error and accidental duplication are slim.

Have the things you are using within reach when you need them. Organize your kitchen so that the equipment you use most and the foods you eat most often are the most accessible. When possible, free up as much counter space as you can so that you have an adequate work area for meal preparation.

COOK-IT-LIGHT TIPS FOR LIGHTER COOKING

Now that you are ready to cook it light, here are some tips for lighter cooking. These guidelines are the very same ones I use in modifying the recipes sent to me for my syndicated column, "Cook It Light." By following the guidelines, you, too, can modify your own recipes.

CALORIE CONTROL

Calories have only four sources—the three food groups, carbohydrates, proteins, and fats—plus alcohol. Carbohydrates and proteins both contain 4 calories per gram. Fats contain 9 calories per gram, or more than twice as many as carbohydrates and proteins; and alcohol contains 7 calories per gram—almost twice as many. It is easy to see that if you want to control calories, it is important to greatly reduce your intake of fat and alcohol, since they are the two major sources of calories with the least amount of nutrition. To really keep your calories under control, it is important to eliminate fat wherever possible with "light" cooking techniques.

REDUCING THE AMOUNT OF FAT

Cook in nonstick cookware or use a nonstick vegetable spray on your pans and baking dishes to prevent sticking rather than butter, margarine, or oil.

Use water, defatted stock, juice, or wine instead of butter, margarine, or oil to prevent sticking or burning when sautéeing.

When sautéeing onions, garlic, or shallots for a sauce, cook them, covered, over low heat, adding a little water, stock, or wine to prevent scorching rather than butter, margarine, or oil. This will save you a whopping 120 calories per tablespoon of sautéeing fat omitted from your final dish.

When making salad dressings, it is not necessary to add the classic two parts of oil to a part of vinegar. You can extend dressing with water, adding only 1 to 2 tablespoonsful of oil per cup, and still have a delicious, flavorful dressing.

To reduce the amount of saturated fat, use a liquid vegetable oil and margarines that are high in polyunsaturated fats. These include safflower oil, corn oil, cottonseed oil, canola oil, and all vegetable oils that are not hydrogenated and that run liquid at room temperature. Do not use coconut oil, palm oil, or chocolate. Most nondairy creamers contain coconut oil or palm oil, so always read the labels. For coconut flavor use coconut extract and for chocolate use powdered cocoa. Buy lean cuts of meat and remove all visible fat. Remove the skin from all poultry. Always refrigerate pan drippings so that the fat congeals on the top and can be removed completely.

REDUCING THE AMOUNT OF CHOLESTEROL

To reduce the amount of cholesterol in the foods you are cooking, the most important single rule is to use less animal protein and more complex carbohydrates. Animal protein includes fish, poultry, meat, dairy products, and eggs. Complex carbohydrates include everything that grows that is not refined—fruits, vegetables, grains, unrefined grain products, nuts, and seeds. Cholesterol is found only in foods of animal origin. There is no cholesterol at all in any foods of plant origin. Foods particularly high in cholesterol include egg yolks, some shellfish, and organ meats such as liver, heart, kidneys, sweetbreads, and brains.

INCREASING THE AMOUNT OF FIBER

The source of fiber is just the opposite of cholesterol. Fiber is found only in foods of plant origin—the complex carbohydrates described previously. There is no fiber in any foods of animal origin or in simple or refined carbohydrates such as sugars, syrups, and refined grains.

CONTROLLING SODIUM

The easiest way to control the amount of sodium in your diet is to avoid using salt whenever possible. According to the American Heart Association, no one needs more than a total of 2000 milligrams of sodium per day. If you are on a sodium-restricted diet, avoid foods particularly high in sodium, such as most cheeses, soy sauce, and many condiments, most snack foods, canned soups, and all stock bases, including bouillon cubes, powdered stock bases, and canned consommé and broth.

It is possible to have intense flavor without any salt at all by using herbs and spices. We taste only four things—sweet, salt, sour, and bitter. Everything else is smell. If you have ever had a bad cold and told people you couldn't taste, what you really meant was that you could not smell. You could still taste just fine; in fact you could still tell someone whether something was sweet, salty, sour, or bitter— you just couldn't tell whether it was strawberry or vanilla or lamb or beef. Therefore flavor, as we describe it, is really smell, not taste.

When using dry herbs and spices, always crush them, using a mortar and pestle, before adding them to any recipe, whether it is a cold preparation, such as salad dressing, or something you are cooking, such as stew. This is an essential step because it releases their aroma and increases the flavor. If you want to know how long you continue to grind them in the mortar, the answer is "until you smell them all over the kitchen." That will tell you a great deal about how much more flavor you are adding to any dish.

Never use wines for cooking that are labeled cooking wine, because they contain salt.

REDUCING THE AMOUNT OF SUGAR

Cut the amount of sugar called for in recipes by one-third to one-half.

Substitute concentrated fruit juice (undiluted orange, apple, or pineapple) for the sweetener in recipes.

Reduce ordinary table sugar (sucrose) by at least one-third by using fructose, which is one and one-half times sweeter.

Raise the level of perceived sweetness without adding any sweetener by using vanilla and/or cinnamon.

INCREASING CALCIUM

To increase your calcium intake, use nonfat and low-fat dairy products. The lower the fat content of any dairy product, the higher the calcium content. Also include dark green leafy vegetables, dried fruits, tofu, and all soy products in your diet. Fish and seafood, particularly those with bones, such as sardines, herring, and anchovies, are high in calcium, as is blackstrap molasses. When making fish, poultry, or meat stocks, always add a little vinegar to leach the calcium from the bones and add calcium to the stock.

NUTRITION AT A GLANCE

SUGGESTED % OF CALORIES CONSUMED	BASIC FOOD GROUPS	SOURCES
60% or more	I. *Carbohydrates* A. Complex	Everything that grows and is not refined (fruits, vegetables, and whole grains)
	B. Simple	Sugars, syrups, and refined grains
20% or less	II. *Proteins* A. Animal Protein	Fish, poultry, meat, dairy products, and eggs
	B. Plant Protein	Vegetables, whole grains, legumes, and tofu (soybean curd)
20% or less	III. *Fats* A. Polyunsaturated	1) Most vegetable oils (safflower, corn, and sesame) 2) Seeds
	B. Saturated	1) All fat of animal origin (butter, cream, and lard) 2) Coconut and palm oils and cocoa butter (the fat in chocolate)
	C. Monounsaturated	1) Olive and nut oils 2) Avocados, olives, and nuts

CALORIES PER GRAM	CHOLES-TEROL ?	FIBER ?	GUIDELINES
4	NO	YES	Use five times the amount in volume of complex carbohydrates as animal protein. (This ensures adequate dietary fiber as fiber is found only in foods of plant origin.)
4	NO	NO	Use sparingly.
4	YES	NO	Use ⅕ the amount in volume of animal protein as complex carbohydrates. (This 5 to 1 ratio helps limit cholesterol as cholesterol is found only in foods of animal origin.)
4	NO	YES	Remove poultry skin, trim all visible fat from meat, use only nonfat dairy products, and limit use of egg yolks and organ meats.
9	NO	NO	Use fat sparingly and only for flavor, moisture, and texture.
9	NO	YES	
9	YES	NO	Avoid. These aid in buildup of cholesterol in arteries.
9	NO	NO	
9	NO	NO	
9	NO	YES	These are classified in the fat category because the fat content is so high.

STOCKS & SOUPS

MAKING YOUR OWN STOCK is the single most important step toward becoming a truly fine cook. It always amazes me how many people I know who consider themselves accomplished amateur chefs go to great lengths to buy all fresh, natural, and even exotic ingredients for their dinners, yet still treat stock as the unimportant stepchild on the ingredients' list, routinely using stock bases or canned stocks. Unlike all other quality ingredients, stock cannot be purchased. You must make it yourself. Any really professional chef would die if anyone intimated that any stock was being used in his kitchen that had not been made there.

All stock bases and canned stocks and broth that are not labeled low sodium contain large amounts of salt as well as monosodium glutamate (MSG), artificial coloring, and fat. Stock bases and canned stocks and broth that are labeled low sodium generally taste so bad that it doesn't really matter what's in them because water is a better ingredient!

If you want a low-sodium stock that is truly delicious, making your own is the answer. Making your own stock will not only improve your cooking; it will make all of your dishes healthier and infinitely less expensive. The best news is that it is easy and fast.

I have had so many readers tell me that they don't have time to make their own stock that I finally did a column called "Fifteen-Minute Stock," which I have incorporated into my recipe for chicken stock in this section to show you step-by-step how easy it really is.

When making your own stock, never allow the pot to actually come to a full boil, especially when clarifying (when it starts to boil reduce the heat and simmer the stock). In classic cuisine someone was always designated to make sure this didn't happen. Thus the old cliché: "A watched pot never boils." Don't add salt or much seasoning so that you can adjust the salt and seasonings for every individual recipe. Another tremendous bonus to making your own stock is that you can make it very high in calcium by adding a little vinegar to the water when you put the stockpot on. The vinegar leaches the calcium from the bones, making each cup of stock almost as rich in calcium as milk and practically calorie-free. Almost all of the calories and cholesterol in stock are in the fat, so after totally defatting your stock you do not have to worry about either one of them.

Once you have defatted your stock, freeze it in containers of a volume you most often use. I store my own in ice cube trays. When the stock is solidly frozen, I remove the cubes from the trays and place them in plastic bags. Two cubes equal ¼ cup, so measuring is very simple.

Stock is the base for most soups. Therefore, it goes without saying that your soups will improve dramatically when made with your own stock.

Soups are uniquely different from one culture to another, and I have included a variety of these national and ethnic recipes. Soups also run the gamut from light, practically calorie-free first courses to hearty main dishes.

Almost everyone likes soup. For most of us, various kinds of soup conjure up memories from childhood—perhaps there is a cold fruit soup you loved because you thought it tasted like a dessert or a wonderful seafood chowder your mother always served for Sunday-night supper.

Soups can be elegant and extremely expensive to make, or inexpensive and delicious combinations of your favorite leftovers.

Just remember, no matter what kind of soup you're making, the quality of any dish is totally dependent upon the quality of the ingredients used; and no ingredient in soup is more important than stock.

FIFTEEN-MINUTE CHICKEN STOCK

Making your own stock is essential not only to good light cooking but for any kind of tasty cooking, whether it's healthy or not. You will notice in the recipe that the carrots are scraped and the leaves are removed from the celery, but that the onions and garlic do not have to be peeled. The reason for this is that the outside of the carrot has oxidized and therefore tends to add a bitter taste to the stock, as do the leaves of the celery. Any ingredient that adds a bitter taste should be avoided in any recipe. The onions do not need to be peeled because the onion skins do not affect the taste of the stock; in fact, brown onion skins add a little desirable color. After the chicken stock has cooked for an hour or more, you may want to throw in a whole chicken and cook it for your dinner or have it to dice for a salad or casserole the next day. It will take the chicken less than an hour to cook, and overcooking can make it tough and dry; so as soon as it is tender, remove it from the stockpot.

> 3 to 5 pounds chicken bones, parts, and giblets, excluding the
> liver
> 2 carrots, scraped and chopped
> 2 celery ribs, without leaves, chopped
> 1 onion, unpeeled, quartered
> 3 parsley sprigs
> 2 to 4 garlic cloves, halved
> 1 bay leaf
> 12 peppercorns
> ¼ cup vinegar
> Cold water to cover

Buy chicken parts for stock from a butcher or save chicken carcasses in the freezer until ready to make stock.

Put all the ingredients into a large pot with a lid. Add cold water to cover and bring slowly to a boil. Preparation to this point takes about 5 minutes.

Reduce the heat, cover, leaving the lid ajar, and simmer for 3 hours or more. Longer cooking makes the stock more flavorful. Remove from the heat and allow to stand until cool enough to handle. Remove the chicken parts and vegetables and discard. Strain the stock and cool to room temperature. This second step takes 5 minutes more. Refrigerate, uncovered, overnight or until the fat has congealed on top.

Remove the fat and store the stock in the freezer in containers of a volume you most often use (see page 21).

This final step completes the 15 minutes of preparation time. You now have a high-calcium, non-fat, practically calorie-free stock that costs you just a few cents per serving and takes less than 15 minutes to make.

Makes approximately 10 cups (2½ quarts)

1 CUP CONTAINS APPROXIMATELY (CALCIUM VARIES
DEPENDING ON BONES USED): N* TOTAL CALORIES
N CALORIES IN FAT / CHOLESTEROL VARIES / N MG SODIUM
CALCIUM VARIES

*Note: N is used throughout this book to mean "negligible."

BEEF STOCK

Basically, beef stock is made exactly the same way you make chicken stock. The only difference is the first step, where you brown the bones and vegetables prior to starting the stock. The reason for browning the ingredients is to give a rich, dark color to the stock. Pale meat stocks do not make sauces and gravies look as rich and appetizing. Also, a foam or scum rises to the surface of a meat stock and must be removed at least once and sometimes several times when the stock first comes to a boil.

Veal knuckles are ideal to use for the bones. The optional addition of the beef or veal makes for a richer stock.

3 pounds beef or veal bones
1 pound beef or veal, any cut (optional)
1 tomato, halved
3 carrots, scraped and chopped
2 celery ribs, without leaves, chopped
1 large unpeeled onion, quartered
3 parsley sprigs
3 garlic cloves, halved
1/4 teaspoon dried thyme, crushed in a mortar and pestle
1/4 teaspoon dried marjoram, crushed in a mortar and pestle
1 bay leaf
12 peppercorns
1/4 cup vinegar
Cold water to cover

Place the bones, meat, and vegetables in a roasting pan in a 400°F oven until well browned, about 40 minutes, turning frequently to brown evenly.

Remove from the roasting pan and place in a large pot with a lid. Add all the other ingredients and cover with cold water by 1 inch. Bring slowly to a boil. Simmer slowly for 5 minutes and remove any scum on the surface. Reduce the heat, cover, leaving the lid ajar, and simmer for 2 to 6 hours. Cooking longer makes the stock more flavorful.

Remove from the heat and allow to stand until cool enough to handle. Remove the bones, meat, and vegetables and discard. Strain the stock and cool to room temperature.

Refrigerate, uncovered, overnight or until the fat has congealed on top. Remove the fat and store the stock in the freezer in the size containers you most often use.

Makes approximately 10 cups (2½ quarts)

1 CUP CONTAINS APPROXIMATELY (CALCIUM VARIES
DEPENDING ON BONES USED): N TOTAL CALORIES
N CALORIES IN FAT / 1 MG CHOLESTEROL / SODIUM VARIES
CALCIUM VARIES

FISH STOCK

There is nothing better than a good fish stock for either a seafood soup such as Halászlé (page 40), the Hungarian fish soup, or a seafood stew such as Bouillabaisse (page 150), the classic French fisherman's stew that originated in Marseilles. I also like to use fish stock for poaching fish or to moisten the pan for sautéeing or braising fish or seafood. When fish heads are not available, I often make a shellfish stock using shrimp, crab, or lobster shells.

3 quarts water
¼ cup vinegar
2 pounds fish heads, bones, and trimmings
2 onions, sliced
5 parsley sprigs
1 carrot, sliced
½ teaspoon dried marjoram, crushed in a mortar and pestle
¼ teaspoon peppercorns
½ teaspoon salt
1 tablespoon freshly squeezed lemon juice

Bring all the ingredients to a boil and simmer for 40 minutes. Line a strainer with damp cheesecloth and strain the stock through it, discarding the bones and vegetables. Cool to room temperature. Refrigerate. Freeze the stock not needed immediately, using containers that will most nearly fit your requirements.

Makes about 2 quarts

1 CUP CONTAINS APPROXIMATELY (CALCIUM VARIES
DEPENDING ON BONES USED): N TOTAL CALORIES
N CALORIES IN FAT / 1 MG CHOLESTEROL / SODIUM VARIES
CALCIUM VARIES

COURT BOUILLON

Court bouillon is actually a fancy name for seasoned water and is used as a substitute for fish stock for poaching fish and seafood. I much prefer using fish stock or even chicken stock for cooking fish or seafood, but you don't always have it on hand when you need it. Court bouillon is certainly a better substitute than just plain water!

> 6 cups water
> 1/3 cup white vinegar
> 1 lemon, including peel, sliced
> 2 celery ribs, without leaves, sliced
> 2 carrots, sliced
> 1 onion, sliced
> 2 whole garlic cloves, peeled
> 2 bay leaves
> 12 peppercorns

Combine all the ingredients in a large pot and bring to a boil. Reduce the heat and simmer, uncovered, for 45 minutes.

Strain through two layers of damp cheesecloth and store in the freezer in the size containers you will require.

Use for cooking shrimp, crab, or lobster or to poach any fish. This court bouillon may be used many times, straining after each use.

Makes 6 cups

1 CUP CONTAINS APPROXIMATELY: N TOTAL CALORIES
N CALORIES IN FAT / 0 MG CHOLESTEROL / SODIUM VARIES
CALCIUM VARIES

DASHI

Dashi is a Japanese fish stock that is used for many Japanese soups and stews. It is an essential ingredient for Miso Soup (page 28), which happens to be a favorite of mine. You can buy Dashi stock base in Japanese grocery stores, but they all contain monosodium glutamate (MSG). This is a quick and easy way to make your own

Dashi and avoid preservatives or MSG. Dried seaweed is available in all Oriental grocery stores.

> *6 cups water*
> *1 pound fish and fish bones*
> *1 carrot, chopped*
> *1 onion, chopped*
> *2 parsley sprigs*
> *4 peppercorns*
> *¼ teaspoon salt*
> *2 teaspoons freshly squeezed lemon juice*
> *2 tablespoons dried seaweed*

Bring all the ingredients to a boil in a large saucepan. Reduce the heat and simmer, uncovered, for 1½ hours.

Strain off the liquid and discard the solids. Store the stock in the refrigerator or freezer in a tightly covered container.

Makes 4 cups

1 CUP CONTAINS APPROXIMATELY (CALCIUM VARIES
DEPENDING ON BONES USED): N TOTAL CALORIES
N CALORIES IN FAT / 1 MG CHOLESTEROL / SODIUM VARIES
CALCIUM VARIES

VEGETABLE STOCK

Vegetable stock is an essential ingredient for running a purely vegetarian kitchen where chicken, beef, and fish stock cannot be used. Basically you can make vegetable stock from almost any combination of vegetables as long as you eliminate any ingredient that might add bitterness, such as carrot peelings or celery leaves. All of the vegetarian dishes I serve at the Canyon Ranch Spa in Tucson are made with vegetable stock. To ensure consistency in the taste range of our vegetarian entrées, I had to develop a recipe for our vegetable stock so it always tasted the same. Try my recipe and then experiment with your own favorite vegetables. Use your imagination and your leftover vegetables and you can create lots of your own vegetable stock recipes.

> *1 pound cabbage, shredded (4 cups)*
> *2 pounds onions, chopped (6 cups)*
> *1 pound carrots, scraped and chopped (4 cups)*
> *2 pounds celery, without leaves, chopped (6 cups)*
> *¼ pound parsley, chopped (2 cups)*
> *2 bay leaves*
> *2 teaspoons dried marjoram, crushed*
> *1 teaspoon salt*
> *1 gallon water*

Combine all the ingredients in a large pot and bring to a boil. Reduce the heat and simmer for 1 hour, covered.

Strain and refrigerate the stock in a tightly covered container or store in the freezer in the size containers most used for individual recipes. Freeze some in an ice cube tray to use in sautéeing. Discard the vegetables or puree them as a side dish.

Makes approximately 3 quarts

1 CUP CONTAINS APPROXIMATELY: N TOTAL CALORIES
N CALORIES IN FAT / 0 MG CHOLESTEROL
SODIUM VARIES / CALCIUM VARIES

MISO SOUP

The first time I ate Miso Soup was in a private home just outside Tokyo and I loved it. The next day I ordered it in a restaurant and found that it was much too salty. I learned that they had used a prepared base for the Dashi (Japanese fish stock), which is the basic ingredient of this soup, whereas my hostess the day before had made her own Dashi. I asked for the recipe so that I could make it myself when I got home. It is possible to buy miso in all Japanese markets and some health food stores.

> *2 cups Dashi (see page 26)*
> *2 tablespoons miso*
> *¼ pound tofu, cut into ¼-inch cubes (½ cup)*
> *¼ cup chopped scallion tops*
> *½ cup enoki mushrooms*

Combine the Dashi and miso and bring to a boil. Simmer for 10 minutes over low heat.

While the soup is simmering, place 2 tablespoons of the cubed tofu, 1 tablespoon of the chopped scallion tops, and 2 tablespoons of the enoki mushrooms in each of four bowls. Pour ½ cup hot soup into each bowl and serve immediately.

Makes 4 servings

EACH SERVING CONTAINS APPROXIMATELY:
50 TOTAL CALORIES / 20 CALORIES IN FAT
1 MG CHOLESTEROL / 105 MG SODIUM / 45 MG CALCIUM

SHERRIED CONSOMMÉ

This is a quick and easy method for clarifying consommé. The classic clarification method involves adding more vegetables and raw chicken to the cold stock and then bringing it just to the boiling point, but never allowing it to come to a full boil, then simmering it for an hour before straining it. If it is allowed to actually come to a full boil, the stock will not be clear. I have called for sherry to be added to the consommé in this recipe; however, it is good just plain or with a dash of Madeira substituted for the sherry.

4 cups defatted chicken stock (see page 22)
2 tablespoons sherry
Finely chopped parsley for garnish

Line a colander or strainer with two or three layers of damp cheese-cloth. Ladle the stock through the cheesecloth and allow it to drain until all of it has seeped through.

Reheat to serving temperature, add the sherry, and mix thoroughly. Top each serving with chopped parsley.

Makes four 1-cup servings

EACH SERVING CONTAINS APPROXIMATELY:
50 TOTAL CALORIES / 15 CALORIES IN FAT
1 MG CHOLESTEROL / 105 MG SODIUM / 10 MG CALCIUM

EGG DROP SOUP

Egg Drop Soup is served in every Chinese restaurant and is a light and delicious first course for any Chinese meal. It is sometimes called Egg Flower Soup because the egg whites literally look like flowers strewn through the soup. I often serve it on spa menus with Oriental entrées of all types because, along with the fact that it is traditional, it is so low in calories.

3 cups defatted chicken stock (see page 22)
3 egg whites
1 teaspoon reduced-sodium soy sauce
2 tablespoons finely chopped chives or scallion tops

Bring the chicken stock to a boil. Beat the egg whites with a fork until frothy, then pour them into the boiling chicken stock, stirring constantly with a wire whisk. Continue to stir the soup rapidly until the eggs are shredded and look like long strings. Add the soy sauce and mix well.

Ladle ¾ cup soup into each of four consommé cups and sprinkle the top of each serving with chopped chives or scallion tops.

Makes four ¾-cup servings

EACH SERVING CONTAINS APPROXIMATELY:
35 TOTAL CALORIES / 10 CALORIES IN FAT
1 MG CHOLESTEROL / 180 MG SODIUM / 5 MG CALCIUM

GAZPACHO

This classic cold Mexican soup is a favorite not only throughout Mexico but throughout most of the rest of the world as well. I used to serve it at the Canyon Ranch Spa in Tucson only as a first course for some of our Mexican meals. It was so popular that guests started asking for it all the time, and it is now available as an optional appetizer for every meal. It can also be used as a sauce, like a salsa, over salads, beans, rice, or even fish, poultry, or meat. Because of its many possible uses and the fact that it keeps for days in the refrigerator, I have given you a recipe that makes 6 cups. If you want to make a smaller amount, it is easy to cut the recipe in half.

> *1 cucumber, peeled, seeded, and diced (¾ cup)*
> *½ pound red and green bell peppers, seeded and diced (1 cup)*
> *½ medium onion, chopped (¾ cup)*
> *1 large tomato, peeled and diced (1½ cups)*
> *3 cups V-8 juice*
> *1 garlic clove, finely chopped (1 teaspoon)*
> *¼ teaspoon freshly ground black pepper*
> *½ teaspoon Worcestershire sauce*
> *3 tablespoons freshly squeezed lemon juice*
> *Dash Tabasco*
> *Chopped fresh cilantro for garnish*

Combine all the ingredients except the chopped cilantro and mix thoroughly. Prepare a day in advance and store, tightly covered, in the refrigerator.

To serve, spoon ¾ cup cold Gazpacho into each chilled bowl and garnish with 1 tablespoon of chopped cilantro.

Makes 6 cups

A ¾ CUP SERVING CONTAINS APPROXIMATELY:
35 TOTAL CALORIES / 5 CALORIES IN FAT
0 MG CHOLESTEROL / 200 MG SODIUM / 25 MG CALCIUM

GINGERED CARROT SOUP

I really like most soups better served the day after they are made; however, this recipe is an exception. It is much better when it is very fresh. Since I like it best cold, I always make it several hours before I want to serve it so it has enough time to chill thoroughly. It is wonderful served before curried or Oriental-style entrées.

1 teaspoon corn-oil margarine
¼ cup chopped onion
2 tablespoons freshly peeled and chopped ginger
2 cups defatted chicken stock (see page 22)
1 medium potato, peeled and cubed (1 cup)
6 small carrots, peeled and sliced (2 cups)
¾ cup skim milk
¼ teaspoon salt
¼ teaspoon ground cinnamon

Melt the margarine in a large saucepan. Add the onion and ginger and cook over moderate heat until tender, about 5 minutes.

Add the stock, potato, and carrots and bring to a boil. Reduce the heat and simmer, covered, for about 30 minutes.

Pour the vegetable mixture into a blender container. Add the milk, salt, and cinnamon and blend until very smooth.

This soup is good served either hot or cold. If reheating, do not boil.

Makes four 3/4-cup servings

EACH SERVING CONTAINS APPROXIMATELY:
110 TOTAL CALORIES / 20 CALORIES IN FAT
1 MG CHOLESTEROL / 230 MG SODIUM / 85 MG CALCIUM

CREAMY CAULIFLOWER SOUP

This soup is wonderful served either hot or cold. When served cold, it tastes very much like Vichyssoise, the famous French leftover. Vichyssoise is made by pureeing leek and potato soup and adding heavy cream. To be able to get the same effect with a fraction of the calories is wonderful.

1/2 medium onion, finely chopped (3/4 cup)
2 leeks, finely chopped, white part only (2 cups)
1/4 cauliflower head, finely chopped (1 1/2 cups)
1 bay leaf
1 cup defatted chicken stock (see page 22)
2/3 cup skim milk, heated
1/4 teaspoon salt
1/8 teaspoon freshly ground black pepper
Chopped chives for garnish

Combine the onion, leeks, cauliflower, bay leaf, and chicken stock and bring to a boil. Reduce the heat and cook, covered, for 10 minutes.

Remove the bay leaf. Pour the cauliflower mixture into a blender container, add all the other ingredients, and blend until smooth.

To serve, ladle 3/4 cup hot soup into each bowl and sprinkle with the chopped chives.

Makes four 3/4-cup servings

EACH SERVING CONTAINS APPROXIMATELY:
70 TOTAL CALORIES / 10 CALORIES IN FAT
2 MG CHOLESTEROL / 190 MG SODIUM
95 MG CALCIUM

FRESH TOMATO SOUP

This soup is particularly good in the summertime, when tomatoes are in season and are available vine-ripened. It is another soup that is good either hot or cold. I like to serve it hot in mugs before a cold supper on a summer evening.

> *1 tablespoon corn-oil margarine*
> *2 tablespoons minced onion*
> *6 medium-ripe tomatoes, peeled, seeded, and chopped (4 cups)*
> *1/2 cup defatted chicken stock (see page 22)*
> *1/2 teaspoon salt*
> *1/8 teaspoon white pepper*
> *1 cup skim milk*

Melt the margarine in a large saucepan. Add the onion and cook until soft and clear.

Add the tomatoes and cook, covered, over medium heat, stirring occasionally, until the tomatoes are very soft, about 15 minutes.

Place the cooked tomatoes and onion in a blender container with the chicken stock, salt, and pepper. Blend until a smooth, creamy consistency is reached. Add the milk and mix well.

Return the soup to the saucepan and bring to serving temperature over medium heat. Do not boil.

Makes four 1-cup servings

EACH SERVING CONTAINS APPROXIMATELY:
120 TOTAL CALORIES / 35 CALORIES IN FAT
1 MG CHOLESTEROL / 345 MG SODIUM / 100 MG CALCIUM

FRENCH ONION SOUP

For anyone who has ever eaten a steaming-hot, still-bubbling rame-kin of onion soup au gratin in a French bistro, this soup will conjure up wonderful memories—with lots less calories!

4 pieces French bread, thinly sliced (¹/4 inch thick, 4 inches in diameter)
1 teaspoon corn-oil margarine
1 medium onion, sliced very thin vertically (2 cups)
2 tablespoons dry white wine
¹/4 teaspoon freshly ground black pepper
¹/4 teaspoon salt (omit if using salted stock)
2 cups defatted chicken stock or beef stock (see page 22 or 23)
2 ounces Swiss cheese, grated (¹/2 cup)

Place the bread on a cookie sheet in a preheated 300°F oven for approximately 5 minutes. Let it dry out but not brown.

Melt the margarine in a skillet. Add the onions and cook, covered, over very low heat until soft, about 10 minutes. Remove the lid, turn up the heat, and brown the onions, stirring constantly; do not allow them to burn. When brown, reduce the heat and add the wine. Cook until most of the wine has been absorbed. Add the pepper, salt, and stock and mix well. Simmer for 5 minutes.

Pour ¾ cup soup into each of four ovenproof bowls. Place a slice of French bread on top of each bowl and allow to stand until the bread is saturated with soup and has expanded. Sprinkle 2 table-spoons of the cheese over each serving.

Place in a preheated 325°F oven for 30 to 40 minutes or until the cheese is lightly browned.

Makes 4 servings

EACH SERVING CONTAINS APPROXIMATELY:
155 TOTAL CALORIES / 60 CALORIES IN FAT
15 MG CHOLESTEROL / 290 MG SODIUM / 150 MG CALCIUM

BLACK BEAN SOUP

Everyone argues about the origin of Black Bean Soup. The Cubans claim it, as do the Puerto Ricans and several other islands in the Caribbean; however, there is no argument that everyone likes it, and almost everyone develops a slightly different seasoning for it. This is my version, which I developed for a Pritikin cruise through the Panama Canal on a Sitmar ship several years ago. It is classically served with rice as an entrée course; however, it can be served in a cup as a first course, and many people love it for breakfast. It freezes so well that I have given a recipe for twelve soup-size servings or four to six entrée servings, depending upon the size of your appetite. It is a particularly popular entrée with athletes who are carbohydrate-loading before competition.

> 1 pound dry black beans, washed and sorted
> 6 cups water
> 1 medium green bell pepper, seeded and finely chopped (1 cup)
> 1/2 jalapeño pepper, seeded and minced (1 tablespoon)
> 2 cups chicken, beef, or vegetable stock (see page 22, 23, or 27)
> 1 medium onion, chopped (1 1/2 cups)
> 3 garlic cloves, finely chopped (1 tablespoon)
> 1 tablespoon ground cumin
> 1 teaspoon salt (reduce to 1/2 teaspoon if using salted stock)
> 1/4 teaspoon freshly ground black pepper
> 1/4 cup red wine vinegar
> 1/2 cup sherry
> 1/2 cup chopped scallions for garnish
> 3/4 cup Light Cheese (page 52)

Soak the beans overnight in water to cover. Drain. Rinse and drain again.

Combine the beans, water, bell pepper, and jalapeño pepper in a large saucepan. Bring to a boil. Cover. Reduce the heat and simmer for 1 1/2 hours or until the beans are tender.

Heat 1/4 cup of the stock. Add the onions and garlic and cook until the onions are translucent and the stock has been absorbed.

Remove 1 cup of the beans from the pot. Blend in a blender container and return to the pot.

Stir the onions, garlic, the remaining 1¾ cups stock, the cumin, salt, pepper, and vinegar into the beans. Bring to a boil. Reduce the heat and simmer, uncovered, until thick, about 45 minutes.

Add the sherry and simmer for 5 minutes more.

To serve, spoon into bowls and sprinkle 1 tablespoon scallions over the top of each bowl. Top with a tablespoon of Light Cheese.

Makes 9 cups

A ¾ CUP SERVING CONTAINS APPROXIMATELY:
185 TOTAL CALORIES / 20 CALORIES IN FAT
5 MG CHOLESTEROL / 145 MG SODIUM / 110 MG CALCIUM

VARIATION:

For a Cuban-style main dish serve over cooked rice. Top with chopped onions and serve Light Cheese (page 52) or Light Sour Cream (page 53) on the side.

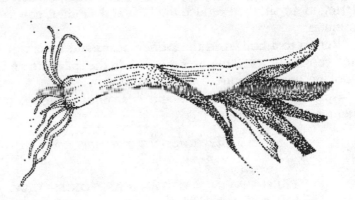

MINESTRONE SOUP

This hearty Italian soup makes a wonderful main dish served with a green salad with Light Italian Dressing (see page 72) and crusty bread.

2 cups defatted beef, chicken, or vegetable stock (see page 23, 22, or 27)

¾ cup beer

1 small carrot, peeled and sliced (½ cup)

½ medium onion, chopped (¾ cup)

1 celery rib, without leaves, chopped (½ cup)

½ cup chopped cabbage

One 16-ounce can tomatoes, undrained (2 cups)

¼ teaspoon salt (omit if using salted stock)

⅛ teaspoon freshly ground black pepper

¾ teaspoon dried rosemary, crushed in a mortar and pestle

¾ teaspoon chili powder

1 garlic clove, finely chopped (1 teaspoon)

1 cup canned kidney beans, undrained

½ cup Italian green beans, cut into 1-inch pieces

½ cup very thin dry spaghetti, broken into 1-inch pieces

2 ounces imported Parmesan cheese, freshly grated (½ cup)

In a large pot, combine the stock, beer, carrots, onions, celery, cabbage, tomatoes, salt, pepper, rosemary, chili powder, and garlic. Bring to a boil, then reduce the heat and simmer, covered, for 30 minutes.

Return to a boil. Add the kidney beans and Italian green beans and cook for 5 to 10 minutes more. Add the spaghetti and continue cooking until al dente, 5 to 6 minutes.

Add the Parmesan cheese and heat until melted, stirring constantly.

Makes eight 1-cup servings

EACH SERVING CONTAINS APPROXIMATELY:
120 TOTAL CALORIES / 20 CALORIES IN FAT
5 MG CHOLESTEROL / 295 MG SODIUM / 115 MG CALCIUM

MANHATTAN CLAM CHOWDER

3 cups defatted chicken stock or fish stock (see page 22 or 25)
1/2 garlic clove, chopped (1/2 teaspoon)
1/2 medium onion, chopped (3/4 cup)
1 medium potato, peeled and cubed (1 cup)
1/2 celery rib, diced (1/4 cup)
1 small carrot, peeled and diced (1/4 cup)
1/2 green bell pepper, seeded and diced (1/4 cup)
One 8-ounce can peeled and chopped tomatoes, undrained
1/2 cup clam juice
1/8 teaspoon caraway seeds
1/2 teaspoon dried thyme, crushed in a mortar and pestle
1/2 bay leaf, crumbled
1/8 teaspoon freshly ground black pepper
One 6 1/2-ounce can chopped clams, undrained

Combine 2 cups of the chicken or fish stock, the garlic, 1/2 cup of the onions, and 1/2 cup of the potatoes in a large pot. Bring to a boil. Reduce the heat and cook, covered, for 30 minutes. Pour into a blender container and puree until smooth.

Pour the puree back into the pot and add the remaining stock, onions, and potatoes and all the other ingredients except for the clams. Simmer, uncovered, for 45 minutes.

Just before serving, add the clams plus all the juice from the can and heat through.

Makes four 1-cup servings

EACH SERVING CONTAINS APPROXIMATELY:
115 TOTAL CALORIES / 15 CALORIES IN FAT
35 MG CHOLESTEROL / 280 MG SODIUM / 60 MG CALCIUM

HALÁSZLÉ
(Hungarian Fish Soup)

The first time I ever had this soup, I was sitting in a courtyard on the Buda side of the Danube in Budapest looking across the river at the magnificent buildings on the Pest waterfront. I couldn't decide whether I was more impressed with my surroundings or my fabulous soup. I asked to meet the chef, who fortunately spoke English, and talked him into revealing his recipe.

3/4 pound firm white fish (traditionally carp or perch)
Juice of 1 lemon
Salt
1 1/2 medium onions, thinly sliced (3 cups)
1 leek, white part only, chopped (1 cup)
2 garlic cloves, finely chopped (2 teaspoons)
2 small tomatoes, peeled and diced (1 cup)
2 celery ribs, without leaves, finely chopped (1 cup)
1/2 teaspoon dried marjoram, crushed in a mortar and pestle
1 1/2 teaspoons mild Hungarian paprika
1/4 teaspoon hot Hungarian paprika or dash cayenne pepper
   (optional)
4 cups defatted chicken stock or fish stock (see page 22 or 25)
1/8 teaspoon salt (omit if using salted stock)

Wash the fish in cold water and pat dry. Place in a glass baking dish and squeeze the lemon juice over it. Lightly salt both sides. Cover the dish tightly and place in the refrigerator until ready to cook.

In a deep kettle, combine the onions and leeks and cook, covered, for 5 minutes, adding a little water or stock if necessary to prevent scorching. Add the garlic, tomatoes, celery, marjoram, mild paprika, and hot paprika or cayenne pepper (if using). Mix thoroughly and cook for 5 minutes more.

Add the stock and salt and bring slowly to a boil. Reduce the heat and simmer for 30 minutes.

Cut the fish into bite-size pieces and add to the simmering soup. Continue cooking for 8 to 10 minutes more or until the fish has turned white.

Makes four 2-cup servings

EACH SERVING CONTAINS APPROXIMATELY:
190 TOTAL CALORIES / 40 CALORIES IN FAT
1 MG CHOLESTEROL / 265 MG SODIUM / 100 MG CALCIUM

JEANNE JONES' CREAM OF MUSHROOM SOUP

One of the most frequently used ingredients in recipes my readers send to me to be modified is condensed cream soup, usually cream of mushroom soup. Condensed soups, while a real convenience in our busy home kitchens, are not really worth eating when you consider the trade-off in higher fat, cholesterol, and sodium. There are 2540 milligrams of sodium in one can of commercial soup and only 624 milligrams of sodium in the same amount of my soup. Commercial soups also contain preservatives and MSG.

In order to modify these recipes I had to create a viable substitute for commercially canned cream soups. It had to be easy enough to make to still be convenient, similar in both taste and texture, and within my guidelines to "Cook it Light." Once you have tried my recipe and its variations, you will never want to go back to using canned soups again.

> *1 tablespoon corn oil margarine*
> *3 tablespoons unbleached flour*
> *¾ cup chicken stock (see page 22)*
> *½ cup skim milk*
> *¼ teaspoon salt*
> *Dash of garlic powder*
> *Dash of freshly ground black pepper*
> *¼ cup fresh cooked or canned mushrooms, finely chopped*

Melt the margarine in a skillet. Add the flour and stir over medium heat for 1 minute. Do not brown. Add the chicken stock and skim milk. Using a wire whisk, stir the mixture over medium heat until it comes to a boil. Add the seasonings (omit the salt if using salted stock) and the mushrooms and continue to cook for 1 minute more. To serve as soup, dilute to taste with water, stock, or skim milk.

Makes 1¼ cups condensed soup

1¼ CUPS OF CONDENSED SOUP CONTAINS
APPROXIMATELY: 250 TOTAL CALORIES
110 CALORIES IN FAT / 2 MG CHOLESTEROL
625 MG SODIUM / 165 MG CALCIUM

VARIATIONS

Cream of Chicken Soup: Omit mushrooms and add ¼ cup finely chopped cooked chicken.

Cream of Celery Soup: Omit mushrooms and add ¼ cup finely chopped celery.

MOCK TURTLE SOUP

One of the readers of my "Cook It Light" column sent this recipe to me on the back of an envelope, where he had written it during World War II. In fact it said to use the meat "if you have the stamps for it." When I wrote back to him, I told him that we all certainly hoped that nothing in this country would ever be rationed again but that vegetarian Mock Turtle Soup is also very good. The original recipe also called for browned flour, which I omitted because I felt it gave the soup a muddy look and kept the flavors from being sharp. I explained that the egg white is supposed to be chopped finely enough to look like turtle meat in the soup and that since sherry is always served with real turtle soup, it is appropriate that it also be served with Mock Turtle Soup.

½ lemon, unpeeled, thinly sliced, and seeded
½ pound very lean ground beef

3 cups water

One 8-ounce cup canned diced tomatoes, undrained

2 tablespoons apple cider vinegar

1 tablespoon fructose or 4 teaspoons sugar

2 small carrots, peeled and grated (1 cup)

1 celery rib, without leaves, finely diced (½ cup)

¼ cup uncooked brown rice

Dash freshly ground black pepper

⅛ teaspoon salt

2 tablespoons pickling spice, tied in a cheesecloth bag

1 hard-cooked egg, white only, finely chopped

2 tablespoons sherry (optional)

Cut the lemon slices in half.

Combine all the ingredients, except for the egg white and sherry, in a large pot. Bring to a boil. Reduce the heat, cover, and simmer for 1 hour. Remove the lid and cook for an additional 30 minutes. Remove the bag of spices.

Add the finely chopped egg white and mix thoroughly. Add the sherry just before serving if desired.

Makes four 1-cup servings

EACH SERVING CONTAINS APPROXIMATELY:
205 TOTAL CALORIES / 60 CALORIES IN FAT
40 MG CHOLESTEROL / 245 MG SODIUM / 45 MG CALCIUM

ALBONDIGAS (MEATBALL) SOUP

Albondigas, or Mexican Meatball Soup, is a popular soup throughout Mexico. It can be served either as a soup course or as the main course for a meal. If using it as the main course, serve larger portions and serve it with warm corn tortillas. As a variation, try Albondigas made with pasta instead of rice.

½ pound very lean ground beef
2 cups defatted chicken stock (see page 22)
1½ cups defatted beef stock (see page 23)
1 cup chopped onions
½ teaspoon dried oregano, crushed in a mortar and pestle
¼ teaspoon crushed red pepper flakes
1 cup thinly sliced carrots
2 tablespoons chopped cilantro
2 tablespoons uncooked brown rice
½ pound fresh spinach, shredded (2 cups)
4 cilantro sprigs for garnish
4 lime wedges for garnish

Preheat the oven to 400°F.

Form eight small meatballs from the ground beef. Place on a rack in a broiler pan in the preheated oven for 10 minutes. Remove from the rack and pat with paper towels to remove any remaining fat.

Combine the chicken and beef stocks, meatballs, onions, oregano, and pepper flakes in a large saucepan. Bring to a boil, then add the carrots, cilantro, and rice. Simmer for 30 to 40 minutes or until the rice is tender.

Remove the stems and veins from the spinach and shred finely. Add the spinach to the soup and continue to cook for 5 minutes more.

Spoon into bowls and garnish each serving with a sprig of cilantro and a lime wedge (to be squeezed into the soup before eating).

Makes four 1-cup servings

EACH SERVING CONTAINS APPROXIMATELY:
185 TOTAL CALORIES / 70 CALORIES IN FAT
40 MG CHOLESTEROL / 140 MG SODIUM / 60 MG CALCIUM

BORSCHT

The Russians have many different types of Borscht, ranging all the way from hearty meat-and-vegetable entrée-type soups to Beet Borscht, which is a totally vegetarian soup that can be served either hot or cold as a first course. I happen to like beets very much and have been experimenting with borscht for years. To date, this is my favorite version of it, and I like it best served cold before Chicken Stroganoff (page 169), with Strawberries Romanoff (page 226) for dessert, for a real Russian menu.

> *2 large beets (¹/2 pound)*
> *1¹/2 garlic cloves, finely chopped (1¹/2 teaspoons)*
> *¹/4 teaspoon salt*
> *2 teaspoons fructose or 1 tablespoon sugar*
> *1¹/3 cups buttermilk*
> *4 teaspoons plain nonfat yogurt*

Scrub the beets thoroughly, being careful not to break the skin. Cut off the roots and tops. Place the beets and chopped garlic in a large saucepan. Add water to cover and bring to a boil. Reduce the heat, cover, and simmer for 20 minutes.

Remove the beets from the water, reserving 1 cup of liquid. Slip the skins off the beets and discard. Chop the beets and place in a blender container. Add the reserved cooking liquid and all the other ingredients, except for the yogurt, and blend until smooth.

Serve either hot or cold. Garnish each serving with a teaspoon of yogurt.

Makes four ³/4-cup servings

EACH SERVING CONTAINS APPROXIMATELY:
70 TOTAL CALORIES / 5 CALORIES IN FAT
5 MG CHOLESTEROL / 270 MG SODIUM
115 MG CALCIUM

SAUCES & DRESSINGS

IN RESPONSE to all the letters I have received asking questions about basic sauces, I am including a very large and varied sauce and salad dressing section. Actually, to design any menu for any meal, all you need is a salad dressing and a sauce or two. You can simply pour good dressing over lettuce, sauce a grilled or poached piece of fish, poultry, or meat, add a vegetable, and pour a fruit sauce over a simple custard—and you have an elegant meal.

Making rich-tasting, creamy-textured sauces without the added butter and other fats always associated with rich sauces is really easy once you learn the tricks.

Reduction is the key. Reducing a sauce in volume to intensify the flavor or thicken the texture is simply a matter of cooking it longer, uncovered, to reduce the volume—it just boils away. If a recipe tells you to reduce by one-half, you literally boil the liquid away until you are left with only half as much as you started with. I often use this technique to intensify flavor and then pour the sauce into a blender in order to get the creamy texture I want.

46

Also defatting pan drippings just as you defat stock gives you a rich flavor base to work with in making sauces and gravies. The juices or drippings that accumulate in the bottom of the pan when you cook poultry or meat are often poured over the finished dish or made into a very-high-fat gravy. In either case you are adding calories along with cholesterol and saturated fats, which do nothing to improve the taste of the finished product.

You really can have your gravy and a healthy dish at the same time by just removing the fat. It only takes a few minutes in the freezer for the fat to congeal on top of the drippings. Remove all the fat and then reheat the drippings to pour the *au jus* over the dish. Or turn the defatted drippings into a tasty sauce or gravy, using the recipes in this section. If you don't plan to use the drippings for the meal you're preparing, put them in the refrigerator to defat later and store in the freezer. Defatted pan juices add a wonderful flavor to many other dishes and also improve the taste of soups and basic stocks.

The vegetable sauces in this section are among my favorite recipes for low-calorie spa cooking. They are colorful, nutritious, and extremely low in calories. In fact, I like to pour these vegetable sauces on the plate and then put the other vegetables, fish, poultry, or meat I am serving on top of them. I also use Cream of Rice to make a completely fat-free, quick-and-easy white sauce as a base for many dishes. And for dairy-free creamy sauces I use tofu (soybean curd), which also adds a great deal of protein and calcium to the dish you are serving it on.

All of my salad dressings are lower in calories, cholesterol, and sodium than their commercial counterparts. The only time I ever use oil in salad dressing is either for flavor or texture, and you will find it DOESN'T TAKE VERY MUCH. For example, in the tofu sauces a small amount of oil is needed for texture or "mouth feel," so I often use unflavored oil. Whenever I am using oil for flavor, I use the most flavorful one obtainable so that only a small amount will give me the result I want in taste. When using olive oil, I always use extra-virgin olive oil, or the "first press" of the olives; this has the strongest, cleanest flavor. When using sesame oil, I call for dark or roasted sesame oil, again because of its strong flavor. Always buy the best-quality oils available and store them tightly covered in a cool place.

Some of my dressings contain no oil at all and therefore practically no calories. You may want to make these up by the quart to use as your "house" salad dressings.

I routinely use oil-free salad dressing as my Jeanne Jones' signature dressing for the menus I create in spas, hotels, and restaurants. I do this for several important reasons. In commercial kitchens dressings are not always thoroughly mixed before being ladled onto salads, and since the oil always rises to the top, it is possible for a dressing very low in calories (because it contains so little oil) to have all the oil at the top spooned onto a salad, therefore making it very high in calories for that particular serving. Even when the dressing is put into a dish or pitcher on the side, unless it is well mixed before being poured into the serving container, it could still contain more oil than it would have if it had been thoroughly mixed first. I learned this firsthand a few years ago when I ordered one of my own salad creations, which is routinely served with the dressing on the side. I was sure it was the wrong dressing because it was over half oil and asked the waiter to replace it. After returning to the kitchen he assured me that it was the right dressing. I then went back to check with the chef myself, and indeed it was out of the right container—it just had not been mixed thoroughly. And therefore, even though the dressing recipe contained very little oil, I had been served the oil off the top rather than the proper mix of dressing. Another reason for having a house dressing that is oil-free and therefore fat-free is that every tablespoon of oil contains 120 calories. These calories can be "traded off" for other fat calories that make more difference in the taste and texture of the salad, such as toasted nuts and seeds or diced avocados.

Along with the recipe for my signature dressing I have included enough variations that it can be used in any flavor range. I have also included how you would use different types of vinegar and oil to get specific flavors. Just remember, with these dressings containing oil for flavor enhancement, how important it is to always mix the dressing thoroughly before using it.

LIGHT GRAVY

Once you have started making Light Gravy, I don't think you will ever like greasy gravy again. The taste is creamier and the flavor sharper without the fat, and Light Gravy works wonders on your waistline. Another bonus provided by this recipe is that you will never again have to contend with lumpy gravy. Even the complete novice cook will get satin-smooth gravy every time! I have given you a choice of stock, milk, or water in this recipe because it really depends upon the intensity of the flavor you want and the type of gravy you are making. If you want a gravy closer to a classic brown sauce, then use defatted stock along with a little red and white wine. If you want a creamy gravy, then use milk, and for a still creamier gravy use nonfat dry milk and mix it with less water than called for on the package directions, or canned skimmed evaporated milk. For a very light gravy, water works well, particularly if the pan drippings themselves are richly flavored. In some cases you might even find that using fruit juice adds an interesting flavor to your gravy, especially when using it for poultry or lean cuts of pork. Your own light gravies will be limited only by your imagination.

> *1 cup defatted stock (see page 22, 23, or 27), skim milk, or*
> *   water*
> *2 tablespoons uncooked Cream of Rice*
> *1 cup defatted poultry or meat drippings*
> *Freshly ground black pepper to taste*
> *Seasonings of your choice, such as fennel, thyme, or sage*

Heat the stock, milk, or water to the boiling point in a small saucepan. Add the cream of rice and stir over the heat for 30 seconds. Remove from the heat, cover, and let stand for 5 minutes.

Pour the mixture into a blender container and blend until smooth. Add the drippings and blend again.

Pour back into the saucepan and reheat. For a thicker gravy, cook over medium heat until it reduces to the desired consistency.

Season lightly to match whatever herb or spice is being used in cooking the poultry or meat (for example, use ¼ teaspoon fennel when serving with Roast Turkey with Fennel, page 180). Stock makes a richer, more intense-flavored gravy than water. Milk makes a creamier gravy.

Makes 2 cups

¼ CUP CONTAINS APPROXIMATELY: 25 TOTAL CALORIES
N CALORIES IN FAT / 1 MG CHOLESTEROL / 25 MG SODIUM
40 MG CALCIUM

EASY, FAT-FREE WHITE SAUCE

Like Light Gravy (preceding recipe), this white sauce is not only truly easy to make but foolproof. You will have smooth, creamy white sauce every time—and no fat!

> 1½ *cups skim milk*
> ¼ *teaspoon salt*
> *Dash white pepper (optional)*
> 3 *tablespoons uncooked Cream of Rice*

Bring all the ingredients except the Cream of Rice to a boil in a small saucepan. Add the Cream of Rice and stir for 1 minute. Remove from the heat, cover, and allow to stand for 5 minutes.

Pour into a blender container and blend until smooth. You may store any unused white sauce in the refrigerator to reheat when needed.

Makes 1½ cups

¼ CUP CONTAINS APPROXIMATELY: 40 TOTAL CALORIES
N CALORIES IN FAT / 1 MG CHOLESTEROL
125 MG SODIUM / 75 MG CALCIUM

WHITE SAUCE

This version of a classic approach to white or béchamel sauce is exceptionally easy and is much lower in fat than the traditional recipes. It is also practically cholesterol-free because I have used pure corn-oil margarine, which is a polyunsaturated fat and contains no cholesterol, and skim milk has only a trace. It is also very low in sodium and works well as a base for any recipe calling for a creamy-type sauce, such as the Mornay Sauce variation that follows.

> *1 tablespoon corn-oil margarine*
> *3 tablespoons whole wheat pastry flour, sifted*
> *2½ cups skim milk, heated to simmering*
> *⅛ teaspoon salt*

Melt the margarine over low heat. Add the flour and cook for 2 minutes, stirring constantly. DO NOT BROWN.

Remove from the heat and add the milk slowly, stirring with a wire whisk. Add the salt and cook slowly over low heat for 15 to 20 minutes, stirring occasionally.

Makes 2 cups

¼ CUP CONTAINS APPROXIMATELY: 50 TOTAL CALORIES
15 CALORIES IN FAT / 1 MG CHOLESTEROL / 75 MG SODIUM
95 MG CALCIUM

VARIATION:

Mornay Sauce: When the sauce has thickened, add ⅛ teaspoon white pepper, ⅛ teaspoon freshly grated nutmeg, and ½ cup grated Swiss or Gruyère cheese (2 ounces). Add more skim milk for a thinner sauce.

LIGHT CHEESE

Light Cheese is one of the staples of my light cuisine. In fact it even has several aliases—Breakfast Cheese, Fitness Cheese, Mock Crème Fraîche—depending upon how it's used in a menu. By any name it is a delicious, nutritious, and satisfying condiment that can be used as a spread for toasted bagels, waffles, and pancakes or a topping for soups, salads, and vegetables. I particularly like it on baked potatoes with chopped scallions and freshly ground black pepper. I also love it for breakfast on whole wheat toast with the Apple Butter on page 61.

1/3 cup plain nonfat yogurt
2 cups part-skim ricotta cheese

Blend the yogurt and ricotta in a food processor with a metal blade until it is *satin smooth.* Refrigerate in a tightly covered container. Make it at least a day before using if possible. Keeps 5 days.

Makes 2 1/4 cups

2 TABLESPOONS CONTAIN APPROXIMATELY:
40 TOTAL CALORIES / 20 CALORIES IN FAT
10 MG CHOLESTEROL / 35 MG SODIUM
85 MG CALCIUM

GARLIC SPREAD

2 bulbs fresh garlic (1/2 cup cloves)
1 cup Light Cheese (see recipe above)
1/8 teaspoon salt
1/4 teaspoon oregano, crushed in a mortar and pestle

Bake the garlic in a preheated 350°F oven for 40 minutes.

Peel the garlic and combine all the ingredients in a food processor with a metal blade. Blend until satin smooth.

Makes 1¼ cups

1 TABLESPOON CONTAINS APPROXIMATELY: 20 CALORIES
10 CALORIES IN FAT / 5 MG CHOLESTEROL / 30 MG SODIUM
40 MG CALCIUM

LIGHT SOUR CREAM

1 cup low-fat cottage cheese
2 tablespoons buttermilk
1½ teaspoons freshly squeezed lemon juice

Put all the ingredients into a blender container and blend until completely smooth. Even when you think it's smooth enough, blend a little longer for a better result.

Makes 1 cup

¼ CUP CONATINS APPROXIMATELY: 45 TOTAL CALORIES
5 CALORIES IN FAT / 3 MG CHOLESTEROL / 240 MG SODIUM
45 MG CALCIUM

VARIATIONS:

To 1 cup add:

Curry Dip: ½ teaspoon curry powder, ⅛ teaspoon ground ginger, and 2 teaspoons grated onion.

Latin Dip: ½ teaspoon chili powder, ¼ teaspoon ground cumin, ¼ teaspoon garlic powder, and dash of Tabasco (optional).

CINNAMON-APPLE YOGURT SAUCE

I developed this sauce originally for a gingered fruit compote, which is a dessert on my menu in the Neiman-Marcus restaurant in Newport Beach, California. However, I like it so much that I use it as a topping for breakfast cereal and fresh fruits of all types.

> *1 cup plain nonfat yogurt*
> *1 teaspoon vanilla extract*
> *3 tablespoons frozen unsweetened apple juice concentrate, undiluted*
> *1/2 teaspoon ground cinnamon*

Combine all the ingredients and mix well. Refrigerate in a tightly covered container.

Makes 1 1/4 cups

2 TABLESPOONS CONTAIN APPROXIMATELY:
25 TOTAL CALORIES / 5 CALORIES IN FAT
0 MG CHOLESTEROL / 40 MG SODIUM
50 MG CALCIUM

VARIATION:

To serve warm add 1 tablespoon of cornstarch per 1 cup of yogurt to prevent the yogurt from separating.

SALSA

Salsa is as essential to the Mexican menu as tortillas, beans, and rice. In Mexico, restaurants serve one salsa to the tourists and make another they call kitchen salsa to eat themselves. The difference is that the kitchen salsa has many more chili peppers and therefore is much hotter and thus more desirable to the Mexican palate. Salsa can be made with many different kinds of peppers; however, jalapeños are usually more available in the markets in this country. In this recipe I suggest an amount of chili pepper and garlic but really leave it to your personal taste; since I lived in Mexico for two years, my personal preference might be a bit too close to the Mexican kitchen salsa.

3 medium tomatoes, finely diced (2 cups)
1/2 medium onion, finely diced (3/4 cup)
2 tablespoons finely chopped cilantro
1/2 jalapeño pepper, seeded and finely chopped (or to your taste)
1/2 garlic clove, finely chopped (1/2 teaspoon) (or to your taste)
3/4 teaspoon ground cumin
3/4 teaspoon dried oregano, crushed in a mortar and pestle
1/8 teaspoon salt
1 tablespoon freshly squeezed lemon juice
1 tablespoon freshly squeezed lime juice

Combine all the ingredients. Cover and refrigerate for at least 2 hours before serving.

Makes 1 1/2 cups

1/4 CUP CONTAINS APPROXIMATELY: 15 TOTAL CALORIES
N CALORIES IN FAT / 0 MG CHOLESTEROL / 40 MG SODIUM
10 MG CALCIUM

LIGHT PESTO SAUCE

In order to make classic Italian pesto sauce, it is necessary to have fresh basil, which is not available in all places at all times of the year. Therefore, when basil is available, it is a good idea to make it in quantity and freeze it in ice cube trays. As well as being a tasty sauce for pasta of all types, pesto sauce is good on sandwiches or as a spread on toasted Italian bread as an hors d'oeuvre. It also makes a delicious salad dressing. In fact, my favorite picnic salad is rotelle or fusille pasta combined with a colorful assortment of bite-size cooked vegetables topped with toasted pine nuts. Cold cooked chicken or water-packed tuna is also good in this pesto pasta salad.

1/4 cup pine nuts
2 cups tightly packed fresh basil, all stems removed (1/2 pound)
2 cups tightly packed fresh spinach, all stems and veins removed (1/2 pound)
4 garlic cloves, finely chopped (4 teaspoons)
1/4 pound imported Parmesan cheese, freshly grated (1 cup)
1/4 teaspoon salt
1/4 cup extra-virgin olive oil
1/2 cup water

Place the pine nuts in a preheated 350°F oven for 8 to 10 minutes. Watch carefully, as they burn easily. Combine the pine nuts and all the other ingredients except the water in a food processor with a metal blade. Mix until a smooth paste is formed. Add the water and mix thoroughly.

Refrigerate in a tightly covered container or freeze in containers of appropriate size.

Makes 2 1/2 cups

2 TABLESPOONS CONTAIN APPROXIMATELY:
50 TOTAL CALORIES / 40 CALORIES IN FAT
3 MG CHOLESTEROL / 110 MG SODIUM
65 MG CALCIUM

SZECHUAN PEANUT SAUCE

Szechuan Peanut Sauce is the topping for one of my own favorite recipes in this book, Oriental Noodles with Szechuan Peanut Sauce (page 135). When I first put this cold pasta dish with a cold peanut sauce on the menu at one spa, everyone in the kitchen thought I was crazy—until they tasted it. Then guess what happened? They routinely doubled the amount they thought they would need so they could eat what was left over themselves. All I can say is that if you don't think you will like it, please try it. I also use this sauce as a dip with cold blanched vegetables and rice crackers.

> 6 tablespoons unhomogenized peanut butter
> 1/2 cup plain nonfat yogurt
> 1 1/2 teaspoons fructose or 2 teaspoons sugar
> 1 teaspoon low-sodium soy sauce
> 1/4 teaspoon dark sesame oil
> 1/2 garlic clove, finely chopped (1/2 teaspoon)
> 1/4 teaspoon crushed red pepper flakes (or to taste)
> 2 tablespoons rice wine vinegar

Combine all the ingredients in a blender container and blend until smooth. Refrigerate in a tightly covered container.

Makes 1 cup

1/4 CUP CONTAINS APPROXIMATELY: 180 TOTAL CALORIES
110 CALORIES IN FAT / 1 MG CHOLESTEROL
125 MG SODIUM / 95 MG CALCIUM

CREOLE SAUCE

Creole Sauce can be used as a filling for omelets, to spice up soups, to dress salads, or as a sauce on other vegetables, fish, poultry, or meat. It is an ingredient of my own Cajun/Creole–type dish, which is Chicken Jambalaya (page 177). This recipe makes just enough for the jambalaya recipe, but you may want to double it so you can have it on hand as a sauce for other dishes.

1 *small tomato, peeled and chopped (³/4 cup)*
¹/2 *medium onion, finely chopped (³/4 cup)*
¹/2 *medium green bell pepper, seeded and chopped (¹/2 cup)*
1 *celery rib, without leaves, chopped (¹/2 cup)*
1 *garlic clove, finely chopped (1 teaspoon)*
1 *bay leaf*
¹/8 *teaspoon white pepper*
¹/4 *teaspoon salt (omit if using salted stock)*
¹/4 *teaspoon sweet paprika*
¹/4 *teaspoon cayenne*
¹/4 *teaspoon freshly ground black pepper*
¹/2 *teaspoon dried oregano, crushed in a mortar and pestle*
¹/2 *teaspoon dried thyme, crushed in a mortar and pestle*
¹/2 *teaspoon dried basil, crushed in a mortar and pestle*
³/4 *cup defatted chicken stock (see page 22)*
¹/2 *cup tomato sauce*
¹/2 *teaspoon fructose or ³/4 teaspoon sugar*
¹/4 *teaspoon Tabasco (or to taste)*

Combine the tomatoes, onion, pepper, celery, and garlic in a large skillet. Add all the seasonings and mix well. Sauté over low heat, stirring occasionally, until the onion becomes translucent, about 5 to 10 minutes.

Add the chicken stock, tomato sauce, fructose or sugar, and Tabasco. Bring to a boil. Reduce the heat and simmer, uncovered, stirring occasionally, until the vegetables are cooked and the sauce thickens slightly, about 20 minutes. Remove the bay leaf.

Cool to room temperature and store in the refrigerator in a tightly covered container. Or freeze in appropriate-size containers.

Makes 2 cups

¹/2 CUP CONTAINS APPROXIMATELY: 45 TOTAL CALORIES
5 CALORIES IN FAT / 1 MG CHOLESTEROL / 355 MG SODIUM
35 MG CALCIUM

MARINARA SAUCE

This is the easiest-to-make, best-tasting, and lowest-calorie marinara sauce you have ever eaten. The recipe makes just enough for Cioppino (page 149), the famous San Francisco Italian seafood stew. It is also an ingredient for Pasta Primavera (page 131), but it has a wide variety of uses on its own. It is wonderful on any pasta and is also delicious on fish, poultry, and meat dishes.

5 cups tomato sauce
2¹/₂ cups water
2 medium onions, finely chopped (3 cups)
2 garlic cloves, finely chopped (2 teaspoons)
1 teaspoon dried oregano, crushed in a mortar and pestle
1 teaspoon dried basil, crushed in a mortar and pestle
¹/₄ teaspoon dried rosemary, crushed in a mortar and pestle
¹/₄ teaspoon dried thyme, crushed in a mortar and pestle
1 bay leaf, broken
¹/₈ teaspoon freshly ground black pepper
¹/₂ teaspoon salt
¹/₂ teaspoon fructose or ³/₄ teaspoon sugar

Combine all the ingredients and bring to a boil. Reduce the heat and simmer, uncovered, for at least 2 hours.

Cool to room temperature and refrigerate or freeze in containers of appropriate size.

Makes 4 cups

¹/₂ CUP CONTAINS APPROXIMATELY:
70 TOTAL CALORIES / 5 CALORIES IN FAT
0 MG CHOLESTEROL / 1060 MG SODIUM
50 MG CALCIUM

PRUNE SAUCE

This prune sauce is a marvelous substitute for cranberry sauce with turkey for holiday dinners.

> 1 cup dried pitted prunes
> 1 1/2 teaspoons grated lemon zest
> 2 tablespoons freshly squeezed lemon juice
> 1/8 teaspoon ground mace
> 12 whole cloves
> 3 whole allspice
> 1 peppercorn
> 1/2 cup frozen unsweetened apple juice concentrate, undiluted, thawed
> 2 tablespoons apple cider vinegar

Put the prunes in a medium saucepan with water to cover. Add the lemon zest, lemon juice, and mace. Tie the cloves, allspice, and peppercorn in a cheesecloth bag and add this to the prune mixture. Cook, uncovered, over moderate heat for 10 minutes.

Stir in the apple juice concentrate and cook over low heat until the prunes are mushy and the mixture syrupy, about 20 minutes. Stir in the vinegar and cook for 5 minutes more. Remove the spice bag. Keeps for weeks tightly covered in the refrigerator.

Serve with poultry or meat.

Makes 1 1/2 cups

2 TABLESPOONS CONTAIN APPROXIMATELY:
65 TOTAL CALORIES / N CALORIES IN FAT
0 MG CHOLESTEROL / 60 MG SODIUM / 15 MG CALCIUM

EASY STRAWBERRY JAM

This recipe is truly so easy and yet so delicious that I did not want to leave it out of the book. However, I really couldn't decide what section it belonged in because even though I use it as an ingredient for Strawberry-Yogurt Parfait (page 227), it is also a wonderful sauce with poultry, as well as a spread on toast, pancakes, and waffles for breakfast. For this reason it has ended up here along with Apple Butter (following recipe), which is also rather difficult to categorize.

> *1 cup thawed frozen unsweetened strawberries (1 1/2 cups un-*
> *thawed)*
> *1 tablespoon fructose or 1 1/2 tablespoons sugar*

Combine the strawberries and the fructose or sugar and mix well. It will keep 3 to 4 days in the refrigerator or can be frozen.

Makes 1 cup

1/4 CUP CONTAINS APPROXIMATELY: 25 TOTAL CALORIES
N CALORIES IN FAT / 0 MG CHOLESTEROL / 1 MG SODIUM
5 MG CALCIUM

APPLE BUTTER

This is the recipe I use most frequently myself—I have it with Light Cheese (page 52) on my toast almost every morning for breakfast. It is also an ingredient in another of my favorite recipes, Our Famous Sugar-Free Bran Muffins (page 215), which calls for 1 cup of Apple Butter for a dozen muffins. Try this recipe for breakfast and I can almost guarantee your instant conversion to a healthy breakfast condiment for the whole family. It is even good with yogurt or ice cream as a dessert.

> *1/4 pound dried unsulfured sliced apples (2 cups)*
> *1 teaspoon ground cinnamon*
> *1/2 teaspoon ground allspice*
> *1/8 teaspoon ground cloves*
> *2 cups unsweetened apple juice*

Combine all the ingredients in a large saucepan and bring to a boil. Reduce the heat and simmer, covered, for 20 minutes, stirring occasionally. Remove from the heat and cool slightly.

Pour into a blender container and blend until smooth. Cool to room temperature and refrigerate in a tightly covered container. It will keep for months.

Makes 2 cups

2 TABLESPOONS CONTAIN APPROXIMATELY:
35 TOTAL CALORIES / N CALORIES IN FAT
0 MG CHOLESTEROL / 5 MG SODIUM / 10 MG CALCIUM

APPLE CHUTNEY

This chutney is fabulous, easy to make, and keeps for months. It can also be canned, using the classic sterilization procedures, and kept for years. It is free of preservatives and contains less sugar than commercial chutneys. It is also much less expensive. I like to serve it with any curried dish, and it is an ingredient of the Curried Chutney Dressing (page 77).

> *4 cups dried unsulfured apples, diced*
> *1 cup dried figs, finely diced*
> *1 cup golden raisins, finely diced*
> *1 medium onion, finely chopped (1½ cups)*
> *1½ cups fructose or 2 cups sugar*
> *1¼ teaspoons ground ginger*
> *¼ cup pickling spice, tied in a cheesecloth bag*
> *2 cups water*
> *2 cups apple cider vinegar*

Combine all the ingredients in a large saucepan and bring to a boil. Reduce the heat and simmer slowly, uncovered, for 2 hours.

Cool to room temperature. Remove and discard the cheesecloth bag containing the spices. Refrigerate the chutney in a tightly covered container. It will keep for months.

Makes 4¾ cups

¼ CUP CONTAINS APPROXIMATELY: 175 TOTAL CALORIES
N CALORIES IN FAT / 0 MG CHOLESTEROL / 10 MG SODIUM
25 MG CALCIUM

JALAPEÑO CHUTNEY

Like Apple Chutney (preceding recipe), Jalapeño Chutney can be
canned or just covered tightly and stored in the refrigerator. It
keeps for months. It is an ingredient in Southwestern Pasta Salad
(page 93) and Pasta Salad with Seafood (page 94). It is also a good
sauce on fish, poultry, or meat.

> *1 cup water*
> *2 cups apple cider vinegar*
> *3 medium tomatoes, chopped (2 cups)*
> *6 tomatillos, chopped (1½ cups)*
> *¾ cup fructose or 1 cup sugar*
> *1 medium onion, chopped (1½ cups)*
> *½ cup canned green California chilies, seeded and chopped*
> *1 cup golden raisins*
> *½ cup chopped fresh cilantro*
> *2 fresh jalapeño peppers, seeded and chopped (¼ cup)*
> *1 teaspoon ground cumin*

Combine all the ingredients in a large saucepan and simmer, uncovered, for 3 hours.

Cool to room temperature, then refrigerate in a tightly covered
container. It will keep for months.

Makes 4 cups

2 TABLESPOONS CONTAIN APPROXIMATELY:
50 TOTAL CALORIES / N CALORIES IN FAT
0 MG CHOLESTEROL / 20 MG SODIUM / 10 MG CALCIUM

BARBECUE SAUCE

This recipe can be used both as a marinade prior to grilling and as a sauce in which to cook poultry or meat. One of the favorite dishes of guests at the Canyon Ranch Spa in Tucson is the barbecued chicken that is cooked in this sauce. The chicken is baked in a 350°F oven for 15 minutes, then removed, skinned, and put back in the pan, topped with barbecue sauce. It is then baked, covered, for another 20 minutes and is absolutely delicious served with corn on the cob and a fresh green vegetable. This sauce is also good as a spread for sandwiches and as a dip for hot grilled vegetables.

1 medium onion, finely chopped (1 1/2 cups)
2 tablespoons water
1/2 cup tomato sauce
1/2 teaspoon lemon zest, grated
2 tablespoons freshly squeezed lemon juice
1 1/2 tablespoons Worcestershire sauce
1 tablespoon apple cider vinegar
3/4 teaspoon dry mustard
1/8 teaspoon salt
6 tablespoons frozen unsweetened apple juice concentrate
1/4 teaspoon Liquid Smoke

Combine the onions and water in a small saucepan and cook about 10 minutes until the onions are soft and translucent. Add all the other ingredients except for the Liquid Smoke. Mix well and bring to a boil. Reduce the heat to medium and cook, uncovered, until thick, about 30 minutes.

Remove from the heat, add the Liquid Smoke, and mix well. Pour into a blender container and blend until smooth.

Cool to room temperature, then refrigerate in a tightly covered container.

Makes 1 1/2 cups

1/4 CUP CONTAINS APPROXIMATELY: 55 TOTAL CALORIES
N CALORIES IN FAT / 0 MG CHOLESTEROL / 60 MG SODIUM
20 MG CALCIUM

LEMON BARBECUE SAUCE

This is an especially good marinade for chicken prior to barbecuing. Marinate for several hours, then barbecue over low coals for 25 to 30 minutes or until done, turning frequently and basting occasionally with the rest of the sauce.

> *1 garlic clove, minced (1 teaspoon)*
> *1/2 teaspoon salt*
> *2 tablespoons extra-virgin olive oil*
> *2 tablespoons defatted chicken stock (see page 22)*
> *1/2 cup freshly squeezed lemon juice*
> *2 tablespoons grated onion*
> *1/2 teaspoon freshly ground black pepper*
> *1/2 teaspoon dried thyme, crushed in a mortar and pestle*

Combine the garlic, salt, and oil in a small bowl. Stir in the remaining ingredients and chill for 24 hours.

Makes 3/4 cup

THE ENTIRE RECIPE CONTAINS APPROXIMATELY:
290 TOTAL CALORIES / 245 CALORIES IN FAT
0 MG CHOLESTEROL / 1115 MG SODIUM / 45 MG CALCIUM

CRANBERRY CATSUP

What else would you serve with a turkey burger? I served this during the Christmas season last year at the Four Seasons Hotel and Resort in Dallas and it was a big hit. Cranberry Catsup is also a good condiment served with any kind of poultry and a wonderful spread on cold turkey sandwiches as well as hot turkey burgers. I made it for Christmas gifts this past year, and many of my friends asked for more. Instead of refills I am sending them recipes!

1/2 pound raw cranberries
1/2 cup chopped onion
1/4 cup water
1/4 cup frozen unsweetened apple juice concentrate, undiluted
1/4 cup white vinegar
1/8 teaspoon ground cloves
1/2 teaspoon ground cinnamon
1/2 teaspoon ground allspice
1/2 teaspoon salt
1/8 teaspoon white pepper

Place the cranberries and onions in a small saucepan with the water and cook until tender. Stir every few minutes to keep it from burning. Pour into a food processor with a metal blade and blend until smooth.

Place the mixture back in the saucepan and add the remaining ingredients. Cook until thick, stirring while cooking, approximately 10 minutes.

Makes 1 1/4 cups

2 TABLESPOONS CONTAIN APPROXIMATELY:
25 TOTAL CALORIES / N CALORIES IN FAT
0 MG CHOLESTEROL / 140 MG SODIUM / 10 MG CALCIUM

VEGETABLE SAUCE

As I mentioned in the introduction, vegetable sauces are the most nutritious and lowest in calories of all sauces. Fortunately they are also tasty and beautiful and can be very elegant. I like brightly colored vegetable sauces, such as beet, carrot, broccoli, and spinach. (If you are using spinach, remove the fibrous central veins *before* you chop and measure it.) When using them as presentation sauces, I sometimes pour them on the plate as a liner for the entire bottom of the plate and then place the entrée items on top of the sauce, using the sauce as a colorful background or frame for the other items being served. Sometimes I make the sauces thicker by adding less vegetable stock and pipe more than one color sauce out of pastry tubes over the other items on the plate like a painting. Leftover vegetable sauces can be thinned a bit with additional stock and make wonderful soups.

> *1½ cups peeled and chopped colorful vegetables*
> *½ White Rose potato, peeled and diced (½ cup)*
> *½ medium onion, chopped (¾ cup)*
> *1 tablespoon chopped shallots*
> *½ teaspoon freshly squeezed lemon juice*
> *⅛ teaspoon salt*
> *Dash freshly ground black pepper*
> *Vegetable stock to cover (see page 27)*

Combine all the ingredients in a medium saucepan and bring to a boil. Reduce the heat and simmer for 30 minutes. Cool slightly.

Pour all the ingredients into a blender container and blend until satin smooth. If the sauce is too thick, add a little more vegetable stock. Season as desired.

Makes about 1½ cups

¼ CUP CONTAINS APPROXIMATELY: 30 TOTAL CALORIES
N CALORIES IN FAT / 0 MG CHOLESTEROL / 60 MG SODIUM
15 MG CALCIUM

VARIATION:

Beet Sauce: To keep Beet Sauce from tasting bitter, first cut the stems off the beets and wash them well. Then place them in a saucepan and cover with cold water. Bring to a boil, reduce the heat, and simmer for 20 minutes. Drain. Peel and chop the beets and proceed with the recipe.

MAYO-NOT

Mayonnaise it is NOT! But it is a wonderful dairy-free, cholesterol-free, low-calorie substitute that works well in recipes calling for mayonnaise. It is not good as a substitute spread on bread because the oil content is so low, but it is a good dairy-free base for sauces calling for sour cream or cottage cheese, and it is of great value to people on nondairy diets.

> *1/2 pound tofu, cubed (1 cup)*
> *1 tablespoon canola or corn oil*
> *1 tablespoon freshly squeezed lemon juice*
> *1/2 teaspoon salt*

Place all the ingredients in a blender container and blend until smooth. Refrigerate in a tightly covered container. It will keep 1 week.

Makes 1 cup

¼ CUP CONTAINS APPROXIMATELY: 75 TOTAL CALORIES
54 CALORIES IN FAT / 0 MG CHOLESTEROL
300 MG SODIUM / 60 MG CALCIUM

VARIATIONS:

Horseradish Sauce: Add 2 teaspoons prepared horseradish, 1½ teaspoons Worcestershire sauce, ½ teaspoon garlic powder, and dash Tabasco.

Vanilla/Cinnamon Sauce: Add 4 teaspoons fructose or 2 tablespoons sugar, 1½ teaspoons vanilla extract, and ½ teaspoon ground cinnamon.

ROASTED RED PEPPER SAUCE

This brilliantly colored, spicy sauce makes a beautiful presentation sauce for, and is an ingredient in, the Vegetable Terrine (page 112).

5 large red peppers
1 tablespoon apple cider vinegar
1 tablespoon extra-virgin olive oil
1/2 teaspoon salt

Broil the peppers until blackened on all sides, turning frequently. Place the peppers in a plastic bag for 25 to 30 minutes (this makes them easier to peel). Peel, core, and seed the peppers.

Combine all the ingredients in a blender container and blend until smooth.

Makes 1 1/2 cups

1/4 CUP CONTAINS APPROXIMATELY: 35 TOTAL CALORIES
25 CALORIES IN FAT / 0 MG CHOLESTEROL
165 MG SODIUM / 5 MG CALCIUM

WALNUT-DILL SAUCE

This is an excellent nondairy cream sauce made with tofu. It is an ingredient in my recipe for Poached Salmon (page 157). In this recipe I combine the sauce with toasted walnuts, which offers a wonderful balance in texture with the smooth creaminess of the sauce, and I suggest either plating the sauce under the salmon or spooning it over the top and garnishing it with sprigs of fresh dill. This presentation would work with other seafood, including water-packed tuna or poultry. I also serve this sauce on a vegetarian plate at the Four Seasons Hotel and Resort in Dallas.

1/2 pound tofu (1 cup)
1/2 teaspoon salt
1/2 teaspoon dried dillweed, crushed in a mortar and pestle
1/4 teaspoon dried tarragon, crushed in a mortar and pestle
1/4 cup water
2 teaspoons white vinegar
1 tablespoon freshly squeezed lemon juice
1 tablespoon walnut oil
1/8 cup tightly packed fresh dill

Combine all the ingredients in a blender container and blend until satin smooth. Refrigerate in a tightly covered container.

Makes 1 1/4 cups

1/4 CUP CONTAINS APPROXIMATELY: 60 TOTAL CALORIES
45 CALORIES IN FAT / 0 MG CHOLESTEROL
210 MG SODIUM / 65 MG CALCIUM

CREAMY CURRY SAUCE AND DRESSING

When I was developing a creamy dressing for the Canyon Ranch Spa in Tucson, the dietitian asked me if I could make it nondairy as well as creamy because we have so many guests with dairy allergies that it would be nice to have a creamy dressing that all the guests could enjoy. Since curry is always a very popular flavor range, I created this Creamy Curry Sauce and Dressing using tofu as the base. The Canyon Ranch guests love it, and I hope you will too.

1/2 pound tofu, cubed (1 cup)
1/4 cup water
1/2 teaspoon salt
3/4 teaspoon fructose or 1 teaspoon sugar
3/4 teaspoon curry powder
1/8 teaspoon ground ginger

1 tablespoon freshly squeezed lemon juice
1 tablespoon canola or corn oil

Combine all the ingredients in a blender container and blend until smooth. Refrigerate in a tightly covered container.

Makes 1 1/4 cups

2 TABLESPOONS CONTAIN APPROXIMATELY:
35 TOTAL CALORIES / 20 CALORIES IN FAT
0 MG CHOLESTEROL / 120 MG SODIUM
50 MG CALCIUM

JEANNE JONES' LIGHT DRESSING

This is my own signature dressing, which I mentioned in the introduction to this section. I have used it on menus at the restaurant at Neiman-Marcus in Newport Beach, California, all of the Four Seasons hotels, and the Canyon Ranch Spa in Tucson. It is also the dressing I keep in my own refrigerator. I make the basic dressing in large quantities and then add the variations to it as I need them. Further variations are possible within the four categories I have given you by changing the type of vinegar used in the recipe and adding 1 tablespoon of oil per cup of dressing for additional flavor. For example, by using raspberry vinegar and adding walnut oil (Raspberry-Walnut Vinaigrette Dressing, page 72), the entire personality of the dressing changes, and the oil adds only about 8 calories per tablespoon. Remember, however, when using any oil in your salad dressing, it must be mixed thoroughly before serving because it all rises to the top. Also remember when using any oil for flavor to make every calorie count by using the most flavorful oil available; for example, if you wish to add olive oil to your Italian Dressing, use extra-virgin olive oil so you can really taste the small amount you are using. For a creamy-type dressing, add plain nonfat yogurt, Light Cheese (page 52), low-fat cottage cheese, or tofu and blend until smooth.

½ cup red wine vinegar
¼ teaspoon freshly ground black pepper
½ teaspoon salt
1 tablespoon fructose or 4 teaspoons sugar
2 garlic cloves, finely chopped (2 teaspoons)
2 teaspoons Worcestershire sauce
1 tablespoon Dijon-style mustard
2 tablespoons freshly squeezed lemon juice
1 cup water

Combine all the ingredients and mix well. Refrigerate in a container with a tight-fitting lid. It will keep for months.

Makes 2 cups

2 TABLESPOONS CONTAIN APPROXIMATELY:
5 TOTAL CALORIES / 0 CALORIES IN FAT
0 MG CHOLESTEROL / 85 MG SODIUM / 10 MG CALCIUM

VARIATIONS:

Italian: Add 1 teaspoon each of crushed dried tarragon, oregano, and basil.
Cumin: Add ½ teaspoon ground cumin.
Curry: Add 1 teaspoon curry powder.
Tarragon: Add 1 tablespoon crushed dried tarragon.

RASPBERRY-WALNUT VINAIGRETTE DRESSING

½ cup raspberry vinegar
¼ teaspoon salt
¼ teaspoon freshly ground black pepper
1 tablespoon fructose or 4 teaspoons sugar
2 garlic cloves, finely chopped (2 teaspoons)
2 teaspoons Worcestershire sauce
1 tablespoon Dijon-style mustard

1 tablespoon freshly squeezed lemon juice
2 teaspoons dried tarragon, crushed in a mortar and pestle
1 cup water
2 tablespoons walnut oil

Combine the vinegar and salt and mix until the salt is thoroughly dissolved. Add all the other ingredients and mix well. Refrigerate in a tightly covered container. ALWAYS MIX WELL BEFORE USING.

Makes 2 cups

2 TABLESPOONS CONTAIN APPROXIMATELY:
20 TOTAL CALORIES / 15 CALORIES IN FAT
0 MG CHOLESTEROL / 55 MG SODIUM / 5 MG CALCIUM

POPPY SEED DRESSING

1/2 pound tofu (1 cup)
1/4 cup frozen unsweetened apple juice concentrate, undiluted
1/4 teaspoon salt
1 1/2 teaspoons dry mustard
2 tablespoons reduced-calorie mayonnaise
1/2 cup rice wine vinegar
1/2 medium onion, chopped (3/4 cup)
1 1/2 cups chopped orange
4 teaspoons poppy seeds

Combine all the ingredients except for the poppy seeds in a blender container and blend until smooth. Pour into a bowl. Add the poppy seeds and mix well. Refrigerate in a tightly covered container.

Makes 3 cups

2 TABLESPOONS CONTAIN APPROXIMATELY: 25 CALORIES
10 CALORIES IN FAT / 0 MG CHOLESTEROL / 40 MG SODIUM
30 MG CALCIUM

CAPER DRESSING

1/4 cup rice wine vinegar or champagne wine
1/2 teaspoon salt
1/8 teaspoon freshly ground black pepper
1 shallot, finely chopped (1 tablespoon)
1 tablespoon minced capers
1 teaspoon Dijon-style mustard
1/2 cup water
2 tablespoons canola or corn oil

Combine the vinegar or wine and salt and mix until the salt is completely dissolved. Add all the other ingredients except the oil and mix well. Whisk the mixture constantly while adding the oil.

Refrigerate in a tightly covered container. MIX THOROUGHLY BEFORE EACH USE.

Makes 1 cup

2 TABLESPOONS CONTAIN APPROXIMATELY:
35 TOTAL CALORIES / 30 CALORIES IN FAT
0 MG CHOLESTEROL / 230 MG SODIUM / 5 MG CALCIUM

MANDARIN DRESSING AND MARINADE

This dressing and marinade is used for two of the most popular recipes in this book—as a salad dressing on the Chinese Chicken Salad (page 97) and to cook the prawns for Polynesian Prawns (page 152). It also works perfectly for wok cooking and adds enormously to the flavor of stir-fries of all types.

1/2 cup rice wine vinegar
3 tablespoons dark sesame oil
1 tablespoon reduced-sodium soy sauce
One 6-ounce can (3/4 cup) frozen unsweetened pineapple juice
  concentrate, undiluted
2 teaspoons chopped peeled ginger
1 garlic clove, chopped (1 teaspoon)
1/8 teaspoon crushed red pepper flakes

Combine all the ingredients in a blender container and mix well. Refrigerate in a tightly covered container. MIX WELL BEFORE EACH USE.

Makes 1 1/2 cups

2 TABLESPOONS CONTAIN APPROXIMATELY:
65 TOTAL CALORIES / 30 CALORIES IN FAT
0 MG CHOLESTEROL / 85 MG SODIUM / 10 MG CALCIUM

LIGHT RANCH DRESSING

This is a recipe I developed in answer to a letter from one of my readers, who wanted a ranch dressing mix that was lower in sodium and without preservatives and that she could make herself. After lots of experimenting, I finally came up with a mix I really like. In fact, in my column I suggested that it be made in large quantities and put in little jars for hostess gifts along with the recipe for making the dressing. This dressing is also a good sauce for cooked vegetables, and I like it very much on fish and seafood.

RANCH DRESSING MIX:

1/4 cup dried parsley
3 tablespoons dried minced onion
2 teaspoons dried chives
1 teaspoon salt
1/2 teaspoon garlic powder
1/2 teaspoon ground celery seed
1/4 teaspoon black pepper

1/4 cup reduced-calorie mayonnaise
3/4 cup buttermilk

Combine the dressing mix ingredients in a small jar and mix well. Store in a dry place (makes ½ cup of mix).

Combine 1 tablespoon of the dressing mix with the mayonnaise in a bowl and mix thoroughly using a wire whisk. Add the buttermilk slowly, stirring constantly until well mixed. Refrigerate in a tightly covered container.

Makes 1 cup

2 TABLESPOONS CONTAIN APPROXIMATELY:
20 TOTAL CALORIES / 10 CALORIES IN FAT
1 MG CHOLESTEROL / 50 MG SODIUM / 30 MG CALCIUM

BLEU CHEESE DRESSING

This is my own favorite recipe for bleu cheese dressing. Fortunately it is also lower in calories, cholesterol, and sodium than any other bleu cheese dressing I have ever liked. If you prefer Roquefort, Gorgonzola, or Stilton to bleu cheese, just substitute the same amount.

1/2 cup reduced-calorie mayonnaise
1 cup buttermilk
1 garlic clove, very finely chopped (1 teaspoon)
2 ounces bleu cheese, crumbled (1/2 cup)
1/4 cup low-fat cottage cheese

Combine all the ingredients except the cottage cheese in a bowl and mix thoroughly with a wire whisk. Stir in the cottage cheese. Refrigerate in a tightly covered container. It will keep 1 week.

Makes 2 scant cups

2 TABLESPOONS CONTAIN APPROXIMATELY:
35 TOTAL CALORIES / 20 CALORIES IN FAT
5 MG CHOLESTEROL / 95 MG SODIUM / 45 MG CALCIUM

CURRIED CHUTNEY DRESSING

1/3 cup reduced-calorie mayonnaise
1/3 cup plain nonfat yogurt
1 1/2 teaspoons curry powder
1 tablespoon fructose or 4 teaspoons sugar
1/8 teaspoon crushed red pepper flakes
Dash freshly ground black pepper
1/2 garlic clove, finely chopped (1/2 teaspoon)
1 shallot, finely chopped (1 tablespoon)
1/8 teaspoon Worcestershire sauce
1/4 teaspoon freshly squeezed lemon juice
1 1/2 teaspoons reduced-sodium soy sauce
1 tablespoon red wine vinegar
1/4 cup Apple Chutney (page 62)

Combine all the ingredients except the Apple Chutney in a blender container and blend until smooth. Pour in a bowl, add the chutney, and mix well.

Refrigerate in a tightly covered container.

Makes 1 cup

2 TABLESPOONS CONTAIN APPROXIMATELY:
50 TOTAL CALORIES / 15 CALORIES IN FAT
0 MG CHOLESTEROL / 85 MG SODIUM / 20 MG CALCIUM

THOUSAND ISLAND DRESSING

This is the dressing I use on the famous Ranch Burger at the Canyon Ranch Spa in Tucson. On our All-American Day I serve the Ranch Burger with Oven Fries (page 122) (no fat) and Coleslaw (page 86) and Carob-Yogurt Sundae (page 227) for dessert, and it is one of the most popular lunches with all the guests.

> 1 cup reduced-calorie mayonnaise
> 1/2 cup chili sauce
> 1/4 cup sweet relish
> 2 tablespoons white vinegar
> 1/4 teaspoon salt
> 1/4 teaspoon fructose or 1/2 teaspoon sugar
> Dash white pepper
> 1 tablespoon freshly squeezed lemon juice

Combine all the ingredients and mix well. Refrigerate in a tightly covered container.

Makes 2 scant cups

2 TABLESPOONS CONTAIN APPROXIMATELY:
35 TOTAL CALORIES / 20 CALORIES IN FAT
0 MG CHOLESTEROL / 80 MG SODIUM / 5 MG CALCIUM

SALADS

IN THE BEGINNING, salads consisted only of a few edible plants and herbs sprinkled with a bit of salt. In fact the word *salad* actually comes from the word *salt*. This is an amazing fact in today's fitness-conscious society where salad is considered the epitome of good nutrition and salt is decidedly on the other end of the spectrum.

What makes this original concept of salads seem even more strange to me is that it is the salt that wilts the greens when a salad is dressed too soon before serving. The advantage of a salt-free dressing is that you can literally dress the greens hours before serving and still have them crisp and attractive in appearance when they are presented.

The widely held notion that salads are somehow low in calories is indeed a myth in itself. Today salads do not only include leafy raw vegetables and herbs; literally anything you can eat can be an ingredient in a salad. Because of this a salad offers enormous variety in meal planning. It can be a small, almost calorie-free side dish, an appetizer such as a cold jelled terrine or marinated celery root or artichoke hearts, the entrée course, or an entire meal in itself.

At what point during the meal the salad is served has a great deal to do with geographical location. Californians routinely serve salad as a first course; it is often waiting for you at the table when you are seated to a meal. New Yorkers are more likely to serve a small salad on the side with the entrée. And the French prefer the salad after the entrée.

When preparing salad greens it is important to wash and dry them thoroughly before storing them in bags or wrapping them in towels in the refrigerator. Wet salad greens dilute the dressing, and therefore you will be inclined to use more dressing on the salad. The thorough washing of the greens is one of the single most important steps in salad preparation. Nothing is worse than to be served a "gritty" salad; it can even be dangerous. I know several people who have broken teeth biting down on a small rock in an innocent-looking salad.

Cold steamed vegetables can also be marinated for an antipasto salad with an Italian meal or served for hors d'oeuvres with any type of meal. When I prepare cold marinated vegetables, I use one of my oil-free dressings (in the Sauces & Dressings section), so they are very low in calories. Also, if serving them as finger food, they don't leave you with greasy hands. When marinating vegetables, marinate all but the green vegetables (broccoli, snow peas, asparagus, and so on); add them to the mixture just before serving because green vegetables lose their color in the marinade.

My favorite light salad, which can be served either as a first-course salad or after the entrée with equal integrity, is a Salad of young greens with Raspberry-Walnut Vinaigrette Dressing (page 72). Since all salad greens grow from the inside out, young greens are the hearts or centers of lettuce heads as well as the young tender leaves on sprigs of greens such as watercress and arugula. When serving this salad after the meal, you might want to add a small wedge of warm cheese and sprinkle it with a few toasted nuts. In fact, I am so fond of toasted nuts and seeds on salads that I think it was because of them that I was first motivated to create a completely fat-free salad dressing so I could better afford the calories of the nuts and seeds.

Always buy nuts and seeds raw and toast them yourself. The commercially toasted or roasted varieties contain oil and often salt and preservatives. Even though many nuts such as walnuts, almonds, and pine nuts can be eaten without toasting them, they don't have nearly as much flavor, and since nuts and seeds have approximately 50 calories per tablespoon, you want to get as much taste per calorie as possible.

Keep your raw nuts and seeds in the refrigerator so the oils in them won't turn rancid and the bugs won't attack them. Then toast them as you need them so they are always crisp and have that wonderful toasted taste. The only exception is for peanuts; I buy the dry-roasted unsalted variety because raw peanuts take so long to toast.

Toasting nuts and seeds is easy. Place them in a preheated 350°F oven for 8 to 10 minutes or until golden brown. Watch them carefully because they burn easily.

When preparing spinach, it is necessary to fill the sink or a large tub or bowl with water and submerge the spinach completely, tearing off one leaf at a time in order to make certain that all the sandy dirt is removed. During the rainy season it is often necessary to wash lettuce and cabbage in the same manner because they tend to be caked with sand and dirt that cannot be removed any other way. With spinach it is also necessary to remove the stems and large veins that run down the backs of the leaves to take the bitter taste out of it. If you don't like spinach or spinach salad because of a slightly bitter aftertaste, you may find you have discovered a whole new vegetable when you eat it with the stems and veins removed. If you have ever wondered why spinach salads are always more expensive on menus than lettuce when spinach is less expensive to buy at your supermarket, it is because it takes so long to prepare it properly, and the cost of labor has to be added to the price.

Today salads can be served at any temperature or combination of temperatures. In fact my own favorite salad in this section is the Breast of Chicken Salad with Goat Cheese and Warm Mushroom Dressing (page 99), which is a delightful combination of tastes, temperatures, and textures to which a salad lends itself better than any other menu category. When serving cold salads, always chill the salad plates briefly in the freezer.

Another warm salad I particularly like is a grilled vegetable salad. It is easy to make and a wonderful way to use up leftover vegetables. You can either start with raw vegetables or use blanched vegetables. I prefer to use blanched vegetables because they don't require as much cooking time since they are already partially cooked and therefore don't dry out as much when cooking over a grill or under a broiler. I like to serve skewers of grilled vegetables plated on a creamy tofu or vegetable sauce as an appetizer or salad course. Skewered grilled vegetables are also a nice accompaniment to grilled fish, poultry, or meat.

Never put nuts or seeds on a salad or any other dish until you are ready to serve it. Otherwise the moisture will soften them and you won't get the delightful crunchiness that so enhances the texture of any dish.

There is no question that salads are my favorite food category; I almost always have a salad for lunch. For that reason I have included many different types of entrée salads in this section. Never make the mistake of thinking that just because you're having a salad you're having a low-calorie lunch. One of the most popular salads on most menus is the chef's salad, routinely prepared with lettuce, tomatoes, hard-cooked eggs, and various kinds of meat and cheeses and often served with a heavy Roquefort or bleu cheese dressing. This benign-looking bowl of salad can easily contain 2000 calories; after all, the cheeses are each approximately 100 calories per ounce and the salad dressing is over 100 calories per tablespoon. Along with the calories in the salad are hundreds of milligrams of cholesterol and sodium. In other words, the salad of choice for a healthy life-style is not a chef's salad with Roquefort or bleu cheese dressing!

Salads offer a wonderful way to use leftovers. The next time you're planning a meal, go through the refrigerator to see what you have on hand that needs to be used and then look through my salad dressings to find just the right dressing for your "Clean the Refrigerator Salad." You will be surprised at just how good some of these impromptu improvisations can be.

SALAD GREENS GLOSSARY

ARUGULA: Sprigs of dark green leaves with a strong nutlike flavor. It combines well with mild-flavored lettuces or with equally intensely flavored greens, such as watercress.

BELGIAN ENDIVE (French endive, Witloof): Six- to 8-inch heads of crisp-tender yellow-white leaves with a green tinge. Delicately bitter flavor. Use whole or in bite-size pieces of julienne cut. Mixes well with other greens. Expensive but little waste.

BIBB LETTUCE (Limestone): Small, cup-shaped leaves held together loosely. Dark green crisp-tender leaves are succulent; considered by some to be the aristocrat of lettuces. The whole leaves are ideal "bowls" for salad mixtures. Mixes well with other greens.

BOSTON LETTUCE (Butterhead): Soft, small head with delicate leaves. Outer leaves are green and inner are light yellow and buttery. Mixes well with other greens.

CHICORY (American or Curly Endive): Yellow-white stem with curly, fringed tendrils. Somewhat bitter taste. The outer leaves are darker and stronger flavored than the inner. A prickly texture to add to tossed salad. An attractive garnish.

CHINESE CELERY CABBAGE: Celery-colored, white-ribbed leaves in a tightly packed head. Serve alone, as a base for salad mixtures, or mix with other greens. The flavor is between celery and cabbage, as the name implies.

DANDELION GREENS: The wild variety is available in most places and is also especially grown for salads. The youngest leaves are the most tender. Slightly bitter.

ESCAROLE (Batavian Endive): The leaves are less curly and broader than endive and are a paler green; they should snap easily. Combine with other greens.

FENNEL (Anise): The stalks are similar to celery and grow from a bulbous root with lacy, fernlike leaves. The licoricelike flavor is more intense in the leaves, which are usually used as an herb. Substitute for celery in stuffings and casseroles. Slices of the bulb provide a uniquely different taste in salads.

FIDDLEHEAD: A fern often said to taste like asparagus, it is best in early spring when very young. Grows along stream banks.

FIELD LETTUCE (Lamb's Lettuce, Corn Salad, Mâché): Small, smooth green leaves in a loosely formed head. Tangy flavor. Good for tossed salads or as cooked greens.

ICEBERG LETTUCE (Crisphead Lettuce): Large, compact heads with crisp leaves tightly packed. The outer leaves are a medium green and the inner leaves are a paler green. Slice, shred, or tear to add crunch to any salad. Longer shelf life than most lettuces.

ITALIAN PARSLEY: The sprigs have a flat, broad leaf rather than the tight, curly leaf of regular parsley, with a slightly milder flavor. A good garnish for Italian dishes.

LEAF LETTUCE: Loose, smooth leaves growing from a central stalk. Green or red-tipped. The curly leaves make a good undergarnish for molded salads or fruit or vegetable arrangements.

MINT: Usually considered an herb, but important as a salad green in the Middle East, where it is an essential ingredient for the classic salad, tabbouleh.

NAPA CABBAGE: Similar to Chinese celery cabbage, but the head is shorter and the base broader. Use for the same purposes, alone or with other greens.

NASTURTIUM FLOWERS AND LEAVES: The leaves, stems, and flowers are all edible and interesting additions to salads. The leaves and stems have a pungent, peppery flavor. The flowers have a milder flavor and are a wonderful edible garniture.

PARSLEY: Dark green sprigs of tightly crimped leaves with a strong, refreshing flavor. Usually thought of as a garnish, parsley is good in soups and for flavoring stocks. It is also good in salads of all types.

RADICCHIO: Small, cabbage-type head with red leaves. Flavor slightly bitter. Use as a garnish or mix with other greens to provide color and a different taste to a salad.

ROMAINE LETTUCE (Cos Lettuce): An elongated head of loose dark green leaves that are firm and crisp. The pungent flavor adds tang to salads. Classically used for Caesar Salad.

SORREL: Many edible varieties, both cultivated and wild. The arrow-shaped green leaves have a sour, almost bitter taste; the very young leaves are best. Best mixed with milder greens. Most frequently used in soups and sauces.

WATERCRESS: Dark green glossy leaves, dime-size, on crisp sprigs. The leaves and the tender part of the stems are spicy and peppery. Good additions to tossed salads. Also often used as a garnish.

PARSLEY SALAD

This salad may take longer to prepare than any other salad in this section because the parsley must be thoroughly washed and thoroughly dried and then just the tips or curly parts of the parsley picked off for the salad one by one. There is no really fast way to do this and do it properly, but believe me, it is worth the time it takes because it is one of the best and most unusual salads you will ever taste. You can add drained water-packed tuna or diced cooked chicken or turkey and serve this as a luncheon or light supper entrée as well.

1/2 cup Light Tarragon Dressing (page 72)
1/2 teaspoon fructose or 3/4 teaspoon sugar
1/4 cup sun-dried tomatoes packed in olive oil, thoroughly drained and julienne cut
2 cups tightly packed parsley tips, stems removed (4 loosely packed cups)
1/4 pound imported Parmesan cheese, freshly grated (1/2 cup)

Combine the dressing and fructose or sugar and mix thoroughly.
Combine the sun-dried tomatoes, parsley, dressing, and half the Parmesan cheese and toss well. Place on four chilled plates and garnish each with a tablespoon of the remaining cheese.

Makes four 1-cup servings

EACH SERVING CONTAINS APPROXIMATELY:
160 TOTAL CALORIES / 80 CALORIES IN FAT
20 MG CHOLESTEROL / 640 MG SODIUM / 470 MG CALCIUM

SPINACH SALAD WITH TOASTED WALNUTS

I love spinach salad and I like spinach best with toasted walnuts. I had this as an entrée salad with shrimp on my menu at the restaurant at Neiman-Marcus in Newport Beach, California. It is also good with drained water-packed tuna or diced cooked chicken or turkey.

1/4 cup chopped walnuts
1 pound fresh spinach, deveined and torn into bite-size pieces (4 cups)
1/4 cup Raspberry-Walnut Vinaigrette Dressing (page 72)

Place the walnuts in a preheated 350°F oven for 8 to 10 minutes. Watch carefully, as they burn easily. Set aside.

Place 1 cup spinach on each of four chilled plates and spoon 1 tablespoon dressing over the top. Top with 1 tablespoon toasted walnuts.

Makes four 1-cup servings

EACH SERVING CONTAINS APPROXIMATELY:
70 TOTAL CALORIES / 50 CALORIES IN FAT
0 MG CHOLESTEROL / 70 MG SODIUM
65 MG CALCIUM

COLESLAW

This is a delightfully different coleslaw. I know many people who don't like regular coleslaw but are crazy about this recipe. It is wonderful to make in large quantities for backyard barbecues or picnics, and it goes well with any type food.

DRESSING:

> 1/4 cup reduced-calorie mayonnaise
> 1 1/2 tablespoons white vinegar
> 1 1/2 teaspoons Dijon-style mustard
> 1 1/2 teaspoons fructose or 2 teaspoons sugar
> 1/2 teaspoon caraway seeds
> 1/8 teaspoon salt
> Dash white pepper
>
> 6 ounces green cabbage, shredded (1 1/2 cups)
> 3 ounces red cabbage, shredded (3/4 cup)
> 1/2 cup peeled and grated carrots
> 1 small tart green apple, cored, peeled, and grated (3/4 cup)
> 1/4 cup finely chopped red onion

Combine the dressing ingredients and mix thoroughly.

Combine the dressing with all the other ingredients and again mix well. Chill for several hours before serving.

Makes four ¹/₂-cup servings

EACH SERVING CONTAINS APPROXIMATELY:
60 TOTAL CALORIES / 20 CALORIES IN FAT
0 MG CHOLESTEROL / 125 MG SODIUM
35 MG CALCIUM

CELERY ROOT SALAD

The most interesting thing about celery root is that it is not really celery root at all but the root of the celeriac plant. This root is delicious raw or cooked. In fact this recipe can be made with raw celery root as well as cooked as the recipe suggests. I like it best cooked and then chilled to serve as an appetizer.

1 small celery root, peeled and grated (1¹/₄ cups)
1 teaspoon freshly squeezed lemon juice
1¹/₂ tablespoons Dijon-style mustard
2 tablespoons water
1 tablespoon white vinegar
Dash freshly ground black pepper
¹/₄ teaspoon dried tarragon, crushed in a mortar and pestle
4 lettuce leaves to line plates
2 teaspoons chopped parsley
1 tablespoon finely chopped capers

Combine the celery root and lemon juice and steam over boiling water for 2 minutes. Rinse in cold water. Drain thoroughly and set aside.

In a small bowl, whisk the mustard, water, vinegar, pepper, and tarragon and blend well. Toss the dressing with the celery root. Cover and refrigerate for at least 2 hours.

To serve, place a lettuce leaf on each of four chilled plates. Spoon ½ cup of the celery root mixture on each plate. Top each serving with chopped parsley and a pinch of chopped capers.

Makes 4 servings

EACH SERVING CONTAINS APPROXIMATELY:
35 TOTAL CALORIES / 5 CALORIES IN FAT
0 MG CHOLESTEROL / 125 MG SODIUM
50 MG CALCIUM

POTATO SALAD

DRESSING:

½ cup plain nonfat yogurt
¼ cup reduced-calorie mayonnaise
2 tablespoons apple cider vinegar
½ teaspoon Dijon-style mustard
½ teaspoon prepared mustard

3 medium red potatoes, cooked, and diced (3 cups)
1 tablespoon finely chopped parsley
1½ celery ribs, without leaves, chopped (3/4 cup)
½ cups chopped scallions
¼ cup chopped green bell pepper
½ teaspoon celery seed
¼ teaspoon salt
¼ teaspoon freshly ground black pepper
¼ cup sweet pickle relish
2 hard-cooked egg whites, chopped (optional)

Combine the dressing ingredients and mix well. Set aside.

Combine all the salad ingredients and mix well. Fold the dressing into the potato mixture and refrigerate for several hours. Stir the salad before serving.

Makes four 1-cup servings

EACH SERVING CONTAINS APPROXIMATELY:
190 TOTAL CALORIES / 25 CALORIES IN FAT
1 MG CHOLESTEROL / 355 MG SODIUM
100 MG CALCIUM

WILD-RICE SALAD

I serve this salad as a vegetarian entrée at the Canyon Ranch Spa in Tucson; however, it is also good with water-packed tuna or diced cooked poultry or meat added to it. It is a wonderful portable meal for picnics and al fresco parties of all types. To steam vegetables, see page 106.

> *½ cup chopped walnuts*
> *1 medium onion, finely chopped and steamed (1½ cups)*
> *2 cups broccoli flowerettes, steamed*
> *¾ cup wild rice*
> *1½ cups water*
> *1 tablespoon reduced-sodium soy sauce*
> *1 teaspoon dried thyme, crushed in a mortar and pestle*
> *2 medium carrots, scraped and finely chopped (1 cup)*
> *2 celery ribs, without leaves, finely chopped (1 cup)*
> *½ cup Caper Dressing (page 74)*
> *Lettuce leaves for lining plates*
> *4 cups greens, torn into bite-size pieces (4 cups)*
> *4 sprigs fresh thyme for garnish*

Toast the walnuts in a preheated 350°F oven for 8 to 10 minutes. Watch them carefully, as they burn easily. Set aside. Steam the onion and broccoli and set aside.

Combine the wild rice, water, soy sauce, and thyme and bring to a boil. Reduce the heat and cook, covered, for about 30 to 35 minutes or until all the liquid has been absorbed and the rice is fluffy.

Allow to cool to room temperature and combine the steamed onions, chopped carrots, chopped celery, and the dressing and mix well. Refrigerate until cold before serving.

To serve, add the steamed broccoli (if the broccoli is added sooner, it will lose its color). Toss again thoroughly.

Line four chilled plates with lettuce leaves and cover each with 1 cup of greens. Place 2 cups of the wild-rice mixture over the top of the greens. Garnish with a sprig of fresh thyme. Top with 2 tablespoons of toasted walnuts.

Makes four 2-cup servings

EACH SERVING CONTAINS APPROXIMATELY:
300 TOTAL CALORIES / 115 CALORIES IN FAT
0 MG CHOLESTEROL / 545 MG SODIUM
90 MG CALCIUM

VEGETARIAN DELIGHT SALAD

This salad appears on many of my light-cuisine menus for spas, hotels, and restaurants. Besides being vegetarian, it is also extremely high in vitamins, minerals, and fiber and very low in calories. For those who always like to get as much nutrition as possible per calorie, this salad is a very popular entrée.

1/4 cup raw sunflower seeds
1 pound tofu, cubed (2 cups)
2 cups Light Tarragon Dressing (page 72)
6 cups lettuce and spinach, torn into bite-size pieces

6 *cups bite-size pieces vegetables—a colorful assortment, such as carrots, red and green bell peppers, tomatoes, zucchini, pea pods, mushrooms—steamed crisp-tender (see chart on page 106)*

5 1/2 *ounces part-skim mozzarella cheese, freshly grated (1 1/3 cups)*

16 *tomato slices, halved, for garnish*

Place the sunflower seeds in a preheated 350°F oven for 8 to 10 minutes or until golden brown. Watch carefully, as they burn easily. Set aside.

Cover the tofu with 1 1/2 cups of the Light Tarragon Dressing and allow to marinate for several hours. Drain, reserving dressing for the salad.

When ready to serve, place 1 1/2 cups lettuce and spinach on each of four chilled plates. Arrange 1 1/2 cups vegetables on top of the greens. Place 1/2 cup marinated tofu on top of the vegetables. Sprinkle 1/3 cup cheese and 1 tablespoon sunflower seeds over the top. Arrange the tomato slices around salads in a scallop pattern. Serve 1/2 cup of the remaining Light Tarragon Dressing on the side.

Makes 4 servings

EACH SERVING CONTAINS APPROXIMATELY:
400 TOTAL CALORIES / 195 CALORIES IN FAT
20 MG CHOLESTEROL / 645 MG SODIUM
570 MG CALCIUM

CURRIED WALDORF SALAD

If you like Waldorf Salad, you're going to *love* Curried Waldorf Salad. I served this salad for a holiday party and it was the hit of the menu. The next day I combined the leftover Curried Waldorf Salad with some leftover chopped turkey and it was a delicious luncheon salad.

14 raw almonds
3 celery ribs, without leaves, chopped (1½ cups)
2 red Delicious apples, cored and diced (1½ cups)
2 golden Delicious apples, cored and diced (1½ cups)
¼ cup chopped chives or scallion tops (½-inch pieces)
¼ cup dried currants
¼ cup reduced-calorie mayonnaise
¼ cup plain nonfat yogurt
1 teaspoon curry powder
⅛ teaspoon ground cumin
1 pinch each of:
    ground ginger
    ground cinnamon
    ground allspice
    ground cloves

Chop the almonds coarsely and toast them in a preheated 350°F oven for 8 to 10 minutes or until lightly browned. Watch carefully, as they burn easily. Set aside.

Combine the celery, apples, chives or scallion tops, and currants in a bowl. In a separate bowl, whisk together the mayonnaise, yogurt, curry powder, cumin, ginger, cinnamon, allspice, and cloves.

Add the dressing to the apple mixture and mix well.

Makes four 1-cup servings

EACH SERVING CONTAINS APPROXIMATELY:
165 TOTAL CALORIES / 65 CALORIES IN FAT
0 MG CHOLESTEROL / 70 MG SODIUM / 90 MG CALCIUM

CITRUS SALAD WITH POPPY SEED DRESSING

2 large oranges (3 cups sectioned)
1 small red onion, peeled and thinly sliced (1 cup)

¹/₂ cup Poppy Seed Dressing (page 73)
Green lettuce leaves for lining plates
4 mint sprigs for garnish

Peel the oranges and divide them into sections, removing the membranes and seeds. Separate the sliced onions into rings.

Arrange the orange sections and onion rings on four chilled plates that have been lined with the green lettuce leaves. Dribble 2 tablespoons of dressing over each salad. Garnish with a sprig of mint.

Makes 4 servings

EACH SERVING CONTAINS APPROXIMATELY:
85 TOTAL CALORIES / 5 CALORIES IN FAT
0 MG CHOLESTEROL / 20 MG SODIUM
75 MG CALCIUM

SOUTHWESTERN PASTA SALAD WITH JALAPEÑO CHUTNEY

Both vegetarian and pasta salads are increasingly popular on all menus, as are Southwestern dishes of all types. Therefore, this Southwestern vegetarian pasta salad has met with great success on the Four Seasons Hotel and Resort menu in Dallas. There it is served with Southwestern Corn Bread (page 205).

1/2 cup Jalapeño Chutney (page 63)
3/4 teaspoon ground cumin
3/4 teaspoon chili powder
1 1/2 teaspoons balsamic vinegar
1 3/4 cups dry rotelle pasta, cooked al dente
1 1/2 teaspoons extra-virgin olive oil
1/2 cup chopped scallions
1 large tomato, peeled, seeded, and diced (1 cup)
1 1/2 cups cooked canned or frozen corn kernels
1 small green bell pepper, seeded and diced (1/2 cup)
1 small red bell pepper, seeded and diced (1/2 cup)
2 chayote squash, peeled and diced (1 cup)
1/4 cup chopped fresh cilantro
2 ounces Monterey Jack cheese, grated (1/2 cup)

Combine the chutney, cumin, chili powder, and vinegar and mix well. Combine the pasta and oil and mix well. Combine both the mixtures and again mix well. Add all the other ingredients except the cheese and mix well.

Spoon 1 1/2 cups of salad on each of four chilled plates. Top each serving with 2 tablespoons of grated cheese.

Makes 4 servings

EACH SERVING CONTAINS APPROXIMATELY:
350 TOTAL CALORIES / 80 CALORIES IN FAT
40 MG CHOLESTEROL / 120 MG SODIUM
160 MG CALCIUM

PASTA SALAD WITH SEAFOOD

I have this salad on my light-cuisine menu at the famous Hotel del Coronado across the bridge from San Diego, California. I like the look of the pasta shells with the seafood salad. This salad is also good made with chicken or turkey and when using poultry, I use rotelle pasta because it absorbs the flavor of the marinade even better than the shells.

> *¹/₄ cup rice wine vinegar*
> *1 tablespoon extra-virgin olive oil*
> *1 cup Jalapeño Chutney (page 63)*
> *1 small bunch scallions, chopped (³/₄ cup)*
> *3 medium tomatoes, peeled, seeded, and diced (2 cups)*
> *¹/₂ pound dry medium-size pasta shells, cooked (4 cups)*
> *Green leaf lettuce leaves for lining plates*
> *8 ounces diced cooked shrimp or other seafood, such as crab, lobster, scallops, water-packed tuna, or a combination (2 cups)*
> *4 large whole shrimp, cooked and butterflied, for garnish (optional)*

Combine the vinegar, oil, and chutney and mix well. Add the scallions, 1½ cups of the tomatoes, and the pasta and again mix well. Chill overnight.

Line four plates with the green lettuce leaves. Combine pasta mixture and seafood and mix well. Place 1½ cups of the salad on each plate. Top each serving with a butterflied shrimp if desired. Sprinkle the top with the remaining diced tomato.

Makes 4 servings

EACH SERVING CONTAINS APPROXIMATELY:
465 TOTAL CALORIES / 60 CALORIES IN FAT
130 MG CHOLESTEROL / 180 MG SODIUM
110 MG CALCIUM

PITA POCKET SANDWICH WITH TOFU SALAD

This pita pocket sandwich is a favorite poolside lunch at Fess Parker's Red Lion Resort in Santa Barbara, California. It is also often requested for the bicycle picnic lunches packed for guests to take with them along the beautiful stretch of beach in front of the resort. You may want to double the recipe for those with hearty appetites.

1/2 pound tofu, drained and mashed (1 cup)
1/8 teaspoon freshly ground black pepper
1/8 teaspoon red pepper flakes
1/2 teaspoon turmeric
3/4 teaspoon curry powder
1 1/2 teaspoons reduced-sodium soy sauce
1/2 teaspoon Pommery mustard
2 tablespoons reduced-calorie mayonnaise
1/2 celery rib without leaves, finely chopped
1/2 cup water chestnuts, finely chopped
1/2 cup scallions, finely chopped
1/2 cup cauliflower, steamed crisp-tender and finely chopped
4 whole pita pockets, halved
8 tablespoons mung bean sprouts
1 medium tomato, peeled, seeded, and chopped (1 cup)
1 cup alfalfa sprouts
Lettuce leaves for garnish

Combine the tofu, pepper, red pepper flakes, turmeric, curry powder, soy sauce, mustard and mayonnaise and mix well. Add the celery, water chestnuts, scallions, and cauliflower and mix well.

To make the pita sandwiches, spoon 1/3 cup salad into each pita pocket. Add 1 tablespoon of mung bean sprouts, 2 tablespoons of diced tomatoes, and 2 tablespoons alfalfa sprouts. Place on a lettuce-lined plate, or in a sandwich bag to take with you.

Makes 8 pita sandwiches

EACH SANDWICH CONTAINS APPROXIMATELY:
170 TOTAL CALORIES / 30 CALORIES IN FAT
0 MG CHOLESTEROL / 245 MG SODIUM
95 MG CALCIUM

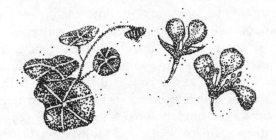

CHINESE CHICKEN SALAD

This is, hands down, the best-selling salad at the La Valencia Hotel in La Jolla, California, where it is on my light-cuisine menu. You can also use turkey, water-packed tuna, or shrimp in this salad, or a combination of any of them.

1/4 cup raw almonds, chopped
1 head Napa cabbage
1 pound raw mushrooms, sliced (4 cups)
3/4 pound cooked chicken breast, julienne cut (3 cups)
1 cup chopped scallion tops
1 cup snow peas, strings removed, ends notched in a V shape and
*   blanched*
1 cup fresh bean sprouts
1 cup water chestnuts, julienne cut
1 cup Mandarin Dressing (page 75)
1/4 cup julienne-cut red and yellow bell peppers for garnish
4 scallion flowers for garnish

Place the chopped almonds in a preheated 350°F oven for 8 to 10 minutes or until golden brown. Watch carefully, as they burn easily. Set aside.

Place 3 Napa cabbage leaves on each of four chilled plates for garnish. Shred the rest; you should have 4 cups. Combine the shredded cabbage, mushrooms, chicken, scallions, snow peas, bean sprouts, water chestnuts, and Mandarin Dressing and toss thoroughly.

Spoon 3 cups of the salad mixture onto each plate and top each with 1 tablespoon toasted almonds and 1 tablespoon red and yellow bell peppers. Plant a scallion flower on the top of each serving.

To make a scallion flower, cut the bulb end off the scallion just below the green top. Cut the root end off of the bulb and shred the bulb by slicing it through first in half, then in quarters, then in eighths and so on until it looks shredded. To open the scallion flower, drop it in ice water and allow it to "bloom" before using.

Makes four 3-cup servings

EACH SERVING CONTAINS APPROXIMATELY:
420 TOTAL CALORIES / 140 CALORIES IN FAT
70 MG CHOLESTEROL / 295 MG SODIUM
180 MG CALCIUM

CURRIED CHICKEN SALAD IN PINEAPPLE BOATS

Most salads are better if assembled just before serving, but with this salad it is essential to literally wait until the last minute before combining all of the component parts. The enzymes in the pineapple break down the chicken, so it becomes mushy in texture if prepared ahead of time. This salad is on my menu in the restaurant at Neiman-Marcus in Newport Beach, where I garnish it with sliced red apples for color and serve it with hot Light Cinnamon Popovers (page 203) and Apple Butter (page 61).

  1/2 cup chopped raw walnuts
  1 fresh pineapple
  1 pound papaya, cut into bite-size pieces (2 cups)
  1 cup Curried Chutney Dressing (page 77)
  8 Bibb lettuce leaves for lining plates
  3/4 pound cooked chicken breast, cut to bite-size pieces

Place the walnuts in a preheated 350°F oven for 8 to 10 minutes or until golden brown. Watch carefully, as they burn easily. Set aside.

Cut the pineapple into quarters, leaving the leaves attached at the top. Remove the pineapple from its shell and cut into bite-size pieces to use in the salad. You should have 2 cups. Trim the pineapple leaves, cutting off any dead leaves. Set aside.

Combine the papaya, pineapple, and dressing and toss thoroughly. Line four chilled plates with 2 Bibb lettuce leaves each and place the pineapple boats on top. Just before serving, stir the chicken into the salad mixture. Spoon 1¾ cups into each pineapple boat. Top with 2 tablespoons toasted walnuts.

Makes four 1¾-cup servings

EACH SERVING CONTAINS APPROXIMATELY:
410 TOTAL CALORIES / 145 CALORIES IN FAT
70 MG CHOLESTEROL / 235 MG SODIUM
85 MG CALCIUM

BREAST OF CHICKEN SALAD WITH GOAT CHEESE AND WARM MUSHROOM DRESSING

This is my own favorite salad. I love the combination of taste, temperatures, and textures. I first had a salad similar to this in Paris several years ago and was so intrigued with it that upon my return home I immediately started experimenting with my own version, which I now serve at the Canyon Ranch Spa in Tucson, where I call it Salade Nouvelle. When asked to do a salad course for the International Food Media Conference in New York I cut this salad down in size and eliminated the chicken breast, which worked well as an appetizer rather than a main-course salad.

¼ cup chopped raw walnuts
2 heads radicchio
1¼ pounds arugula, stems removed (3 cups)

1 pound fresh mushrooms, sliced (4 cups)
3/4 cup Raspberry-Walnut Vinaigrette Dressing (page 72)
3/4 pound cooked chicken breast, cut into strips and warmed
1/4 pound goat cheese, crumbled (1 cup)

Toast the walnuts in a preheated 350°F oven for 8 to 10 minutes or until golden brown. Watch carefully, as they burn easily. Set aside.

Separate eight radicchio leaves for lining the plates and set aside. Tear the remaining radicchio leaves and arugula into bite-size pieces. Combine the radicchio and arugula and mix well. Combine the mushrooms and the dressing in a skillet and cook until the mushrooms are just tender, about 5 minutes.

Garnish the outside edge of each of four plates with 2 radicchio leaves. Spread 1½ cups of the radicchio/arugula mixture in the center of each plate. Place 3 ounces of the warmed chicken breast on top. Sprinkle ¼ cup goat cheese over the chicken. Spoon the warm mushrooms and dressing over the top. Sprinkle 1 tablespoon of toasted walnuts over each salad.

Makes 4 servings

EACH SERVING CONTAINS APPROXIMATELY:
315 TOTAL CALORIES / 150 CALORIES IN FAT
85 MG CHOLESTEROL / 470 MG SODIUM
225 MG CALCIUM

FIESTA SALAD

Ole! This salad is a marvelous way to serve a taco in a hurry. All the ingredients are present and you can substitute ground beef, turkey, or even seafood for the chicken; or you can use beans and have a vegetarian fiesta salad. No matter what ingredients you choose, you will find this south-of-the-border salad a big hit with guests of all ages at fiestas large or small.

4 corn tortillas, cut into ¼-inch ribbons
1 head lettuce, finely chopped (6 cups)
1 cup Light Cumin Dressing (page 72)
½ pound cooked chicken, diced (2 cups)
2 cups Salsa (page 54)
1 cup corn kernels, cooked
2 ounces Cheddar or Monterey Jack cheese, grated (½ cup)
¼ cup sour cream
Green chili strips for garnish
Cilantro sprigs for garnish

Spread the tortilla ribbons on a cookie sheet. Bake in a preheated 400°F oven for 10 to 15 minutes, or until crisp and a golden brown. Stir occasionally to brown evenly. DO NOT USE THE BROILER!

For each serving, mix the chopped lettuce, dressing, and diced chicken and divide evenly onto each serving plate. Top each with ½ cup Salsa, ¼ cup corn kernels, 2 tablespoons grated cheese, and 1 tablespoon sour cream. Garnish with 2 strips of chili crossed over the top and 4 sprigs of cilantro. Arrange the tortilla ribbons around the edge of each salad.

Makes four 2½-cup servings

EACH SERVING CONTAINS APPROXIMATELY:
345 TOTAL CALORIES / 105 CALORIES IN FAT
70 MG CHOLESTEROL / 455 MG SODIUM
215 MG CALCIUM

VEGETABLES &
VEGETARIAN ENTRÉES

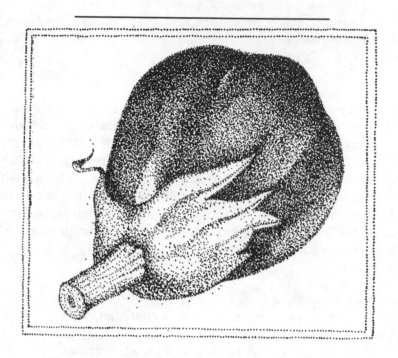

ACCORDING TO THE American Cancer Society the new superstars are the cruciferous vegetables, named for their cross-shaped flowers. They may actually help to prevent cancer. They include broccoli, brussels sprouts, cabbage, cauliflower, and kohlrabi. Many of these vegetables have had star billing in the nutrition world for a long time. Vegetable stars of longer standing that still rate top billing in the medical world include spinach, carrots, garlic, onions, and potatoes. Of these ten top stars of the vegetable world, the only one that is not a relatively common "everyday vegetable" is kohlrabi. The kohlrabi looks like a large turnip but is actually a member of the cabbage family. It can be used in recipes to replace either turnips or potatoes and adds a strong but pleasant turniplike flavor.

Other tips for using some of the star-billed vegetables include the following:

102

- Treat broccoli as two separate vegetables, that is, use the stems and flowerettes separately. People often cut off the top part or flowerette cluster of the broccoli and throw the stems away. However, the stems, when sliced crosswise, have a beautiful star-shaped pattern. Slice them thinly and steam them. Season them as you like and serve them as your vegetable. Very few people will know what vegetable they are eating. When using broccoli stems in this manner I call them broccoli stars. I also like to chill them and serve them in salads. They are a beautifully colorful addition and have a nice crunchy texture.
- Remember to remove the stems and veins from spinach leaves and to scrape carrots in order to get rid of the bitterness in these two vegetables.
- Always keep onions in the refrigerator. When onions are cold, they do not release the tear-producing gases for which they are so famous.
- When shredding potatoes to make hash browns or latkes, always soak them in cold water to wash away some of the potato starch. This gets rid of the gummy, chewy texture.

In this section I have given you recipes for everything from small side dishes to hearty entrées. When planning your menus, don't decide which specific vegetables you are going to serve for each meal before going to the market. Then when you're shopping, select the freshest and most attractive vegetables available. The good news is that the freshest, best-looking, and most nutritious fruits and vegetables are the ones in season and therefore they are also the least expensive.

Many of the entrées in this section are designed for vegetarians in that they contain nothing of animal origin, such as chicken stock, beef stock, or gelatin. However, there are some exceptions where stock is necessary for flavor or gelatin for texture. No vegetarian eats any part of an animal necessitating its death. Most vegetarians eat only animal by-products, such as dairy products and eggs. Vegan vegetarians, however, do not eat anything that is not of plant origin. In fact strict vegans will not even eat honey because it is made by bees. Lacto-vegetarians add dairy products, but do not eat eggs because they believe this is still a form of potential life. Lactoovo-vegetarians include both dairy products and eggs in their diet.

Also included in the vegetable category are grains and legumes (dried beans). Legumes are an excellent source of plant protein and contain valuable vitamins and minerals, and lots of fiber. When combined with grains they form a complete protein and are therefore a high-quality but very inexpensive food. Some of the more popular legumes include lentils, kidney beans, garbanzo beans (chick-peas), pinto beans, lima beans, black-eyed peas, and white beans, which are usually called navy beans because they were discovered in America and taken by ship to the rest of the world; also soybeans and all soybean products, such as tofu or soybean curd and soy milk. Even peanuts are part of the legume family and are often called the underground legumes.

When cooking beans, it is important to soak them overnight for faster cooking, removing any beans that float to the top. Then you can either cook them in their own water or drain them and cook them in fresh water or stock. Some people feel that draining the beans and starting with fresh liquid reduces some of the flatulence-producing properties. One pound of dried beans measures approximately 2 cups. After soaking they approximately double in volume, becoming 4 cups. To cook 4 cups of soaked beans, use 4 cups of water or stock. Bring the beans to a boil and then simmer them, covered, until they are tender—about 2 hours for most beans—checking on them from time to time and adding more water or stock as necessary to prevent the beans from scorching. In cooking beans I have found that the heavier the cooking pot the less likely I am to need additional liquid.

If you want beans in a hurry and don't have time to soak them overnight, cover them with cold water and bring them to a boil. Allow them to simmer for about 2 minutes and then remove them from the heat and cover them tightly, allowing them to soak for 1 hour and proceed as usual.

Most cooks use fewer varieties of grains than any other food category. Grains are wonderful from the nutrition standpoint and can add wonderful variety to your meals. Start experimenting with all of the different whole grains available on the market, such as rice, cracked wheat (bulgur), buckwheat groats (kasha), rye, millet, barley, and oats, using the package directions as your guide.

How people like their rice cooked usually depends upon their background. There are those who feel that if every grain is not separated from every other grain, the rice is ruined. There are others who feel this "fluffy" rice has no substance and want a gummy, almost chewy texture to their rice. Actually if you fall into the second category, you are less likely to be disappointed with the rice in most places because it is infinitely easier to achieve gummy rice than fluffy rice.

Brown rice, which still has its valuable bran layer, is nutritionally superior to its polished white counterpart, which has had most of the fiber removed. Short-grain brown rice has a nuttier flavor and tends to stick together more than long-grain brown rice, which is better for pilaf or just plain cooked brown rice. The short-grain variety is good for soups, casseroles, and puddings. When cooking brown rice, remember that it takes about one-third longer than white rice, so when substituting it in recipes, always allow a longer cooking time. The time can be shortened by soaking the rice prior to cooking it.

Steaming vegetables is the best method for cooking them because they retain more of their nutrients as well as their texture and color. All you need is a collapsible steamer basket and a pan with a tight-fitting lid. Add water to the pan to just below the basket level. Bring to a rapid boil, put the vegetables in the basket, and cover the pan. Set the timer, using the following steaming chart as a guide. This will give you al dente, or crisp-tender, vegetables every time. Remember, the minute you can smell a vegetable cooking, you are overcooking it. Overcooking vegetables destroys their texture and color as well as many valuable vitamins and minerals— and it smells up your house! Just as soon as the vegetables have cooked the prescribed time, remove the steamer basket from the pan and place it under cold running water. This stops the cooking process and preserves the color and texture.

This is the way most restaurants cook their vegetables; they then reheat them to serving temperature as orders come into the kitchen or refrigerate them to serve cold.

Vegetables can be reheated easily in a pan with a little water, defatted stock, juice, or wine instead of butter, margarine, or oil, and seasoned to taste. Be careful when reheating vegetables not to overcook them. Cold steamed vegetables make wonderful hors d'oeuvres and have a brighter color when used in salads than raw vegetables.

Other "light" approaches to cooking vegetables include stir-frying them without oil in the same way you would reheat steamed vegetables. Stir-fry them in either a wok or a skillet in water, defatted stock, juice, or wine. You can also blanch or parboil vege-

STEAMING TIMES FOR FRESH VEGETABLES

VEGETABLE	TIME (MINUTES)	VEGETABLE	TIME (MINUTES)
Artichokes	30	Onions:	
Asparagus	5	green tops	3
Beets, quartered	15	whole	5
Broccoli:		Parsley	1–2
branches	5	Pea pods	3
flowerettes	3–5	Peas	3–5
Brussels sprouts	5	Peppers:	
Cabbage,		chili	2–3
quartered	5	bell	2
Carrots, ½ inch		Potatoes:	
slices	5	white, sliced	10
Cauliflower:		sweet, sliced	15
flowerettes	3	Pumpkin, cut up	5
whole	5	Rhubarb	5
Celery ribs	10	Romaine lettuce	1–2
Celery root	3–4	Rutabagas	8
Chard	1–2	Shallots	2
Chives	2–3	Spinach	1–2
Cilantro	1–2	Squash:	
Corn kernels	3	acorn, cut up	5
Corn on the cob	3	banana	5
Cucumber, sliced	2–3	chayote	3
Eggplant, cut up	5	Hubbard, cut	
Garlic	5	up	5
Kohlrabi	8–10	summer	3
Leeks	5	zucchini	3
Lettuce	1–2	Tomatoes	3
Mushrooms	2	Turnips,	
Okra	5	quartered	8
		Watercress	1–2

tables by plunging them into rapidly boiling water to cook them rather than cooking them above boiling water as in steaming. This method is generally used when you wish to only partially cook a vegetable before reheating or cooking it on a grill.

Using a microwave oven is still another cooking method. Follow the directions for your own oven for the timing. You can also bake vegetables, or broil or barbecue them. Let your imagination be your guide and learn to enjoy the full range of seasonal fresh vegetables. There really is no such thing as a vegetable that is not good for you.

MARINATED MUSHROOMS

These mushrooms are wonderful in salads or on an Italian antipasto salad. I like to serve them on fancy toothpicks as hors d'oeuvres.

> *1 pound small mushrooms*
> *1/2 cup red wine vinegar*
> *1/3 cup water*
> *2 tablespoons canola or corn oil*
> *3/4 teaspoon fructose or 1 teaspoon sugar*
> *1 tablespoon finely chopped onion*
> *1 tablespoon finely chopped parsley*
> *1/2 teaspoon dried basil, crushed in a mortar and pestle*
> *2 garlic cloves, finely chopped (2 teaspoons)*
> *1/4 teaspoon salt*
> *1/4 teaspoon freshly ground black pepper*

Clean the mushrooms, cutting off the ends of the stems and leaving them whole. Set aside. Place all the other ingredients in a large saucepan and bring to a boil. Add the mushrooms and bring to a boil again. Reduce the heat and simmer, uncovered, for 5 to 10 minutes or until the mushrooms are tender.

Cool to room temperature. Refrigerate in a covered container for several hours before serving.

Makes 3 cups

1/4 CUP CONTAINS APPROXIMATELY:
35 TOTAL CALORIES / 20 CALORIES IN FAT
0 MG CHOLESTEROL / 45 MG SODIUM
5 MG CALCIUM

EGGPLANT RELISH

This relish is excellent as either a spread or a dip. I like to serve it on small rounds of crusty Italian bread garnished with sprigs of Italian parsley as an appetizer or hors d'oeuvre. It can also be served warm as a vegetable side dish. It is particularly good with fish.

1 eggplant, halved (1¹/₂ pounds)
Salt
Nonstick vegetable coating
1 tablespoon extra-virgin olive oil
¹/₄ cup finely chopped shallots
¹/₄ cup finely chopped onion
1 garlic clove, finely chopped (1 teaspoon)
¹/₂ cup chopped parsley
4 teaspoons freshly squeezed lemon juice
¹/₈ teaspoon salt
¹/₈ teaspoon freshly ground black pepper

Sprinkle the cut sides of the eggplant with salt and let stand for 30 minutes. Rinse thoroughly and pat dry.

Spray a cookie sheet with nonstick vegetable coating and place the eggplant on it cut side down. Preheat the oven to 375°F and bake for 40 minutes. Cool.

Heat 1 teaspoon of the olive oil in a large skillet. Add the shallots, onions, and garlic and cook over low heat until soft, about 5 minutes.

Peel and chop the eggplant and add the cooked mixture, the remaining 2 teaspoons olive oil, the parsley, lemon juice, salt, and pepper. Mix well. Chill for at least 2 hours.

Makes 2 cups

¹/₄ CUP CONTAINS APPROXIMATELY:
45 TOTAL CALORIES / 15 CALORIES IN FAT
0 MG CHOLESTEROL / 40 MG SODIUM
40 MG CALCIUM

CREAMED LEEKS

This vegetable side dish is incredibly rich-tasting to be so low in calories. I like it much better than the classic approach to creamed leeks, which are actually done in butter and reduced cream. The delicate flavor of the leek is more pronounced in this lower-fat version.

1 1/2 teaspoons corn-oil margarine
1 pound leeks, white part only, coarsely chopped (4 cups)
1/4 cup low-fat milk

Heat the margarine in a skillet and add the leeks. Cook, covered, for 3 minutes. Add the milk and reduce until the liquid disappears.

Makes four 1/2-cup servings

EACH SERVING CONTAINS APPROXIMATELY:
85 TOTAL CALORIES / 20 CALORIES IN FAT
1 MG CHOLESTEROL / 30 MG SODIUM
85 MG CALCIUM

LEEK AND ONION AU GRATIN

I have given you a recipe for 8 servings of this as a vegetable side dish because it is so good served in larger portions as a vegetarian entrée with a big green salad and fresh fruit for dessert.

1 slice whole wheat bread
1/4 pound mozzarella cheese, grated (1 cup)
1/4 pound Monterey Jack cheese, grated (1 cup)
1 pound leeks, white part only, sliced (4 cups)
3 medium onions, sliced (6 cups)
1/2 cup chopped chives

¹/₂ teaspoon dried oregano, crushed in a mortar and pestle
¹/₂ teaspoon dried basil, crushed in a mortar and pestle
¹/₂ teaspoon dried tarragon, crushed in a mortar and pestle
¹/₄ teaspoon salt
¹/₈ teaspoon freshly ground black pepper
¹/₂ cup vermouth

Preheat the oven to 350°F. Place the bread in a blender and convert to bread crumbs. You should have ½ cup. Combine the grated cheeses with the bread crumbs and set aside.

In a separate bowl, combine all the remaining ingredients except for the vermouth.

Spread half the onion mixture in a 9-by-13-inch glass baking dish. Top with half of the cheese mixture. Repeat the layers. Pour the vermouth over the top.

Cover tightly and bake for 1 hour.

Makes 8 servings

EACH SERVING CONTAINS APPROXIMATELY:
195 TOTAL CALORIES / 70 CALORIES IN FAT
20 MG CHOLESTEROL / 225 MG SODIUM
250 MG CALCIUM

SPINACH TIMBALES

It is important to remove the stems and veins from spinach leaves to get rid of the bitterness of the spinach. To devein a spinach leaf, fold the leaf lengthwise and grasp it near the stem end. Then carefully pull the stem toward the outer end of the leaf, removing the large center vein and the larger side vein along with it. If fresh spinach is not available, you may substitute two packages of frozen spinach, thawed and well drained. It is not necessary to cook frozen spinach because it has already been blanched before freezing. When using frozen spinach, the flavor and texture will not be as good as if you use fresh spinach because it is impossible to remove the stems and veins. These timbales are an excellent side dish with fish, poultry, or meat. They also add variety to a strictly vegetarian plate. They are even good cold, served with cold cuts or as a salad plate. When serving them cold, I like to top them with a little Creamy Curry Dressing (page 70).

> *2 pounds spinach*
> *1 teaspoon corn-oil margarine*
> *1 tablespoon flour*
> *1/2 cup skim milk*
> *1/4 teaspoon salt*
> *1/8 teaspoon ground nutmeg*
> *1/8 teaspoon freshly ground black pepper*
> *3 egg whites, lightly beaten*
> *Nonstick vegetable coating*

Preheat the oven to 400°F. Carefully clean the spinach, removing the stems and veins. Steam the spinach for 2 minutes. Squeeze it dry and chop it finely using the metal blade of a food processor. This should make about 1⅓ cups chopped spinach.

Melt the margarine in a saucepan. Add the flour, stirring constantly, and cook for 3 minutes; do not brown. Add the milk and continue to cook, stirring constantly with a wire whisk, until sauce thickens. Add the seasonings and mix well.

Combine the sauce with the spinach and the beaten egg whites. Mix well.

Spray four 3-inch ramekins with a nonstick vegetable coating. Divide the spinach mixture evenly among the ramekins. Place in a baking pan. Pour boiling water around the ramekins to a depth of ¾ inch. Bake for 20 minutes or until a knife inserted in the center of a timbale comes out clean. Let stand for 5 minutes before unmolding.

To unmold, run a knife around the inside of the ramekin and invert the mold over a serving plate.

Makes 4 timbales

EACH TIMBALE CONTAINS APPROXIMATELY:
50 TOTAL CALORIES / 10 CALORIES IN FAT
1 MG CHOLESTEROL / 235 MG SODIUM
125 MG CALCIUM

TZIMMES

I originally developed this recipe for one of my readers, who requested a low-fat version of his mother's tzimmes recipe to serve for a Jewish holiday. I was delighted when he wrote back and told me his mother liked it so much that she wanted "his" recipe.

5 small carrots, peeled and grated (2 1/2 cups)
1 small sweet potato, peeled and grated (2 cups)
1 apple, peeled and grated (1 cup)
1/2 cup water
1/4 teaspoon salt
1/4 teaspoon freshly grated nutmeg
1 tablespoon matzo meal
2 tablespoons frozen unsweetened apple juice concentrate

Combine all the ingredients in a large saucepan. Cook, covered, over low heat for 1 hour. Serve either hot or cold.

Makes 3 cups

1/4 CUP CONTAINS APPROXIMATELY:
60 TOTAL CALORIES / N CALORIES IN FAT
0 MG CHOLESTEROL / 70 MG SODIUM
10 MG CALCIUM

VEGETABLE TERRINE

This is a recipe I developed working with the talented chefs of the Four Seasons Hotels when we were all in Toronto designing the alternative recipes for their menus. The vegetables I have selected for the recipe will give you a brilliant and beautiful combination of colors and textures; however, it certainly isn't necessary to follow this recipe exactly. A terrine can be an extremely creative way of using the leftover vegetables you have in your refrigerator. The only real trick to this recipe involves using either an electric slicer or a mandolin, a slicing tool available in gourmet shops and commercial restaurant supply stores, because it is very difficult to slice the vegetables thinly enough by hand. Slice all the vegetables but the broccoli with an electric slicer or mandolin.

In this recipe I suggest plating the terrine on the Roasted Red Pepper Sauce simply because the colors contrast each other so wonderfully. It is also good with either Creamy Curry Sauce (page 70) or the Walnut-Dill Sauce (page 69) or any of the vegetable sauces. You may even want to serve it without a sauce, plated on a lettuce leaf with Raspberry-Walnut Vinaigrette Dressing (page 72) on the side.

> *3½ cups defatted chicken stock, chilled (see page 22)*
> *¼ cup loosely packed fresh tarragon, thyme, or basil*
> *1 teaspoon dried tarragon, crushed in a mortar and pestle*
> *2 ounces mushrooms, thinly sliced (½ cup)*
> *1 medium onion, thinly sliced (2 cups)*
> *4 large Napa cabbage leaves*
> *2 small yellow squash, thinly sliced lengthwise (6 ounces)*
> *2 small zucchini squash, thinly sliced lengthwise (½ pound)*
> *1 small red bell pepper, thinly sliced (1 cup)*
> *2 small carrots, scraped and thinly sliced lengthwise (¼ pound)*
> *1 cup broccoli in small flowerettes*
> *2 envelopes unflavored gelatin*
> *2 cups Roasted Red Pepper Sauce (page 69)*
> *Tarragon sprigs for garnish*

Combine 3 cups of the chicken stock, the fresh herbs, and the dried tarragon and bring to a boil. Blanch the mushrooms in stock until just fork tender. Drain, reserving the stock. Return the stock to the saucepan and cook the onions until soft. Drain and again reserve the stock.

Steam the Napa cabbage leaves for 15 seconds or until soft and pliable. Individually steam each of the other vegetables until just crisp-tender. Place each vegetable under cold running water after cooking to preserve the color and texture. Drain well.

Soften the gelatin in the remaining ½ cup of chicken stock (it should be cool) for 5 minutes. Measure 1¾ cups of the remaining heated chicken stock, reserving the rest for future use. Bring to a boil. Remove from the heat and stir in the softened gelatin until it is completely dissolved.

Oil a glass loaf pan. Spoon 2 tablespoons of the stock onto the bottom of the pan. Place 2 of the Napa cabbage leaves on the bottom and one side of the pan, the leafy part on bottom. Trim to fit. Place the other 2 leaves on the opposite side, leafy part hanging over the outside rim. Spoon 2 tablespoons of the stock over the cabbage. Sprinkle the mushrooms over this stock. Layer the remaining vegetables by color, pouring ¼ cup stock between each layer. Fold the cabbage over the final layer and pour the remaining stock over the cabbage. Press down gently with your fingers. Cover with plastic wrap and refrigerate overnight or until completely set.

To serve, unmold the terrine and slice very carefully with a serrated knife. Pour ¼ cup of the Roasted Red Pepper Sauce on each plate and turn the plate so the sauce covers the entire bottom of the plate inside the rim. Place a slice of terrine on the sauce and garnish with a fresh tarragon sprig.

Makes 8 servings

EACH SERVING CONTAINS APPROXIMATELY:
115 TOTAL CALORIES / 50 CALORIES IN FAT
0 MG CHOLESTEROL / 110 MG SODIUM
85 MG CALCIUM

QUICK CHILI

As the title suggests, this recipe takes very little time to make. Because it is a completely vegetarian dish it keeps for a long time in the refrigerator. I have had lots of competing athletes tell me that this chili and a bowl of brown rice comprise one of their favorite carbohydrate-loading meals because it is so easy to make and so inexpensive.

> *3 medium onions, finely chopped (4¹/₂ cups)*
> *2 garlic cloves, finely chopped (2 teaspoons)*
> *¹/₂ cup canned chopped green California chilies, undrained*
> *1 tablespoon chili powder*
> *2 teaspoons dried oregano, crushed in a mortar and pestle*
> *2 teaspoons ground cumin*
> *One 10-ounce can diced tomatoes, drained*
> *2¹/₂ cups dry kidney beans, cooked (6 cups), or one 46-ounce*
>   *can, undrained*

Combine the onions and garlic and cook in a large saucepan, covered, over low heat until soft, adding a little water if necessary to prevent scorching.

Add all the other ingredients except the beans. Mix thoroughly and bring to a boil. Simmer for 10 minutes. Add the cooked beans, mix well, and heat thoroughly.

Makes 6 cups

1 CUP CONTAINS APPROXIMATELY:
280 TOTAL CALORIES / 15 CALORIES IN FAT
0 MG CHOLESTEROL / 100 MG SODIUM
135 MG CALCIUM

RATATOUILLE

Ratatouille, the classic French vegetable stew, is very versatile. It's easy to make, keeps well in the refrigerator for over a week, and is equally good served hot or cold. I like it for hors d'oeuvres cold as a spread with crusty French bread. For a hot hors d'oeuvre or appetizer course, I stuff giant pasta shells with the ratatouille, topped with melted part-skim mozzarella cheese. I also serve ratatouille au gratin as an entrée at the Canyon Ranch Spa in Tucson. I put 1½ cups of the ratatouille in an au gratin dish and top it with ¼ cup grated part-skim mozzarella cheese, then place it in a preheated 350°F oven for about 10 minutes or until the ratatouille is hot and the cheese is melted.

¼ cup water
2 garlic cloves, minced (2 teaspoons)
1 tablespoon extra-virgin olive oil
1 medium onion, thinly sliced (2 cups)
2 green or red bell peppers, seeded and chopped (1½ cups)
1 medium eggplant, cubed (6 cups)
2 zucchini, cut into rounds (4 cups)
4 large tomatoes, cut into wedges
¼ cup finely chopped parsley
¼ teaspoon freshly ground black pepper
½ teaspoon salt
½ teaspoon dried rosemary, crushed in a mortar and pestle
1 teaspoon dried basil, crushed in a mortar and pestle
1 teaspoon dried thyme, crushed in a mortar and pestle
1 teaspoon dried marjoram, crushed in a mortar and pestle

Combine the water and garlic in a large saucepan and cook slowly until the water has evaporated. Add the olive oil and continue cooking until the garlic is soft, without browning it.

Add the onions, peppers, eggplant, and zucchini and cook for 5 minutes, stirring frequently.

Add the tomatoes and all the seasonings and mix well. Continue to cook over low heat, stirring frequently, for 1 hour. If you prefer a real "French-style" ratatouille, continue cooking for another hour or two, just as you would any other stew.

Makes six 1-cup servings

EACH SERVING CONTAINS APPROXIMATELY:
120 TOTAL CALORIES / 30 CALORIES IN FAT
0 MG CHOLESTEROL / 205 MG SODIUM
100 MG CALCIUM

EGGPLANT FLORENTINE

When fresh spinach is not available, this recipe can be made with two packages of frozen chopped spinach, thawed and thoroughly drained; however, as I mentioned in the recipe for Spinach Timbales (page 110), it is not necessary to steam the frozen spinach, and the appearance and flavor of the dish will not be as good as if using fresh spinach. A delicious variation is to use 4 ounces of tofu per serving to replace the eggplant. For a nonvegetarian entrée this dish is also good made with oysters, clams, or scallops instead of eggplant.

1 medium eggplant
Salt
2 pounds fresh spinach (8 cups packed)
2 cups Mornay Sauce (page 51)
1 ounce imported Parmesan cheese, freshly grated (¼ cup)

Peel the eggplant and slice it crosswise into rounds approximately ¼ inch thick. Put these into a glass baking dish and sprinkle with salt on both sides. Cover and allow to stand for 1 hour. Pour off the liquid and rinse the eggplant thoroughly. This step removes the bitterness from the eggplant.

Carefully wash the spinach to remove all grit. Remove the stems and veins. Chop coarsely and steam for 1 minute. Rinse with cold water and set aside.

Steam the eggplant until it can be pierced easily with a fork, about 4 minutes.

Preheat the oven to 350°F. Line the bottom of an 8-by-8-inch baking dish with spinach. Place the eggplant slices on top of the spinach and cover with the Mornay Sauce. Sprinkle evenly with the Parmesan cheese. Bake for 10 minutes, then brown lightly under the broiler.

Makes 4 servings

EACH SERVING CONTAINS APPROXIMATELY:
250 TOTAL CALORIES / 50 CALORIES IN FAT
15 MG CHOLESTEROL / 605 MG SODIUM
680 MG CALCIUM

SPANISH RICE

I serve this dish in spas as a vegetarian entrée, adding lentils to it to make it a complete protein. I also use it as stuffing for bell peppers and acorn squash. I have also served it cold as a rice salad for picnics.

1 1/2 teaspoons extra-virgin olive oil
1 medium onion, chopped (1 1/2 cups)
1 red bell pepper, seeded and chopped (1 cup)
1 cup quick-cooking long-grain brown rice
1 1/4 cups water or vegetable stock (see page 27), heated
1 cup tomato sauce
1/4 teaspoon dried saffron
1/4 teaspoon ground fennel
1/4 teaspoon salt
1/4 teaspoon freshly ground black pepper
1/2 cup frozen peas, unthawed

Heat the olive oil in a medium saucepan over low heat. Add the onions and peppers. Sauté slowly, stirring constantly, until soft, about 10 minutes. Add the rice and cook until the rice is golden, stirring frequently. Add the heated water or vegetable stock, the tomato sauce, saffron, fennel, salt, and pepper and mix well. Cover and cook over low heat for 20 minutes or until the rice is tender and liquid has been absorbed.

Stir in the peas and let stand, covered, for 5 minutes.

Makes 4 cups

1/2 CUP CONTAINS APPROXIMATELY:
130 TOTAL CALORIES / 15 CALORIES IN FAT
0 MG CHOLESTEROL / 260 MG SODIUM
25 MG CALCIUM

RICE PILAF

Like Spanish Rice (page 118), this Rice Pilaf recipe lends itself well to variations. You can add fish, poultry, or meat or drained water-packed tuna for a delicious hot entrée or serve it cold as a rice salad.

> *1 1/2 teaspoons canola or corn oil*
> *3/4 cup long-grain brown rice*
> *1/2 medium onion, thinly sliced (1 cup)*
> *1 tablespoon reduced-sodium soy sauce*
> *1 1/2 teaspoons fresh thyme, finely chopped, or 1/2 teaspoon dried*
> *   thyme, crushed in a mortar and pestle*
> *1 cup defatted chicken stock (see page 22)*

Heat the oil in a heavy skillet. Add the rice and the onion slices and cook, stirring frequently, until brown.

Add the soy sauce and thyme to the chicken stock in a small saucepan and bring to a boil.

Put the rice mixture in a baking pan and add the hot stock. Stir, then cover tightly. Place in a preheated 400°F oven for 40 minutes. Remove and allow to stand for 10 minutes more before removing the cover.

To reheat, add 2 to 3 tablespoons of stock to the cold rice and mix thoroughly. Cover and heat slowly in a preheated 300°F oven for about 25 minutes.

Makes 3 cups

1/2 CUP CONTAINS APPROXIMATELY:
115 TOTAL CALORIES / 15 CALORIES IN FAT
0 MG CHOLESTEROL / 185 MG SODIUM
15 MG CALCIUM

LIGHT POLENTA

The original version of this recipe was served at the International Food Media Conference in New York City, where it was prepared for us by Palio's Restaurant. It was fabulous, but when I saw the recipe I realized that I wouldn't dare eat it very often and decided to try to find a way to make it lower in calories, cholesterol, and sodium. I have also made it easier to prepare so that you can enjoy polenta more often and with less effort!

POLENTA:

2¼ cups water
½ cup yellow cornmeal
1½ teaspoons corn-oil margarine

RICOTTA SAUCE:

1 cup part-skim ricotta cheese
⅓ cup low-fat milk
⅛ teaspoon freshly grated nutmeg

FONTINELLA SAUCE:

4 ounces Fontinella cheese, diced (1 cup)
2 tablespoons low-fat milk
3 spinach leaves, deveined
Fresh herbs for garnish (basil, oregano, thyme, or Italian parsley)

To prepare the polenta, bring the water to a boil. Slowly add the cornmeal, stirring constantly with a wire whisk. Reduce the heat to medium and continue to cook, uncovered, stirring occasionally, for 30 minutes. Remove from the heat and whisk in the corn-oil margarine. Pour ⅓ cup of the mixture into each of four 3-inch ramekins. Keep warm in a very low oven until ready to serve.

Combine the ricotta sauce ingredients in a blender and blend until smooth. Pour into a saucepan and heat to simmering, stirring frequently. DO NOT BOIL.

Heat the Fontinella cheese and milk in the top of a double boiler over simmering water until the cheese has melted. While the cheese is melting, place the spinach leaves in boiling water until soft. Remove from the water and drain thoroughly. Combine the melted cheese and spinach leaves in a blender and blend until smooth.

To serve, spoon ¼ cup of the ricotta sauce on each of four salad-size plates. Unmold a polenta on top of the ricotta sauce. Top with 2 tablespoons of Fontinella sauce and garnish with a sprig of fresh herb, such as basil, oregano, thyme, or Italian parsley.

Makes 4 servings

EACH SERVING CONTAINS APPROXIMATELY:
420 CALORIES / 135 CALORIES IN FAT
40 MG CHOLESTEROL / 360 MG SODIUM
425 MG CALCIUM

SCALLOPED POTATOES

If you like scalloped potatoes but rarely eat them because they are so fattening, you are going to love this recipe. I developed it for one of my readers, who was put on a low-fat diet and missed scalloped potatoes more than anything else. I have since used it on spa menus and received raves from the guests.

> *Nonstick vegetable coating*
> *2 medium White Rose potatoes, peeled and thinly sliced (3 cups)*
> *1 tablespoon flour*
> *¼ teaspoon salt*
> *Freshly ground black pepper to taste*
> *½ medium onion, thinly sliced (1 cup)*
> *1½ teaspoons corn-oil margarine*
> *1 cup low-fat milk*

Preheat the oven to 350°F. Spray a loaf pan or baking dish with nonstick vegetable coating.

Layer one-third of the potatoes in the bottom of the pan and sprinkle with one-half of the flour, ⅛ teaspoon of the salt, and the pepper to taste. Top with one-half of the onions.

Repeat with another layer of potatoes, flour, salt, pepper, and onions.

Top with the final third of potatoes. Dot with margarine and pour the milk over the top. Bake for 1 hour, uncovered. Turn the heat up to 375°F and bake for 30 minutes more.

Makes six ¾-cup servings

EACH SERVING CONTAINS APPROXIMATELY:
100 TOTAL CALORIES / 20 CALORIES IN FAT
5 MG CHOLESTEROL / 120 MG SODIUM
70 MG CALCIUM

OVEN FRIES

If you love French fries, but are fighting fat, try making these Oven Fries. You will be surprised how much more flavorful they are— you can actually taste the potato!

Nonstick vegetable coating
2 unpeeled baking potatoes, cut into strips

Spray a baking sheet heavily with nonstick vegetable coating. Arrange the potato strips so that they do not overlap.

Bake for 1 hour in a preheated 375°F oven, turning every 15 minutes for even browning.

Makes 4 servings

EACH SERVING CONTAINS APPROXIMATELY:
110 TOTAL CALORIES / N CALORIES IN FAT
0 MG CHOLESTEROL / 10 MG SODIUM
10 MG CALCIUM

LIGHT LATKES AND APPLESAUCE

I developed these light latkes originally for a Hanukkah menu in an article in *San Diego Magazine.* The oil traditionally used for frying the latkes is there for the same symbolic purpose, but in an infinitely smaller amount.

> *3 medium potatoes, peeled and grated (2½ cups)*
> *2 tablespoons finely chopped onion*
> *1 egg, lightly beaten*
> *¼ teaspoon salt*
> *⅛ teaspoon baking powder*
> *1½ tablespoons matzo meal or whole wheat flour*
> *1 teaspoon canola or corn oil*
> *1 cup Baked Applesauce (page 231) (optional)*
> *1 cup Light Sour Cream (page 53) (optional)*

Place the grated potatoes in a bowl with water to cover and let stand 12 hours.

Drain the potatoes well in a strainer or colander and press out any excess moisture. Place in a mixing bowl and add the onion and beaten egg. Mix well.

Combine the salt, baking powder, and matzo meal or flour and slowly add to the potato mixture. Mix thoroughly.

Heat a skillet until a drop of water dances around on it before evaporating.

Drop the mixture by tablespoonsful onto the hot, lightly oiled skillet. Cook on one side until well browned; turn over and brown on the other side.

Serve ¼ cup Baked Applesauce and ¼ cup Light Sour Cream with each serving if desired.

Makes 8 latkes

EACH LATKE CONTAINS APPROXIMATELY:
58 TOTAL CALORIES / 12 CALORIES IN FAT
27 MG CHOLESTEROL / 95 MG SODIUM
8 MG CALCIUM

CANYON RANCH STUFFED SPUD

This popular luncheon entrée at the Canyon Ranch Spa in Tucson made its photographic debut in *Vogue* magazine several years ago. The *Vogue* photographers were at the spa to photograph Jane Seymour and her baby daughter. A full-page color picture of Jane and her daughter sharing the Canyon Ranch Stuffed Spud was used in the magazine. This recipe is easy, inexpensive, and surprisingly delicious.

> *2 small baking potatoes*
> *1 medium onion, finely chopped (1 1/2 cups)*
> *1/4 cup buttermilk*
> *1/2 cup low-fat cottage cheese*
> *3 tablespoons grated Parmesan or Romano cheese*
> *2 tablespoons chopped scallions, including the tops*

Wash the potatoes well. Pierce with the tines of a fork and bake in a preheated 400°F oven for 1 hour.

Cut a very thin slice from the top of each potato. Remove the pulp from the potatoes, being careful not to tear the shells. Mash the potato pulp and set aside in a covered bowl. Keep the shells warm.

Cook the onions, covered, over low heat until soft, adding a little water if necessary to prevent scorching. Add the mashed potatoes and all the other ingredients except the chopped scallions. Mix well and heat thoroughly. Stuff the potato mixture back into the warm shells. They will be heaping way over the top!

To serve, sprinkle the top of each Stuffed Spud with 1 tablespoon of chopped scallions. If you have prepared them in advance, reheat in a 350°F oven for 10 to 15 minutes or until hot before adding the chopped scallions.

Makes 2 servings

EACH SERVING CONTAINS APPROXIMATELY:
245 TOTAL CALORIES / 30 CALORIES IN FAT
10 MG CHOLESTEROL / 415 MG SODIUM
220 MG CALCIUM

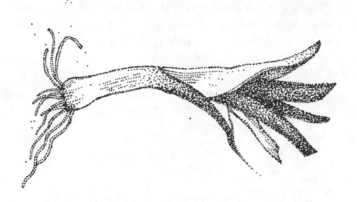

COLCANNON-STUFFED POTATOES

This stuffed potato contains the classic Irish cabbage-and-potato mixture frequently served for Irish get-togethers and is always a real hit on Saint Patrick's Day.

4 medium baking potatoes
4 cups green cabbage, shredded
3 tablespoons corn-oil margarine
1/2 cup skim milk, heated to lukewarm
4 scallions, including 2 inches of tops, finely chopped (3/4 cup)
1/2 teaspoon salt
1/2 teaspoon caraway seeds
Freshly ground black pepper to taste
1/4 cup finely chopped fresh parsley for garnish

Wash the potatoes thoroughly, dry, and pierce with a fork. Bake in a preheated 400°F oven for 1 hour. Remove from the oven and cool slightly.

While the potatoes are cooling, put the shredded cabbage into a pan with water to cover. Bring to a boil. Boil rapidly, uncovered, for 8 minutes. Drain thoroughly and set aside.

When the potatoes are cool enough to handle, split them down the center and carefully remove the pulp from the shells, being careful not to tear the shells. Set the shells aside to refill with the colcannon mixture.

Combine the potato pulp with the margarine. Mash thoroughly. Beat the potatoes, adding milk a little at a time. Add more milk, if necessary, to achieve a creamy consistency.

Add the cabbage to the potato mixture. Add the scallions, salt, caraway seeds, and pepper and mix thoroughly. Refill the potato shells with the colcannon mixture. Garnish each potato with fresh parsley. Note: If making ahead of time and reheating, add the parsley just before serving.

Makes 4 servings

EACH SERVING CONTAINS APPROXIMATELY:
270 TOTAL CALORIES / 80 CALORIES IN FAT
1 MG CHOLESTEROL / 320 MG SODIUM
115 MG CALCIUM

PIZZA

Pizza lovers of the world, rejoice! You can now have your pizza and eat it without guilt. If you really want to be a purist, try serving it with one of the new nonalcoholic beers for your own spa party. Of course you can add any of the suggested toppings touted by all pizza parlors, but this vegetarian version is truly delicious and much lower in calories.

SAUCE:

1/2 medium onion, finely chopped (3/4 cup)
1 garlic clove, finely chopped (1 teaspoon)
1/4 cup finely chopped parsley
1 tablespoon water
One 6-ounce can tomato paste
1/2 teaspoon dried oregano, crushed in a mortar and pestle
1/4 teaspoon dried basil, crushed in a mortar and pestle

¹/₄ teaspoon salt
¹/₈ teaspoon freshly ground black pepper

1 Pizza Crust (page 204)
1 medium onion, sliced (2 cups)
¹/₄ pound mushrooms, thinly sliced (1 cup)
¹/₂ small green bell pepper, seeded and sliced (¹/₂ cup)
¹/₂ small red bell pepper, seeded and sliced (¹/₂ cup)
1 small zucchini, thinly sliced (1 cup)
6 ounces part-skim mozzarella cheese, sliced

Preheat the oven to 425°F.

Sauté the chopped onions, garlic, and parsley in the water until soft. Remove from the heat and add the tomato paste, oregano, basil, salt, and pepper. Mix well.

Spread the sauce over the pizza crust. Arrange the sliced onions, mushrooms, peppers, and zucchini decoratively on top of the sauce. Bake for 10 minutes on the lowest shelf of the oven.

Place the cheese slices on the pizza and bake for an additional 15 minutes. Allow to stand for 3 to 5 minutes before slicing. If the pizza begins to brown too much before the crust is done, place a square of aluminum foil lightly over the top and continue to bake until the bottom crust is lightly browned. Cut into 6 pie-shaped wedges.

Makes 6 servings

EACH SERVING CONTAINS APPROXIMATELY:
260 TOTAL CALORIES / 75 CALORIES IN FAT
20 MG CHOLESTEROL / 395 MG SODIUM
330 MG CALCIUM

QUESADILLA

This quesadilla is one of the most popular items on my menus in spas, hotels, and restaurants alike. Many people have told me this is their favorite Quesadilla served anywhere and much prefer it to the high-calorie version served in Mexican restaurants. I recently co-hosted a party in New York City with Enid Zuckerman, the owner of the Canyon Ranch Spa. I decided to do a Southwestern menu and used this recipe for a Quesadilla, but instead of the vegetarian version, I added lobster and served the Lobster Quesadilla with a Fiesta Salad (page 100).

Corn-oil margarine
Four 12-inch whole wheat flour tortillas
1/4 pound part-skim mozzarella cheese, grated (1 cup)
1/4 pound Monterey Jack cheese, grated (1 cup)
1/2 cup canned green California chilies, seeded and finely chopped
1/2 cup finely chopped scallions
1/2 small head lettuce, shredded, for garnish (2 cups)
1 cup Salsa (page 54)
Fresh cilantro sprigs for garnish

For *each* quesadilla, using a paper towel, rub the inner surface of a large skillet with corn-oil margarine. Place one of the tortillas in the pan and cook until lightly browned on one side. Turn over and sprinkle 1/4 cup of each of the cheeses evenly over the tortilla.

Sprinkle 2 tablespoons of the chilies and 2 tablespoons of the scallions evenly over the cheese. Cook until the cheese is melted. Fold in half and cut into three pie-shaped wedges.

Serve on a plate garnished with 1/2 cup of the shredded lettuce and a ramekin of 1/4 cup fresh Salsa. Place 1 cilantro sprig on each serving.

Makes 4 servings

EACH SERVING CONTAINS APPROXIMATELY:
355 TOTAL CALORIES / 160 CALORIES IN FAT
40 MG CHOLESTEROL / 600 MG SODIUM
450 MG CALCIUM

BEAN BURRITOS

I purposely separated this bean burrito recipe into two steps—the filling and the actual burritos. The reason I did this it is that is just as easy to make 6 cups of the filling as it is to make 2 cups, and it freezes very well. I also like to serve the burrito filling instead of Mexican refried beans as a side dish with all Mexican entrées or just with rice for a vegetarian entrée.

> *1½ cups dry pinto beans*
> *½ medium onion, chopped (¾ cup)*
> *1 garlic clove, minced (1 teaspoon)*
> *½ teaspoon freshly ground black pepper*
> *1 teaspoon salt*
> *1½ medium onions, chopped (2½ cups)*
> *5 medium tomatoes, chopped (3 cups)*
> *¼ cup finely chopped cilantro*
> *⅓ cup canned chopped green California chilies*
> *½ teaspoon cumin*
> *1½ teaspoons chili powder*
> *8 whole wheat flour tortillas*

The day before serving, place the beans, ¾ cup of onion, the garlic and pepper in a heavy kettle. Cover them with boiling water. Simmer, covered, over medium heat for 2½ to 3½ hours, until the beans are tender. Add additional boiling water as needed to ensure ample broth. When the beans are tender, stir in the salt and let them cool. Store in the refrigerator.

The day of serving, drain the beans, reserving 1 cup of broth. Place the beans in a food processor. Add the reserved broth and process until the consistency of refried beans is attained.

In a nonstick pan, cook the 2½ cups of onion and the tomato until soft. Add the beans, cilantro, chilies, cumin, and chili powder. Cook, uncovered, over medium heat, stirring occasionally until the liquid is reduced and the beans do not run when spooned onto a plate.

Wrap the tortillas in foil and warm them in a preheated 375°F oven for 10 minutes. To serve, spoon ½ cup of the bean mixture onto the lower half of each tortilla. Bring the bottom of the tortilla up over the beans. Fold in the sides of the tortilla, then roll it the rest of the way around the beans.

Makes 8 burritos

EACH BURRITO CONTAINS APPROXIMATELY:
240 TOTAL CALORIES / 45 CALORIES IN FAT
0 MG CHOLESTEROL / 595 MG SODIUM
65 MG CALCIUM

MEXICAN SPAGHETTI

I am always trying to figure out new and unusual ways of combining popular and healthy ingredients. Spaghetti is one of the most popular ingredients with people of all ages and so is anything in the Mexican flavor range; so I decided to create Mexican Spaghetti. Whenever I mention Mexican Spaghetti, I am always asked what it is. The recipe is the answer. I like to serve it topped with grated Monterey Jack cheese rather than the Parmesan, which I like better on Italian spaghetti. The Mexican sauce is also good on any other pasta or rice, beans, fish, poultry, or meat.

1 medium onion, finely chopped (1¹/2 cups)
2 garlic cloves, finely chopped (2 teaspoons)
One 28-ounce can solid-pack tomatoes, undrained
One 6-ounce can tomato paste
³/4 cup water
¹/4 cup red wine
1 teaspoon fructose or 1¹/2 teaspoons sugar
1 celery rib, without leaves, chopped (¹/2 cup)
2 tablespoons chopped cilantro
1 bay leaf
1 teaspoon salt
¹/4 teaspoon freshly ground black pepper
³/4 teaspoon ground cumin

1 1/2 teaspoons chili powder
1/2 teaspoon dried oregano, crushed in a mortar and pestle
1/2 teaspoon dried thyme, crushed in a mortar and pestle
2 dashes Tabasco
1/2 pound dry spaghetti (4 cups cooked)
4 cilantro sprigs for garnish

Combine the onions and garlic and cook, covered, in a saucepan over low heat until tender, 8 to 10 minutes, adding a little water if necessary to prevent scorching. Set aside.

In another saucepan, combine the tomatoes, tomato paste, water, and wine. Bring to a boil, then reduce to simmer. Add the onion mixture, fructose or sugar, celery, cilantro, bay leaf, and all the seasonings. Simmer for 1 hour, adding water if too thick. Remove and discard the bay leaf.

Cook the spaghetti in 3 quarts of boiling water until al dente, about 10 minutes. Drain thoroughly.

To serve, place 1 cup spaghetti on each plate and top with 1 cup sauce. Garnish with a sprig of cilantro.

Makes 4 servings

EACH SERVING CONTAINS APPROXIMATELY:
265 TOTAL CALORIES / 10 CALORIES IN FAT
0 MG CHOLESTEROL / 630 MG SODIUM
135 MG CALCIUM

PASTA PRIMAVERA

This Pasta Primavera is a big hit on my menu in the restaurant at Neiman-Marcus in Newport Beach, California. Pasta Primavera is usually served with a cream sauce, but I think it has a lot more zip and decidedly more of an Italian personality served with marinara sauce; and the pine nuts add just the right amount of texture as well as a complementary flavor.

½ cup pine nuts
4 cups flowerettes and julienne-cut fresh vegetables (a colorful assortment: broccoli, cauliflower, etc.)
2 cups Marinara Sauce (page 59), heated
4 cups cooked fettuccine noodles (½ pound dry)
¼ pound imported Parmesan cheese, grated (1 cup)
Chopped fresh basil for garnish
4 sprigs fresh basil for garnish (optional)

Toast the pine nuts in a preheated 350°F oven for 8 to 10 minutes or until lightly browned. Watch carefully, as they burn easily. Set aside.

Steam the vegetables separately until crisp-tender. Rinse with cool water to maintain their color.

When ready to serve, heat the Marinara Sauce. Reheat the fettuccine and the vegetables by dipping them into boiling water.

For each serving, place 1 cup of the pasta on a hot serving plate and cover with ½ cup of the Marinara Sauce. Top with 1 cup of the heated vegetables and sprinkle with ¼ cup of the cheese. Top with 2 tablespoons of the toasted pine nuts and garnish with chopped fresh basil leaves and a whole basil leaf if desired. Serve extra Marinara Sauce on the side if desired.

Makes 4 servings

EACH SERVING CONTAINS APPROXIMATELY:
385 TOTAL CALORIES / 115 CALORIES IN FAT
15 MG CHOLESTEROL / 1300 MG SODIUM
355 MG CALCIUM

LIGHT LASAGNA

If you have been looking for a vegetarian entrée your whole family will love, this is your answer. I can promise you no one is going to ask, "Where's the beef?" Even if you are making this for two or three people, I recommend making the entire recipe and freezing what is left over for future meals.

> *3 medium onions, chopped (4½ cups)*
> *2 garlic cloves, finely chopped (2 teaspoons)*
> *Two 28-ounce cans solid-pack tomatoes, undrained*
> *Four 6-ounce cans Italian tomato paste*
> *1 cup chopped parsley*
> *1 teaspoon salt*
> *½ teaspoon freshly ground black pepper*
> *2 teaspoons dried oregano, crushed in a mortar and pestle*
> *½ teaspoon dried thyme, crushed in a mortar and pestle*
> *½ teaspoon dried marjoram, crushed in a mortar and pestle*
> *½ pound dry lasagna noodles*
> *1 pound part-skim ricotta cheese (4 cups), divided*
>   *into thirds*
> *½ pound part-skim mozzarella cheese, grated (2 cups) and*
>   *divided into thirds*
> *2 ounces imported Parmesan cheese, grated (½ cup) and divided*
>   *into fourths*

Combine the onions and garlic and cook, covered, until tender, adding a little water if necessary to prevent scorching. Add the tomatoes, tomato paste, parsley, salt, pepper, oregano, thyme, and marjoram. Simmer, covered, for 2 hours, stirring occasionally.

Cook the lasagna noodles in boiling water until al dente, about 12 minutes. Drain in a colander and rinse with cold water.

Cover the bottom of a 9-by-13-by-2-inch baking dish with one-fourth of the sauce. Add a layer of lasagna noodles, trimming the edges to fit the dish. Top with a layer of ricotta cheese, then a layer of mozzarella. Sprinkle with Parmesan cheese. Cover with one-fourth of the sauce. Repeat the procedure two more times and sprinkle the remaining Parmesan on top. Bake in a preheated 350°F oven for 45 minutes. Let stand for 10 minutes before serving.

Makes twelve 3-inch-square servings

EACH SERVING CONTAINS APPROXIMATELY:
285 TOTAL CALORIES / 80 CALORIES IN FAT
25 MG CHOLESTEROL / 645 MG SODIUM
370 MG CALCIUM

ACORN SQUASH RAVIOLIS
WITH MARJORAM SAUCE

These raviolis make a wonderful appetizer course as well as an unusually delicious side dish or entrée. The strong marjoram flavor is particularly good with poultry. I recently served these raviolis for a luncheon with cold sliced turkey, and it was a sensational combination.

1 small acorn squash
1/2 teaspoon freshly ground nutmeg
24 wonton skins, halved
1 tablespoon corn-oil margarine
1 medium onion, diced (1 1/2 cups)
1 cup defatted chicken stock (see page 22)
2 cups low-fat milk
1/2 cup fresh marjoram without stems, chopped, or 2 tablespoons
   dried marjoram, crushed in a mortar and pestle
1/4 teaspoon salt
1/8 teaspoon freshly ground black pepper
1/4 cup part-skim ricotta cheese
4 sprigs fresh marjoram or 1/4 cup finely chopped chives for
   garnish

Remove the seeds from the squash and peel with a sharp knife. Cut into 1-inch cubes and cook in boiling water until tender, about 20 minutes. Drain very well. Puree in a food processor with the nutmeg.

To make the raviolis, place 1 teaspoon of squash puree in the center of each wonton skin half. Fold over, moisten the edges with a little water, and seal with your fingertips. Cook for 5 minutes in boiling water, twelve wontons at a time. Drain the wontons and place them on a paper towel without overlapping until ready to serve.

To make the sauce, melt the margarine in a pan. Add the onions and stir. Cover and cook until the onions are very soft; do not brown. Add the chicken stock and reduce by two-thirds. Add the milk and bring to a rolling boil. Add the marjoram, salt, pepper, and ricotta cheese. Stir to blend. Reduce by one-half.

Remove from the heat, pour into a blender, and puree until satin smooth. Return to the pan and heat through.

To serve, divide the raviolis among four plates (twelve on each plate). Pour ½ cup sauce over each serving. Garnish with a sprig of fresh marjoram or finely chopped chives.

Makes 4 servings

EACH SERVING CONTAINS APPROXIMATELY:
335 TOTAL CALORIES / 75 CALORIES IN FAT
15 MG CHOLESTEROL / 255 MG SODIUM
285 MG CALCIUM

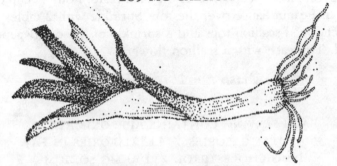

ORIENTAL NOODLES
WITH SZECHUAN PEANUT SAUCE

I will never forget the first time I was in a Szechuan restaurant in New York and had this spectacular cold pasta dish. I recently gave the recipe to a friend who told me he likes it better hot. I prefer it cold, as it is classically served, but there's no law against eating it at any temperature you like. The only problem with this dish is that it will never win a beauty contest or be "the dish most likely to make the cover of *Gourmet Magazine*." Peanut-butter-colored sauce poured over white pasta needs help cosmetically. It is for this reason I suggest topping it not only with chopped scallions, which are traditional, but also with red pepper and a scallion flower. To make a scallion flower, cut the bulb end of the scallion just below the green top. Cut the root off the end of the bulb and shred the bulb by slicing it through first in half, then in quarters, then in eighths, and so on. To open your scallion flower, drop it in ice water and allow it to "bloom" before using it.

10 ounces dry Oriental-style noodles (4 cups cooked)
1¹/2 teaspoons dark sesame oil
1 cup Szechuan Peanut Sauce (page 56)
¹/2 cup chopped scallion tops for garnish
Red bell pepper, seeded and diced, for garnish (optional)
4 scallion flowers for garnish

Cook the noodles al dente according to package directions. Drain and rinse with cold water. Drain again THOROUGHLY.

Combine the noodles and the sesame oil and toss. Refrigerate until cold.

To serve, place 1 cup noodles on each plate. Pour ¼ cup of the Szechuan Peanut Sauce over the top. Sprinkle with 2 tablespoons of the chopped scallion tops and a sprinkle of diced red pepper if desired. Top each with a scallion flower.

Makes four 1¹/4-cup servings

EACH SERVING CONTAINS APPROXIMATELY:
355 TOTAL CALORIES / 115 CALORIES IN FAT
1 MG CHOLESTEROL / 130 MG SODIUM
125 MG CALCIUM

HUEVOS RANCHEROS

When I lived in Mexico City, I was surprised to learn how many versions the Mexicans have for Huevos Rancheros or, as literally translated, ranch-style eggs. After living there for over a year, I developed my own ranchero sauce, which is a sort of combination of all the sauces I liked best. After moving back to this country and becoming involved in the light-cuisine movement, I modified my own recipe further to use only the egg whites. When I was developing recipes for the Pritikin Longevity Center in Santa Monica, California, I made this dish without salt or cheese, and it was one of the menu favorites with all of the participants.

1 medium onion, finely chopped (1½ cups)
2 garlic cloves, finely chopped (2 teaspoons)
⅛ teaspoon salt
⅛ teaspoon freshly ground black pepper
¾ teaspoon dried oregano, crushed in a mortar and pestle
1 teaspoon chili powder
¼ teaspoon ground cumin
1 green bell pepper, seeded and diced (¾ cup)
¼ cup canned chopped green California chilies
2 cups canned tomatoes, drained and chopped (reserve juice)
¼ cup tomato juice (from canned tomatoes)
4 egg whites (½ cup)
2 ounces part-skim mozzarella cheese, grated (½ cup)
4 corn tortillas, heated
Fresh cilantro sprigs for garnish

Sauté the onions and garlic in a medium saucepan over low heat, covered, until soft, adding a little water if necessary to prevent scorching.

Add the salt, pepper, oregano, chili powder, and cumin and mix well. Add the green bell pepper, chilies, tomatoes, and tomato juice. Mix well and cook, uncovered, for 20 minutes.

For each serving, pour ¾ cup of the sauce into a skillet. Put 2 tablespoons of the egg white on top of the sauce (1 egg white). Sprinkle 2 tablespoons of the grated cheese over the egg white. Cook, covered, for about 10 minutes or until the egg white is opaque. Place a hot tortilla on a heated plate. Carefully place the sauce with the egg white and cheese on the tortilla. Spoon 2 tablespoons of the sauce over the top of the cheese. Garnish with a fresh cilantro sprig.

Makes 4 servings

EACH SERVING CONTAINS APPROXIMATELY:
135 TOTAL CALORIES / 15 CALORIES IN FAT
0 MG CHOLESTEROL / 755 MG SODIUM
110 MG CALCIUM

WHITE CHILI

White Chili is one of my own signature recipes. I created it for an all-in-fun cooking contest held by George and Piret Munger for their fellow food professionals and serious amateurs. White Chili won first place for the most original recipe. To make it an entrée and still keep it white I added chunks of tender chicken breast just before serving. It is also good with turkey breast, rabbit, veal, or drained water-packed white albacore or tuna.

It is important to use a heavy saucepan to cook this. The liquid boils too quickly, even over low heat, in a lightweight pan. If you think you have too much liquid left when the chili has finished cooking, stir it up and let it stand, uncovered, until it cools slightly and much of the liquid will be absorbed. Then reheat it to serve.

I purposely wrote this recipe for 8 cups because it doesn't take any more time and it is a wonderful dish for parties and freezes well.

1 pound dry Great Northern beans, soaked overnight and drained
4 cups defatted chicken stock (see page 22)
2 medium onions, coarsely chopped (4 cups)
3 garlic cloves, finely chopped (1 tablespoon)
1 teaspoon salt
1/2 cup canned chopped green California chilies
2 teaspoons ground cumin
1 1/2 teaspoons dried oregano, crushed in a mortar and pestle
1 teaspoon ground coriander
1/4 teaspoon ground cloves
1/4 teaspoon cayenne (or to taste)
1/4 pound Monterey Jack cheese, grated (1 cup) (optional)

Combine the beans, stock, 2 cups of the onions, the garlic, and the salt in a large heavy saucepan or pot and bring to a boil. Reduce the heat, cover, and simmer for 2 hours or until the beans are very tender, adding more stock as needed (more stock should not be needed if you are using a heavy pan or pot).

When the beans are tender, add the remaining 2 cups onions, the chilies, and all the seasonings. Mix well and continue to cook, covered, for 30 minutes.

To serve, spoon 1 cup chili into each serving bowl and top with 2 tablespoons of Monterey Jack cheese if desired.

Makes 8 cups

1 CUP WITHOUT CHEESE CONTAINS APPROXIMATELY:
195 TOTAL CALORIES / 10 CALORIES IN FAT
0 MG CHOLESTEROL / 290 MG SODIUM
105 MG CALCIUM

BROCCOLI-CHEESE PIE

I receive many letters from readers of my column every month requesting modifications of recipes using prepared commercial biscuit mix. In order to create new recipes, it was first necessary to develop a substitute biscuit mix of my own. I call it Magic Biscuit Mix because I truly feel it was a magical breakthrough in recipe development. This recipe is one that I modified for one such reader.

3/4 pound broccoli
1 garlic clove, finely chopped (1 teaspoon)
1/2 cup chopped scallions
6 ounces Cheddar cheese, grated (1 1/2 cups)
1/2 teaspoon dried marjoram, crushed in a mortar and pestle
1/4 teaspoon salt
Nonstick vegetable coating
3 eggs
1 cup skim milk
3/4 cup Magic Biscuit Mix (page 206)
1 tomato, halved and sliced into thin half circles

Preheat the oven to 400°F. Peel tough outer skin from the broccoli stems and chop the broccoli coarsely. Steam until crisp-tender, 4 to 5 minutes. Rinse with cold water and drain thoroughly.

Cook the garlic and scallions in a large skillet, covered, over low heat until tender, about 5 minutes, adding a little water or chicken stock if necessary to prevent scorching. Add the broccoli, cheese, marjoram, and salt and mix well. Turn into a 9- or 10-inch pie plate that you have first sprayed with nonstick vegetable coating.

Combine the eggs, milk, and Magic Biscuit Mix and beat for 1 minute with a hand beater. Pour over the broccoli mixture and bake for 25 minutes.

Remove from the oven and place the tomato circles around the outside edge of the pie plate. Return to the oven and bake for 5 minutes more. Cool for 10 minutes before slicing.

Makes 6 main-dish servings

EACH SERVING CONTAINS APPROXIMATELY:
235 TOTAL CALORIES / 130 CALORIES IN FAT
170 MG CHOLESTEROL / 425 MG SODIUM
340 MG CALCIUM

FISH & SEAFOOD

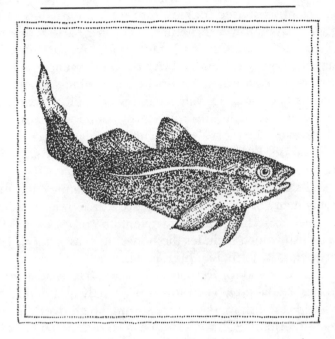

FISH AND SEAFOOD are lower in fat than poultry or meat and are the best sources of animal protein. Not only are fish and seafood lower in fat, most of the fat they do contain is in polyunsaturated form rather than the saturated fats that build up cholesterol and increase the chances of heart disease.

Seafood has long been a very popular item on most menus. In fact the traditional shrimp cocktail is the biggest-selling appetizer item throughout the country. The rapid rise in the popularity of fresh fish in the last couple of years has been awesome. Many restaurateurs have told me that the fresh-fish specials are always the biggest-selling items on their menus.

There was also a time when anyone on a low-cholesterol diet was told to avoid shellfish, but new research shows that shellfish are not nearly as high in cholesterol as was once thought, with the possible exception of shrimp. Even with shrimp, unless you are eating more animal protein than is recommended in a well-balanced healthy diet, the amount of cholesterol per serving can easily be planned

141

into your daily diet without exceeding the cholesterol recommendations of the American Heart Association.

In large part fish owes its new popularity in our diet to the Eskimos, who literally live on fish and seafood. It was only when medical scientists started looking into the eating habits of the Eskimos, who have a lower incidence of coronary artery disease, that they discovered that Omega-3 fatty acids, which include EPA (eicosapentaenoic acid) and DHA (docosahexaenoic acid), were largely responsible for their cardiovascular wellness. Omega-3 fatty acids can also be found in walnuts and walnut oil, wheat germ oil, soybean products, including tofu, most common beans, and seaweed. However, the most abundant and popular source is certainly fish and seafood. Fish particularly high in these fatty acids include salmon, trout, mackerel, haddock, and sardines.

Fish and shellfish are excellent sources of vitamins and minerals and supply many of the minerals that are scarce in most other food sources, such as iodine, zinc, and selenium.

Canned fish, which includes the bones, such as salmon, sardines, and anchovies, is extremely high in calcium.

The rising demand for fresh fish and seafood has had a wonderful effect on its availability. The old rule of supply and demand really does work! Fresh-fish markets have sprung up all over the country, and most supermarkets have a fresh-fish section. If you don't think you like fish, chances are you have never had really fresh fish or properly cooked fish—or maybe neither one.

When buying a whole fresh fish, always look at the eyes. If the fish is really fresh, the eyes will be very clear. As it gets older, the eyes become clouded looking. The scales of a fresh fish will not be separated from the skin. Filleted fresh fish should look moist and never as though it is drying out. Also, fresh fish and seafood do not have the overly strong "fishy" smell many people dislike. If the odor of the fish is too strong, you can count on the fact that the fish is not fresh.

Shellfish are often suspected of coming from contaminated water. Be aware of where the shellfish originates and the water conditions prevailing in that area.

The storage of fresh fish is equally important. Immediately unwrap fish you have purchased and wash it under cold running water. Dry it thoroughly and squeeze fresh lemon juice all over the surface. Store it in a nonaluminum container tightly covered in the refrigerator. If you must keep it for more than a day before serving, place the container on a pan over ice cubes in the refrigerator.

When fresh fish is not available, it is often necessary to buy frozen fish. When using frozen fish, always put it in the refrigerator to thaw so that it thaws slowly. If you force the thawing time, the texture of the fish will be mushy and very unappetizing. After frozen fish has thawed, handle it exactly the same way you would fresh fish. It should not be refrozen.

There are many wonderful canned-fish and seafood products that you can keep in your cupboard and always have on hand. These include canned water-packed tuna, clams packed in clam juice, oysters, salmon, sardines, and anchovies.

When cooking fish the single most important thing to remember is not to overcook it. The minute it turns from translucent to opaque, it is done. Further cooking will only lessen the flavor and make the fish tough and dry. When poaching shellfish such as shrimp and scallops, it will literally take no more than a minute or two in a boiling stock or court bouillon.

Fish lends itself well to many types of cooking procedures, including baking, broiling, poaching, braising, and sautéeing. Before choosing the cooking method you must first decide on the type of fish you are going to use. It is difficult to poach delicately flavored fish such as sole, flounder, or fluke and keep it in one piece. It will also literally fall apart on a grill or under a broiler. It is best to either bake or sauté this type of fish. Poaching and braising are ideal for shellfish and slightly firmer fish such as cod, haddock, pollock, bluefish, trout, perch, snapper, and mackerel.

If you wish to broil or barbecue fish on a grill, it is important to use a very firm fish, such as swordfish, monkfish, tuna, shark, or salmon. Lobster and crab are also good for broiling or grilling.

Many delicately flavored fish are best served with a sauce. In fact good fresh fish, the proper cooking technique, and a good sauce recipe will give you the very best fish dish possible.

CAVIAR-STUFFED PASTA SHELLS

Caviar is an elegant hors d'oeuvre. Two reasons people may avoid using it are its high cholesterol and sodium content and its high price tag. This recipe makes such a little bit of caviar go such a long way that the cholesterol and sodium per portion are greatly reduced, and so is the price! These pasta shells also make a good appetizer course, serving 2 per person and garnishing them with sprigs of parsley or watercress. If you don't like caviar, you can substitute chopped clams or even drained water-packed tuna.

1 cup part-skim ricotta cheese
3 tablespoons plain nonfat yogurt
1 teaspoon freshly squeezed lemon juice
1 1/2 teaspoons finely chopped onion
One 2-ounce jar red caviar
18 giant pasta shells, cooked al dente

Combine the ricotta cheese and the yogurt in a food processor or blender and blend until satin smooth.

Combine the ricotta cheese mixture, lemon juice, onion, and caviar in a mixing bowl and mix thoroughly.

Spoon 1 tablespoon of the caviar mixture into each pasta shell.

Makes 18 pasta shells

EACH SHELL CONTAINS APPROXIMATELY:
50 TOTAL CALORIES / 15 CALORIES IN FAT
15 MG CHOLESTEROL / 90 MG SODIUM
50 MG CALCIUM

CRAB-SHRIMP MOLD

This seafood mold is a revision for one of my readers. The original recipe contained a cup of mayonnaise, for which I have substituted a combination of tofu and ricotta cheese and it works surprisingly well. I used the canned shrimp and crab because they were the ingredients in the original recipe, but you may substitute either leftover fish or drained water-packed canned tuna for the seafood ingredients. If you are serving this for a party, I would suggest making it in a fish-shaped mold. It is good served with rye or whole-grain bread, toasted and cut into quarters, or Herb Bread (page 218).

> *1 envelope unflavored gelatin*
> *2 tablespoons cool water*
> *1/4 cup boiling water*
> *1/2 cup tomato sauce*
> *2/3 cup part-skim ricotta cheese*
> *3/4 cup tofu, cubed*
> *1 tablespoon freshly squeezed lemon juice*
> *1 tablespoon canola or corn oil*
> *1/2 teaspoon salt*
> *1/4 teaspoon fructose or 1/3 teaspoon sugar*
> *1/2 medium onion, finely chopped (3/4 cup)*
> *1 celery rib, without leaves, finely chopped (1/2 cup)*
> *One 4-ounce can shrimp, drained*
> *One 6-ounce can crabmeat, drained*
> *Vegetable oil or nonstick vegetable coating*

Soften the gelatin in the cool water. Add the boiling water and stir until completely dissolved. Pour into a blender container and add the tomato sauce, ricotta cheese, tofu, lemon juice, corn oil, salt, and fructose or sugar and blend until smooth.

Pour the mixture into a bowl and add all the remaining ingredients. Mix well and pour into a mold that is lightly oiled or sprayed with nonstick coating.

Refrigerate overnight before unmolding to serve.

Makes 6 servings

EACH SERVING CONTAINS APPROXIMATELY:
75 TOTAL CALORIES / 30 CALORIES IN FAT
30 MG CHOLESTEROL / 270 MG SODIUM
80 MG CALCIUM

HOT CRAB DIP

This dip is a revision of a much higher calorie version sent to me by a reader. It is a bizarre-sounding list of ingredients but makes an amazingly delicious dip, infinitely lower in calories than the original recipe. It is good served with raw or blanched vegetables, melba toast rounds, or toasted Tortilla Wedges (page 201). It also makes a great open-faced sandwich when spread on toasted whole-grain bread.

1 cup part-skim ricotta cheese
1 garlic clove, minced (1 teaspoon)
2 ounces tofu (¼ cup)
1 teaspoon prepared mustard
2 tablespoons sherry
1 teaspoon freshly squeezed lemon juice
1 teaspoon minced onion
½ pound crabmeat

Place all the ingredients except the crabmeat in a blender container and blend until satin smooth.

Transfer to a pan, add the crabmeat, and heat thoroughly.

Makes 2 cups

¼ CUP CONTAINS APPROXIMATELY:
85 TOTAL CALORIES / 30 CALORIES IN FAT
40 MG CHOLESTEROL / 330 MG SODIUM
110 MG CALCIUM

SCALLOPS IN GINGER SAUCE

This scallop dish is most attractive served in a giant scallop shell and topped with a chive knot. To make the chive knot, take two long pieces of chive and tie them into a knot in the center. Place the chive knot on top of the scallops in the shell. Smaller portions of Scallops in Ginger Sauce also make a nice appetizer. As an entrée, I like to serve it with Rice Pilaf (page 119) and an assortment of colorful fresh vegetables.

> 1 tablespoon corn-oil margarine
> 2 tablespoons chopped peeled ginger
> 4 teaspoons flour
> 1 tablespoon white wine
> 1 cup clam juice or fish stock (see page 25)
> 1 cup skim milk
> 2 tablespoons finely chopped chives
> 2 cups defatted chicken stock or fish stock (see page 22 or 25)
> 1 pound scallops
> 4 whole chives, tied in knots for garnish

Melt the margarine in a medium saucepan. Add the ginger and cook for 1 minute. Stir in the flour.

Combine the wine, the 1 cup clam juice or stock, and the milk and gradually add to the flour mixture, stirring with a wire whisk. Bring the sauce to a boil, whisking constantly. Reduce the heat and simmer, whisking occasionally, until the sauce thickens and is reduced by one-third, about 10 to 15 minutes.

Remove from the heat. Strain the sauce to remove the ginger. Return the sauce to the pan, add the chives, and reheat.

Meanwhile, bring the 2 cups of chicken or fish stock to a boil. Add the scallops, reduce the heat, and simmer just until the scallops become opaque, about 2 to 4 minutes. Drain and divide among 2 to 4 scallop shells.

Spoon ⅓ cup sauce over each serving. Top each with a chive knot.

Makes 4 servings

EACH SERVING CONTAINS APPROXIMATELY:
155 TOTAL CALORIES / 30 CALORIES IN FAT
45 MG CHOLESTEROL / 215 MG SODIUM
110 MG CALCIUM

ITALIAN OYSTER CASSEROLE

This recipe is a lower-calorie version of the one created by Mary Etta Moose, the owner of the famous Washington Square Bar and Grill in San Francisco. This dish can be served either as an entrée with a salad and dessert or in smaller portions as a dressing with turkey during the holidays. Still smaller amounts make an interesting hors d'oeuvre served on oyster shells. No matter how you're serving it, it needs garnish. As good as it is, it is not a particularly attractive dish, and a little chopped parsley and freshly grated imported Parmesan cheese do wonders for its appearance.

1 large eggplant (1½ pounds)
1 tablespoon fennel seeds
1 tablespoon extra-virgin olive oil
1 medium onion, finely chopped (1½ cups)
1 cup finely chopped fennel bulb
3 garlic cloves, finely chopped (1 tablespoon)
1 whole egg
1 egg white
½ teaspoon salt
¼ teaspoon freshly ground black pepper
½ teaspoon dried thyme, crushed in a mortar and pestle
⅛ teaspoon freshly grated nutmeg
½ teaspoon grated lemon zest
2 ounces imported Parmesan cheese, freshly grated (½ cup)
2 tablespoons finely chopped parsley
2 tablespoons finely chopped fennel tops

2 cups cooked brown rice (²/₃ cup uncooked)
1 cup oysters, cut into ¹/₂-inch cubes, plus all the liquid from the
  jar

Pierce holes in an unpeeled whole eggplant with the tines of a fork. Bake for 1 hour in a preheated 400°F oven. When the eggplant is cool enough to handle, peel and cut into ¹/₂-inch cubes. You should have 3 cups.

While the eggplant is cooking, put the fennel seeds in a large dry hot skillet and cook them, stirring constantly, until they are lightly browned. Add the olive oil and mix well. Then add the onions, fennel bulb, and garlic and cook, covered, over low heat until soft, about 10 minutes.

Combine the egg and egg white and mix well. Add the salt, pepper, thyme, nutmeg, lemon zest, ¹/₄ cup of cheese, the parsley, and fennel tops and mix well. Add the cooked rice and mix well. Add the cubed oysters and all of the juice from the oyster jar. Add the eggplant and mix well. Add the onion/fennel mixture to the bowl and again mix well. Pour into a casserole with a tight-fitting lid. Bake in a preheated 350°F oven, covered, for 1 hour; then sprinkle the remaining ¹/₄ cup Parmesan cheese over the top and bake, uncovered, for 15 minutes more.

Makes 6 cups

¹/₂ CUP CONTAINS APPROXIMATELY:
110 TOTAL CALORIES / 30 CALORIES IN FAT
30 MG CHOLESTEROL / 230 MG SODIUM
85 MG CALCIUM

CIOPPINO

Italian fishermen who came to San Francisco at the time of the Gold Rush introduced this spicy shellfish stew, which has since become a San Francisco favorite, where it is served with crusty San Francisco sourdough French bread. Crab and lobster are usually purchased already cooked and therefore they do not need to be poached but simply added in the sauce. This dish is classically presented with all of the shellfish intact in their shells. I suggest serving it with bibs for your guests and big bowls for the shells they discard.

> 4 cups Marinara Sauce (page 59)
> 1 pound assorted raw shellfish (scallops, shrimp, clams, mussels,
>   lobsters, crab, etc.), cleaned
> 2 cups clam juice or fish stock (see page 25)
> 4 whole clams, in their shells (optional), steamed until they open
> Fresh herb sprigs

Heat the Marinara Sauce in a large saucepan. Poach the shellfish in the clam juice or fish stock until it goes from translucent to opaque, about 1 minute. DO NOT OVERCOOK.

Add the clam juice or fish stock to the marinara sauce and mix well.

For each serving, combine 1 cup of the shellfish and 1½ cups of the sauce and place in a large soup bowl garnished with an open clam. Garnish with a sprig of one of the fresh herbs used in making the marinara sauce.

Makes 4 servings

EACH SERVING CONTAINS APPROXIMATELY:
200 TOTAL CALORIES / 20 CALORIES IN FAT
115 MG CHOLESTEROL / 2000 MG SODIUM
110 MG CALCIUM

BOUILLABAISSE

This delicious seafood stew has for centuries been a staple of the fishermen living on the coast of France in and around Marseilles. They use primarily fish for this dish, but when I added a little more shellfish to this savory saffron-scented bowl the guests at the Canyon Ranch Spa in Tucson seemed to like it a lot better; so I am sharing my spa version with you. Also in Marseilles the Bouillabaisse is served over crusty French bread in a bowl, but I like to serve the bread on the side.

> *1 medium onion, finely chopped (1½ cups)*
> *1 leek, white part only, thinly sliced (1 cup)*
> *1 garlic clove, finely chopped (1 teaspoon)*
> *2 medium tomatoes, peeled, seeded, and diced (1½ cups)*
> *2 tablespoons finely chopped parsley*
> *1 celery rib, finely chopped (½ cup)*
> *1 bay leaf*
> *¼ teaspoon dried thyme, crushed in a mortar and pestle*
> *¼ teaspoon dried fennel, crushed in a mortar and pestle*
> *¼ teaspoon dried saffron, dissolved in a little defatted chicken or fish stock*
> *⅛ teaspoon freshly ground black pepper*
> *2 cups defatted chicken stock or fish stock (see page 22 or 25)*
> *1 cup dry white wine*
> *½ pound firm white fish, cut into strips (2 cups)*
> *½ pound shellfish (shrimp, lobster, scallops, etc.), shelled and cleaned*
> *Fresh thyme or fennel for garnish*
> *4 slices crusty French bread*

Combine the onions, leeks, and garlic and cook, covered, over very low heat until soft, about 10 minutes, adding a little stock if necessary to prevent scorching. Add all the other ingredients except the fish, shellfish, garnish, and bread. Mix well and bring to a boil. Reduce the heat and simmer, covered, for 10 minutes.

Add the fish and shellfish and cook until it turns from translucent to opaque, 2 to 5 minutes.

Serve in four casseroles, garnished with sprigs of thyme or fennel. Serve a slice of French bread on the side.

Makes four 2-cup servings

EACH SERVING CONTAINS APPROXIMATELY:
310 TOTAL CALORIES / 45 CALORIES IN FAT
50 MG CHOLESTEROL / 295 MG SODIUM
100 MG CALCIUM

POLYNESIAN PRAWNS

These prawns are as delicious as they are quick and easy to prepare. You can use bite-size shrimp, totally peeled, and put them on toothpicks for hors d'oeuvres or use very large prawns and serve two per person as an entrée with rice and Oriental vegetables. In fact this is a very popular luncheon entrée on my menu at the restaurant at Neiman-Marcus in Newport Beach, California.

1 pound large prawns or shrimp
½ cup Mandarin Dressing and Marinade (page 75)

Peel and devein the prawns, leaving the tails attached.

Bring the dressing to a boil in a large skillet. Add the shrimp and cook, turning frequently, until they turn from translucent to opaque, about 2 minutes.

Makes 4 servings (3 or 4 shrimp each, depending upon size)

EACH SERVING CONTAINS APPROXIMATELY:
175 TOTAL CALORIES / 55 CALORIES IN FAT
160 MG CHOLESTEROL / 245 MG SODIUM
80 MG CALCIUM

LINGUINE WITH CLAM SAUCE

This is one of my favorite "emergency" meals. That is when you have no time to shop, very little time to cook, and unexpected guests coming for dinner. The beauty of this recipe is that everything in it can be kept on hand in your cupboard and refrigerator. Toss whatever salad greens you have on hand with a light dressing and slice up any fruit you may have or open a can of water- or juice-packed fruit and you literally have a meal in minutes.

½ pound dry linguine (4 cups cooked)
One 8-ounce can chopped clams, undrained
1 garlic clove, minced (1 teaspoon)
2 ounces imported Parmesan cheese, grated (½ cup)

Cook the linguine according to the package directions until al dente, or slightly resistant to the bite.

Heat the clams in their juice along with the garlic, until heated through. DO NOT BOIL.

Drain the pasta, toss with the clam and garlic mixture, and the grated Parmesan cheese. Serve on heated plates.

Makes 4 servings

EACH SERVING CONTAINS APPROXIMATELY:
250 TOTAL CALORIES / 45 CALORIES IN FAT
55 MG CHOLESTEROL / 265 MG SODIUM
240 MG CALCIUM

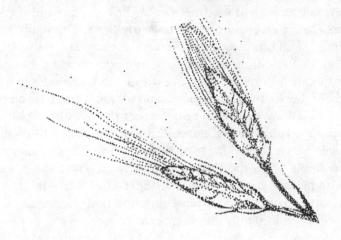

CLAM LASAGNA

I created this clam lasagna for the Four Seasons Hotel and Resort in Dallas. It is as much of a hit with the conference participants as it is with the spa guests. Its uniquely different appearance and taste makes it fun to serve as the entrée for parties. It also works well for a buffet.

Two 6¹/₂-ounce cans minced clams, undrained
1 tablespoon corn-oil margarine
2¹/₂ tablespoons flour
1 cup clam juice
3 garlic cloves, minced (1 tablespoon)
¹/₂ teaspoon each dried basil, oregano, thyme, and marjoram,
    crushed in a mortar and pestle
¹/₄ cup loosely packed finely chopped parsley
¹/₄ teaspoon freshly ground black pepper
3 tablespoons freshly squeezed lemon juice
Vegetable oil for the dish
¹/₂ pound dry lasagna noodles, cooked al dente
2 cups part-skim ricotta cheese
3 pounds fresh spinach, veins and stems removed, blanched or
    steamed for 1 minute
¹/₂ pound part-skim mozzarella cheese, thinly sliced
1 ounce imported Parmesan cheese, freshly grated (¹/₄ cup)

Drain the clams and reserve the liquid. Melt the margarine in a 2-
or 3-quart saucepan over medium heat. Add the flour and cook for
2 minutes, being careful not to brown the flour. Gradually stir in
the reserved clam liquid and the clam juice; there should be 2 cups
total. Continue cooking and stirring until the mixture boils and
thickens, about 5 minutes. Remove from the heat and stir in the
clams, garlic, herbs, parsley, pepper, and lemon juice. Line an oiled
9-by-13-inch baking dish with one-third of the noodles. Spoon the
ricotta cheese evenly over the noodles and top with a third of the
clam sauce. Add a second layer of noodles. Squeeze as much moisture as possible from the spinach and arrange over the noodles.
Cover with half the cheese slices, then spread with half the remaining clam sauce. Top with the remaining noodles, cheese slices, and
clam sauce. Sprinkle with the Parmesan cheese.

Bake, uncovered, in a preheated 350°F oven for 30 minutes or
until bubbly and heated through. Let stand for 10 minutes before
cutting.

Makes 8 servings

EACH SERVING CONTAINS APPROXIMATELY:
370 TOTAL CALORIES / 125 CALORIES IN FAT
75 MG CHOLESTEROL / 425 MG SODIUM
630 MG CALCIUM

FISH EN PAPILLOTE

If you don't have baker's paper, this dish can also be done in aluminum foil, just folding the edges of the foil envelopes to seal them. The thing I like best about it is the marvelous aroma it releases at the table when the envelopes are opened.

1 pound red snapper or any firm, white fish, cut into 4 portions
Salt
Lemon juice, freshly squeezed
2 cups julienne-cut fresh vegetables of your choice
4 teaspoons chopped fresh herbs or 1 teaspoon dried tarragon,
*   crushed in a mortar and pestle*
5 teaspoons corn-oil margarine
4 slices lemon
1/4 cup balsamic vinegar
8 small new potatoes, steamed, baked, or boiled until tender

Wash the fish in cold water and pat dry. Salt lightly, squeeze lemon juice over both sides, and store, covered, in the refrigerator.

Make four 12-by-16-inch ovals of baker's paper, using a bowl for a template. To assemble the servings, place 1/2 cup vegetables in the center of each oval and place a piece of fish on top. Sprinkle 1 teaspoon fresh herbs or 1/4 teaspoon crushed tarragon over the fish and cover with 1 teaspoon of the margarine, a lemon slice, and 1 tablespoon balsamic vinegar. Spread the remaining 1 teaspoon margarine along the edges of the paper, then fold it over and make sure it is sealed by crimping the edges with a tight fold.

Place in a preheated 400°F oven and bake for 5 minutes. Place each envelope on a large dinner plate with two small potatoes on the side. Allow each guest to open the envelope at the table.

Makes 4 servings

EACH SERVING CONTAINS APPROXIMATELY:
220 TOTAL CALORIES / 70 CALORIES IN FAT
1 MG CHOLESTEROL / 35 MG SODIUM
30 MG CALCIUM

RED SNAPPER IN THE STYLE OF VERA CRUZ

This is my favorite Mexican fish dish. I have it on the dinner menu with hot corn tortillas at the Canyon Ranch Spa in Tucson, Arizona.

1½ pounds red snapper or other firm, white fish
½ teaspoon salt
¼ cup freshly squeezed lime juice
1 medium onion, thinly sliced (2 cups)
½ cup whole pimientos, thinly sliced
3 medium tomatoes, peeled, seeded, and diced (2 cups)
¼ cup canned chopped green California chilies
1 tablespoon capers
6 parsley sprigs

Wash the fish thoroughly with cold water. Dry and place in a nonaluminum dish.

Lightly salt and pour the lime juice evenly over the fish. Cover and refrigerate for at least an hour before cooking.

Cook the onions in a heavy skillet, covered, over very low heat until tender, about 10 minutes, adding a little water if necessary to prevent scorching.

Add half of the pimientos and all of the tomatoes, chilies, and capers. Lay 2 of the parsley sprigs over the top and cook, covered, until there is about 1 inch of liquid in the bottom of the pan.

Add the fish and cook for about 5 minutes per side or until it turns from translucent to opaque. Remove the parsley. Serve with the sauce spooned over the top and garnish with the remaining pimientos and sprigs of fresh parsley.

Makes 4 servings

EACH SERVING CONTAINS APPROXIMATELY:
240 TOTAL CALORIES / 45 CALORIES IN FAT
1 MG CHOLESTEROL / 460 MG SODIUM
30 MG CALCIUM

POACHED SALMON IN WALNUT-DILL SAUCE

Not only is salmon the most beautiful fish because of its peachy color, but modern research indicates that it is also one of the most beneficial creatures from the sea because of its Omega-3 fatty acid content. Poached salmon is often served with dill sauce. I like the hint of walnut in this sauce, particularly when it is accompanied by toasted walnuts to reinforce the nutty flavor with a crunchy texture. Both the tofu-based sauce with walnut oil and the walnuts contain Omega-3 fatty acids, making this a really healthy fish dish. To serve, either place the salmon on top of ½ cup of Rice Pilaf (page 119) and pour ¼ cup of the sauce over it with 1 tablespoon of toasted walnuts and a dill sprig or spoon ¼ cup sauce on the plate and place the salmon on top of the sauce, again sprinkling it with walnuts and topping it with a dill sprig. If plating the salmon on the sauce, I like to serve it with boiled new potatoes.

> *¼ cup chopped walnuts*
> *3 cups court bouillon (see page 25)*
> *1 pound fresh salmon, cut into 4 pieces*
> *1 cup Walnut-Dill Sauce (page 69), heated*
> *Fresh dill sprigs for garnish*

Place the walnuts in a preheated 350°F oven for 8 to 10 minutes or until golden brown. Watch carefully, as they burn easily. Set aside.

Bring the court bouillon to a boil and place the salmon in it. When the bouillon returns to a boil, reduce the heat and simmer until the salmon turns from translucent to opaque, about 10 minutes. Do not overcook or the salmon will be dry.

Makes 4 servings

EACH SERVING CONTAINS APPROXIMATELY:
355 TOTAL CALORIES / 225 CALORIES IN FAT
45 MG CHOLESTEROL / 290 MG SODIUM
175 MG CALCIUM

SALMON MOUSSE

The original recipe for this mousse was sent to me by a reader in Miami who had attended a cooking school on Saint Barthélemy in the Caribbean. She loved the taste and texture of the mousse, but wanted to get rid of all the calories. I like my own version so much I now have it on a luncheon menu at the Canyon Ranch Spa in Tucson, Arizona. As a variation, try serving the mousse cold, plated either on Roasted Red Pepper Sauce (page 69), Walnut-Dill Sauce (page 69), or Creamy Curry Dressing (page 70). If you have any leftover mousse, wrap it well and freeze it to serve on crackers for hors d'oeuvres at your next party.

> 1 leek, green part only, cut into very thin strips
> 1 cup part-skim ricotta cheese
> 3 tablespoons plain nonfat yogurt
> 1/2 pound salmon, without bones
> 1/2 pound bass, without bones
> 2 eggs
> 1/2 teaspoon salt
> 1/4 teaspoon freshly ground black pepper
> Corn-oil margarine
> 2 tablespoons raspberry vinegar
> 1 shallot, finely chopped (1 tablespoon)
> 1 cup clam juice or fish stock (see page 25)
> 6 raspberries for garnish (optional)

Cook the leek in boiling water until limp. Drain and put in a bowl of ice water. Drain and set aside.

Combine the ricotta cheese and yogurt in a food processor with a metal blade. Blend until satiny smooth. Add the fish to the ricotta cheese mixture in the food processor along with the eggs, salt, and pepper and blend until satin smooth.

Coat six 3-inch ramekins with the margarine. Fill each ramekin up to 1/4 inch from the top. Set the ramekins in a baking dish filled with hot water to a depth of 3/4 inch. Place the dish with the ramekins in a preheated 350°F oven for 20 minutes.

While the mousse is baking, combine the raspberry vinegar and shallot in a small saucepan. Bring to a boil and reduce completely. Add the clam juice or fish stock and reduce by half.

Remove the ramekins from the oven. Drain each mousse by turning it upside down on a paper towel to remove any melted margarine, then put back in the ramekin.

To serve, unmold the mousse on salad plates. Bring the sauce back to a boil, then remove from the heat. Add 1 tablespoon margarine and shake the pan until the margarine has melted completely. Spoon 1 tablespoon of the sauce over the top of each mousse. To garnish, surround each mousse with strips of leek, which will look like seaweed. If you wish, place a raspberry on top of each mousse.

Makes 6 servings

EACH SERVING CONTAINS APPROXIMATELY:
220 TOTAL CALORIES / 115 CALORIES IN FAT
100 MG CHOLESTEROL / 285 MG SODIUM
170 MG CALCIUM

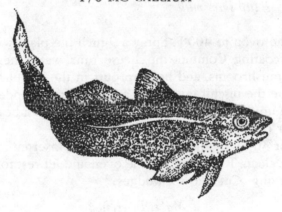

MAGIC TUNA QUICHE

This is another recipe sent to me by a reader who wanted a substitute for the commercially prepared biscuit mix that her recipe called for. I found that it was even lighter with my Magic Biscuit Mix than her original recipe. It makes a nice luncheon or light supper entrée served with my Chinese Chicken Salad (page 97) without the chicken.

> *Nonstick vegetable coating*
> *1/4 pound mozzarella cheese, grated (1 cup)*
> *One 61/2-ounce can water-packed tuna, drained*
> *1/4 cup diced water chestnuts*
> *1/2 cup frozen peas*
> *1/4 cup sliced scallions, including tops*
> *1/4 pound fresh mushrooms, sliced (1 cup)*
> *1/2 cup bean sprouts*
> *3/4 cup Magic Biscuit Mix (page 206)*
> *3 eggs*
> *1 cup skim milk*

Preheat the oven to 400°F. Spray a 9-inch pie plate with nonstick vegetable coating. Combine the cheese, tuna, water chestnuts, peas, scallions, mushrooms, and bean sprouts in the pie plate.

Combine the biscuit mix, eggs, and milk in a blender container and blend until smooth (15 seconds) or mix with a beater (1 minute). Pour over the mixture in the pie plate.

Bake for 30 to 35 minutes or until a knife inserted in the center comes out clean. Remove from the oven and let rest for 5 minutes before serving. Cut into six wedges.

Makes 6 servings

EACH SERVING CONTAINS APPROXIMATELY:
220 TOTAL CALORIES / 85 CALORIES IN FAT
140 MG CHOLESTEROL / 490 MG SODIUM
225 MG CALCIUM

CRAB QUICHE

This crustless quiche makes an excellent appetizer. When serving it for hors d'oeuvres, I cook it in a square pan rather than a round pie pan so that it cuts evenly into small squares. When used as an entrée, the servings are quite small because the ingredients are high in cholesterol and sodium. It makes a wonderful brunch served with fresh fruit on the side and my Herb Bread (page 218).

½ medium onion, finely chopped (¾ cup)
2 cups crabmeat, flaked
½ pound Cheddar cheese, grated (2 cups)
3 eggs, lightly beaten
One 12-ounce can skimmed evaporated milk
½ teaspoon salt

Cook the onions, covered, over very low heat until soft, adding a little water if necessary to prevent scorching.

Line the bottom of a 9-inch pie pan with the crabmeat. Sprinkle the cooked onions over the crabmeat. Sprinkle the grated cheese over the top of the mixture.

Combine the eggs, milk, and salt and mix well. Pour over the other ingredients.

Bake in a preheated 350°F oven for 1 hour. Allow to stand for at least 10 minutes before cutting into eight pie-shaped wedges.

Makes 8 servings

EACH SERVING CONTAINS APPROXIMATELY:
190 TOTAL CALORIES / 75 CALORIES IN FAT
138 MG CHOLESTEROL / 780 MG SODIUM
380 MG CALCIUM

BASS WITH GREEN CHILI SAUCE

1 1/2 pounds bass fillets
Freshly squeezed lemon juice
1/4 cup white wine
1 shallot, minced (1 tablespoon)
1/4 teaspoon salt
1/2 teaspoon freshly ground black pepper
1 pound tomatillos
1/2 cup clam juice or fish stock (see page 25)
1 medium onion, chopped (1 1/2 cups)
1 garlic clove, chopped (1 teaspoon)
2 yellow chilies, finely chopped (2 tablespoons)
1 large green California chili, peeled seeded, and chopped (2
  tablespoons)
1/2 small jalapeño pepper, stem and seeds removed, finely chopped
  (1 teaspoon)
1/4 cup finely chopped cilantro
1/4 teaspoon fructose or 1/2 teaspoon sugar
Corn-oil margarine
1 tablespoon lime juice
Cilantro sprigs for garnish
Twisted lime slices for garnish

Wash the fish in cold water and pat dry. Place in a nonaluminum
baking pan in a single layer. Squeeze lemon juice on the fish. Add
the wine. Sprinkle with shallots, salt, and pepper. Cover and refrigerate.

Husk the tomatillos and pierce each with a fork. Place in boiling
water and simmer until soft, about 12 minutes. Drain and puree in
a food processor with a metal blade or in a blender. Strain to
remove the seeds.

Heat half the clam juice or fish stock in a skillet. Add the onions,
garlic, chilies, and jalapeño pepper. Sauté until soft, about 5 minutes, adding more liquid if necessary to prevent scorching. Combine the onion/chili mixture with the cilantro, fructose or sugar,
and tomatillos in a large saucepan. Bring to a boil, reduce the heat,
cover, and simmer for 10 minutes. Set aside.

To cook the fish, cut a piece of parchment paper to fit the pan containing the fish. Lightly spread one side of the parchment paper with margarine.

In a small saucepan, bring the remaining ¼ cup of clam juice or fish stock to a boil and pour over the fish. Lay the parchment paper directly on the fish, margarine side down.

Preheat the oven to 425°F. Place the fish in the oven and cook until just opaque, about 9 minutes per inch of thickness. Reserve the cooking liquid.

Place the fish on a heated platter and cover with the parchment paper while the sauce is being reheated. Strain the cooking liquid, add it to the sauce, and bring to a boil. Remove the sauce from the heat, add the lime juice, and mix well. You should have 1½ cups of sauce.

To serve, divide the fish among six heated plates. Top each serving with ¼ cup of the sauce. Garnish with a sprig of cilantro and a twisted lime slice.

Makes 6 servings

EACH SERVING CONTAINS APPROXIMATELY:
165 TOTAL CALORIES / 30 CALORIES IN FAT
1 MG CHOLESTEROL / 200 MG SODIUM
25 MG CALCIUM

POULTRY

TO MOST PEOPLE the word *poultry* means chicken. I have always wondered if this has anything to do with the Republican promise in the early 1930s to put a "chicken in every pot" or the fact that chicken soup is the time-honored cure-all for everything from the common cold to a hangover.

White meat is always lower in fat and calories than dark meat, and all poultry is lower in fat without the skin. Unlike the fat in red meat, which is spread throughout the red muscle of the meat, the fat in poultry is concentrated in or just below the skin. That means that just by removing the skin you can remove about half the fat. A half chicken breast (about 3 ounces) with the skin is about 10.8 percent fat. Without the skin it is about 4.5 percent in the same piece of chicken. Also poultry fat is higher in polyunsaturates than the fat in red meat.

The white meat of turkey has about as much fat as the same amount of white chicken meat; however, the dark meat of turkey is higher in fat than the dark meat of chicken. Duck and goose have

50 percent more fat than chicken. These comparisons are all based on cooked poultry without skin. Wild game birds, such as pheasant, duck, and quail, are also very low in fat but are not readily available to most people.

The rising popularity of chicken has had its bad side. To meet the overwhelming demand for billions of chickens each year, the modern poultry farmer can raise a chicken from an egg in just 60 days. In order to do this the birds are fed hormone-packed feeds to speed up their growth, confined to small areas where they can't move freely to prevent weight loss, and given antibiotics to prevent disease.

When ordering chicken, ask for free-range or organically grown chickens that have not been raised as miracles of modern science but have been allowed to grow up naturally in a barnyard. They are more expensive but well worth the price, if you can get them, because the meat is firmer and tastier. The ideal solution is to find a chicken farmer in your area and buy your chickens directly from him. Also if you primarily use chicken breasts for cooking, it is less expensive and less time-consuming to buy the chicken breasts separately and then buy only scrap parts, such as necks and backs, to make your stock, rather than buying a whole chicken and using only the breast meat.

The same guidelines also apply to turkey. Since turkey is no longer considered just a holiday meal, but rather an important food source, I am sure that more and more turkey will need to be produced, causing the same problems facing the chicken population.

When cooking poultry, the single most important thing to remember is not to overcook it. If you are roasting a chicken for a meal, put it breast side down in a flat roasting pan and bake it at 350°F for about 1 hour or until the liquid runs clear when pierced with a knife. When roasting chicken you are going to allow to cool so that you can chop it to use later as an ingredient, remove it from the oven while the liquid is still running a little bit pink. It will continue to cook as it cools and will give you moister, tastier chicken meat to use in other recipes. If you cook it completely before allowing it to cool, the chicken tends to be dry.

When roasting turkey, follow the directions given in my recipe for Roast Turkey with Fennel (page 180) and season it any way you wish.

When sautéeing chicken breasts it literally takes only a very few minutes per side for the chicken breasts to turn from translucent to opaque and spring back when touched with your finger. At this point they are done, still moist, and very tender.

When working with poultry of any kind it is extremely important not to let it stand out at room temperature. Poultry of all types, as well as eggs, quickly build up harmful bacteria when not refrigerated. This is also true of anything containing poultry or eggs as an ingredient, such as mayonnaise and hollandaise sauce.

When freezing chicken or other poultry, I prefer freezing it with the skin left on. Freezing tends to dehydrate everything, so leaving the skin on poultry helps to protect it against this dryness.

Rabbit, while not in the poultry category, does have all white meat, which tastes very much like chicken. Rabbit is lower in fat, cholesterol, and calories than any poultry and is also low enough in sodium to be recommended for people on low-sodium diets. I mention this here because I never know where to put rabbit in a cookbook. It doesn't really fit into any of the major animal-flesh categories, but it substitutes well for poultry in recipes.

Chicken, turkey, and rabbit are three of my favorite ingredients because you can literally use any seasoning range with them successfully. You can always substitute them for each other in any recipe and also use them successfully as substitutes for veal.

GINGERED LEMON CHICKEN

This dish is both quick and easy. For a delicious Oriental-style menu, serve Egg Drop Soup (page 30) as an appetizer and serve the Gingered Lemon Chicken with brown rice and Oriental vegetables such as snow peas and water chestnuts, garnished with julienne-cut carrots and red peppers for color.

1/2 cup coarsely chopped walnuts
*4 chicken breast halves (1 1/2 pounds), boned, skinned, and cut
  into 1/2-inch strips*

1 egg white, *lightly beaten*

2 tablespoons flour

1/4 teaspoon salt

1/2 teaspoon fructose or 3/4 teaspoon sugar

1 tablespoon canola or corn oil

1-inch piece ginger, peeled and very finely chopped (1 1/2 teaspoons)

1 garlic clove, finely chopped (1 teaspoon)

3 scallions, sliced (1/2 cup)

1/2 cup defatted chicken stock (see page 22)

2 teaspoons reduced-sodium soy sauce

1/4 cup sherry

2 tablespoons freshly squeezed lemon juice

Place the walnuts in a preheated 350°F oven for 8 to 10 minutes. Watch carefully, as they burn easily. Set aside.

In a large bowl, coat the chicken with the egg white. Drain well in a colander and return to the bowl.

Combine the flour, salt, and fructose or sugar. Coat the chicken with the flour mixture.

Heat the oil. Add the ginger and garlic and cook over low heat, stirring constantly, until very lightly browned. Add the chicken and cook until just opaque, about 5 minutes, stirring to expose all sides of the chicken to the heat. Stir in the scallions.

Combine the chicken stock, soy sauce, sherry, and lemon juice. Pour over the chicken and mix well. Bring to a boil.

Serve over 1/2 cup rice or Rice Pilaf (page 119). Top each serving with 2 tablespoons toasted walnuts.

Makes four 3/4 cup servings

EACH SERVING CONTAINS APPROXIMATELY:
400 TOTAL CALORIES / 170 CALORIES IN FAT
165 MG CHOLESTEROL / 425 MG SODIUM
50 MG CALCIUM

CHICKEN BOMBAY

This is one of the most popular entrées on my spa menu at the Four Seasons Hotel and Resort in Dallas. It is also a wonderful recipe for parties because you can make the sauce a day or two ahead of time and it is even better than when freshly made. Instead of just plain brown rice, I like to serve the chicken over my Rice Pilaf (page 119) with the Apple Chutney on the side and an assortment of other low-calorie condiments, such as diced tomatoes, finely chopped scallions, peeled and diced cucumbers, chopped hard-cooked egg whites, and diced tropical fruits, such as banana, pineapple, papaya, or mango.

CURRY SAUCE:

1 tablespoon corn-oil margarine
½ medium onion, finely chopped (¾ cup)
1 small green apple, peeled, cored, and finely chopped (¾ cup)
½ garlic clove, finely chopped (½ teaspoon)
1 tablespoon flour
1½ tablespoons curry powder
1 cup defatted chicken stock, boiling (see page 22)
¼ cup skim milk
1 tablespoon nonfat dry milk powder
1 teaspoon freshly squeezed lemon juice
1½ teaspoons grated lemon zest

¼ cup chopped almonds
2 whole chicken breasts, boned, skinned, halved, and butterflied
Juice of ½ lemon
Defatted chicken stock (see page 22)
Dry white wine
2 cups cooked brown rice
½ cup Apple Chutney (page 62)

Heat the margarine in a large skillet. Add the onions, apples, and garlic and cook until the onions are tender and translucent, about 10 minutes.

Combine the flour and curry powder. Mix well and add to the onion mixture, stirring constantly for a few minutes. Add the boiling chicken stock and mix thoroughly. Combine the skim milk with the nonfat dry milk and add to the sauce, mixing well. Add the lemon juice and zest and allow the sauce to simmer slowly, partially covered, for 1 hour or until slightly thickened. This makes 1 cup sauce.

Place the almonds in a preheated 350°F oven for 8 to 10 minutes or until golden brown. Watch carefully, as they burn easily. Set aside.

Sprinkle lemon juice over the chicken. Heat a little chicken stock in a large skillet and reduce until almost dry. Add a little white wine and reduce again. Sauté the butterflied chicken breasts until just done, adding a little more stock as needed to prevent scorching.

To serve, place ½ cup of the cooked rice on each plate and place ½ butterflied chicken breast on top. Spoon ¼ cup of the sauce over each chicken breast. Sprinkle 1 tablespoon chopped toasted almonds over the top of the chicken and serve with 2 tablespoons of Apple Chutney and any other condiments you desire.

Makes 4 servings

EACH SERVING CONTAINS APPROXIMATELY:
565 TOTAL CALORIES / 130 CALORIES IN FAT
100 MG CHOLESTEROL / 380 MG SODIUM
140 MG CALCIUM

CHICKEN STROGANOFF

Chicken Stroganoff is another wonderful dish for a party because it can be made ahead of time and is so easy to serve on a buffet. Whenever I have Chicken Stroganoff on one of my spa menus, I keep the entire theme of the menu Russian, serving Borscht (page 45) as an appetizer and Strawberries Romanoff (page 226) for dessert.

WHITE SAUCE:

1 cup skim milk
2 teaspoons corn-oil margarine
1½ tablespoons flour
⅛ teaspoon salt
2 tablespoons defatted chicken stock (see page 22)
1 medium onion, thinly sliced (2 cups)
½ pound fresh mushrooms, sliced (2 cups)
½ teaspoon dried basil, crushed in a mortar and pestle
¼ teaspoon paprika
¼ teaspoon ground nutmeg
⅛ teaspoon salt
2 tablespoons sherry

½ pound cooked chicken, without skin, cut into strips (2 cups)
¼ cup plain nonfat yogurt
3 cups cooked noodles (10 ounces dry)

Heat the milk in a small saucepan over low heat. In another small saucepan, melt the margarine and add the flour, stirring constantly. Cook the flour and margarine for 3 minutes, then take the mixture off the heat and add the simmering milk all at once, stirring constantly with a wire whisk. Put the sauce back over low heat and cook slowly for 15 minutes, stirring occasionally. If you wish a thicker sauce, cook it a little longer. Add the salt and mix thoroughly. If there are lumps, blend until smooth.

In a large saucepan, heat the chicken stock and cook the onions, covered, over very low heat until soft, adding a little chicken stock if necessary to prevent scorching. Add the mushrooms and continue cooking, covered, until soft. Add the white sauce and all the other ingredients except the chicken, yogurt, and noodles. Simmer, uncovered, for 10 minutes.

Add the chicken and cook until thoroughly heated. Remove from the heat, add the yogurt, and mix thoroughly. On each of four heated plates serve ¾ cup of the mixture in the center of ¾ cup of noodles.

Makes 4 servings

EACH SERVING CONTAINS APPROXIMATELY:
345 TOTAL CALORIES / 65 CALORIES IN FAT
90 MG CHOLESTEROL / 165 MG SODIUM
145 MG CALCIUM

COMPANY CHICKEN

This recipe is a revised version of an old standby sent to me by a reader. It contained two packages of frozen broccoli, two cans of cream of chicken soup, and a cup of mayonnaise. This is a long way "ingredientswise" from the original, but amazingly similar in both taste and appearance.

> *2 whole chicken breasts, halved*
> *2 cups water*
> *1½ pounds fresh broccoli*
> *4 tablespoons corn-oil margarine*
> *3 tablespoons flour*
> *1½ cups defatted chicken stock (see page 22)*
> *¼ cup skim milk*
> *½ pound tofu (1 cup)*
> *1 tablespoon canola or corn oil*
> *2 tablespoons freshly squeezed lemon juice*
> *½ teaspoon salt (omit if using salted chicken stock)*
> *¼ teaspoon ground white pepper*
> *½ teaspoon curry powder*
> *2 ounces low-fat Cheddar cheese, grated (½ cup)*
> *½ cup soft bread crumbs*

Remove the skin and fat from the chicken breasts. Put into a Dutch oven along with the water. Bring to a boil, reduce the heat, and simmer for 25 to 30 minutes or until all the pink is gone from the chicken breasts. Cool and slice thinly.

Cut the broccoli into even-length spears. Steam for 5 minutes or until crisp-tender. Remove from the heat and cool under cold running water. Drain and set aside.

Melt 3 tablespoons of the margarine in a medium saucepan. Add the flour and stir until bubbly. Add the chicken stock and milk. Continue to cook and stir until the mixture thickens and comes to a boil.

In a blender container, combine the chicken stock mixture, tofu, corn oil, lemon juice, salt, pepper, and curry powder. Blend until smooth and velvety.

Arrange the broccoli in the bottom of a 9-by-13-inch glass baking dish. Top with the chicken. Pour the sauce over the chicken and top with the grated cheese. Melt the remaining 1 tablespoon of margarine in a small saucepan. Mix with the bread crumbs. Sprinkle over the top of the casserole.

Bake in a preheated 350°F oven until lightly browned and bubbly, about 30 minutes.

Makes 4 servings

EACH SERVING CONTAINS APPROXIMATELY:
500 TOTAL CALORIES / 230 CALORIES IN FAT
70 MG CHOLESTEROL / 490 MG SODIUM
330 MG CALCIUM

CHICKEN IN BURGUNDY

If you prefer, chicken stock may be substituted for the beef stock in this recipe. I like the flavor this sauce gives the chicken so much that I often double the recipe to have cold leftover chicken for lunch the next day.

2 cups defatted beef stock (see page 23)
½ cup Burgundy
1 teaspoon dried thyme, crushed in a mortar and pestle

1 teaspoon dried marjoram, crushed in a mortar and pestle
1/8 teaspoon freshly ground black pepper
1/2 teaspoon salt (omit if using salted stock)
2 tablespoons chopped parsley
8 to 10 small white onions
5 celery ribs
1 1/2 pounds boned and skinned chicken breasts

Combine the stock, wine, thyme, marjoram, pepper, salt, parsley, and onions in a large saucepan and bring to a boil. Lay the celery ribs over the top of the mixture. Reduce the heat, cover, and simmer for 1 hour. Remove the celery and discard.

Add the chicken breasts to the sauce and poach gently for 5 to 10 minutes or until the chicken is opaque but still slightly pink in the center (it will continue to cook while it is being held).

Remove the chicken and onions to a warm platter and cover lightly with aluminum foil to keep it warm. Bring the heat up and reduce the sauce to 1 cup. Pour over the chicken. Serve with rice or noodles.

Makes 4 servings

EACH SERVING CONTAINS APPROXIMATELY:
260 TOTAL CALORIES / 55 CALORIES IN FAT
100 MG CHOLESTEROL / 460 MG SODIUM
90 MG CALCIUM

CHICKEN IN PINK PEPPERCORN SAUCE

The original recipe for this dish was sent to me by a reader and was loaded with butter and cream. It took me a long time to revise this recipe to my own satisfaction, but now that I have, it is one of my favorites. The only problem with it is that the chicken must be cooked at the last minute for the dish to be truly as superb as it deserves to be.

1 *tablespoon corn-oil margarine*
1 *pound chicken breasts, boned, skinned, and cut diagonally
    into sixteen 1-inch strips (reserve the scraps)*
¼ *cup cognac or brandy*
½ *cup defatted chicken stock (see page 22)*
½ *cup low-fat milk*
1 *tablespoon fresh tarragon, finely chopped, or 1 teaspoon dried
    tarragon, crushed in a mortar and pestle*
2 *tablespoons dry pink peppercorns*
2 *cups Rice Pilaf (page 119)*
2 *cups Creamed Leeks (page 109)*
1 *small tomato, peeled, seeded, and diced (½ cup) for garnish*
2 *teaspoons finely chopped chives for garnish*
4 *fresh tarragon sprigs for garnish*

Melt the margarine in a large skillet. When hot, add the scraps of chicken breast and sauté until brown. Remove the chicken scraps and discard.

Pour the cognac or brandy into the hot skillet to deglaze and reduce until almost dry. Add the chicken stock and reduce by half. Add the milk and reduce by half. Add the tarragon and peppercorns. Set aside.

To serve, cook the chicken strips for 3 to 5 minutes or until tender. On each of four heated plates, arrange ½ cup Rice Pilaf in a ring around the outer edge and ½ cup Creamed Leeks in the center. Fan four strips of chicken over the leeks. Spoon 2 tablespoons sauce over the chicken and leeks and sprinkle 2 tablespoons diced tomato and ½ teaspoon chopped chives on top. Lay a sprig of tarragon across the top of each serving.

Makes 4 servings

EACH SERVING CONTAINS APPROXIMATELY:
465 TOTAL CALORIES / 110 CALORIES IN FAT
75 MG CHOLESTEROL / 400 MG SODIUM
165 MG CALCIUM

MOROCCAN CHICKEN WITH COUSCOUS

This delightfully different Middle Eastern dish can be served with turkey or rabbit as well as chicken. Couscous is a fine, cereal-like pasta popular in the Middle East, where they eat it with their right hand. Unless you are inviting adventurous guests, I suggest serving this dish with a soup spoon.

> *6 cups defatted chicken stock (see page 22)*
> *1 medium onion, finely chopped (1½ cups)*
> *½ teaspoon salt (omit if using salted stock)*
> *½ cup canned garbanzo beans (chick-peas), drained*
> *1 medium turnip, peeled and cut into bite-size pieces (2 cups)*
> *1 medium yam, peeled and cut into bite-size pieces (2 cups)*
> *1 cup canned peeled tomatoes*
> *1½ teaspoons ground coriander*
> *1½ teaspoons ground cumin*
> *1 cup uncooked couscous*
> *¾ pound cooked chicken breast, cut into bite-size pieces (3 cups)*
> *   and kept warm*
> *Chopped chives for garnish*

Combine the stock, onions, and salt and bring to a boil. Reduce the heat and simmer for 1 hour, uncovered. Add the beans, vegetables, and spices and cook for 20 minutes more or until vegetables are just tender. Do not overcook.

Spoon 1½ cups of the liquid from the vegetables into a medium saucepan and bring to a boil, then add the couscous. Mix well and remove from the heat. Allow to stand, covered, for 5 minutes. This yields 3 cups of cooked couscous.

For each serving, combine 1 cup of vegetables and broth with ½ cup warm chicken in a large bowl and sprinkle with chopped chives. Serve ½ cup couscous on the side.

Makes 6 servings

EACH SERVING CONTAINS APPROXIMATELY:
355 TOTAL CALORIES / 45 CALORIES IN FAT
50 MG CHOLESTEROL / 400 MG SODIUM
80 MG CALCIUM

CHICKEN ENCHILADA

For a real "south of the border" Mexican fiesta, serve these enchiladas with Gazpacho (page 31) to start, a lettuce and tomato salad with Light Cumin Dressing (page 72), and a Mexican fruit plate for dessert. All fruits grow somewhere in Mexico! Accompany this menu with either my Make-believe Margaritas (page 257) or the real thing.

> *1 medium onion, finely chopped (1½ cups)*
> *½ cup defatted chicken stock (see page 22)*
> *½ teaspoon salt*
> *1 tablespoon chili powder*
> *½ teaspoon ground cumin*
> *3 large tomatoes, peeled and diced (3 cups)*
> *2 ounces part-skim mozzarella cheese, grated (½ cup)*
> *¼ pound cooked chicken, finely chopped (1 cup)*
> *4 corn tortillas*

Sauté the onions in a large skillet, covered, until tender, adding a little chicken stock if necessary to prevent scorching. Add the salt, chili powder, and cumin and mix well.

Add the tomatoes and chicken stock and mix well. Cook, uncovered, for 5 minutes over low heat. Remove half the sauce and set aside.

To the sauce remaining in the pan, add ½ cup of the cheese and the chicken and mix well.

Spoon ½ cup of the mixture down the center of each tortilla and roll the tortilla around it. Place, fold side down, in a baking dish. Spoon the remaining sauce evenly over the tops of the enchiladas. Then sprinkle 1 tablespoon of the remaining grated cheese over each enchilada.

Bake, uncovered, in a preheated 350°F oven for 25 minutes.

Makes 4 servings

EACH SERVING CONTAINS APPROXIMATELY:
195 TOTAL CALORIES / 55 CALORIES IN FAT
55 MG CHOLESTEROL / 435 MG SODIUM
145 MG CALCIUM

CHICKEN JAMBALAYA

Of all the Cajun and Creole-style recipes that have been so popular in the last couple of years, Jambalaya is still the one I like best. This recipe is easy to make and can be made the day before you plan to serve it, which makes it an ideal dish for company.

2 tablespoons water
1¹/₂ celery ribs, without leaves, chopped (1 cup)
¹/₂ medium onion, finely chopped (³/₄ cup)
1 green bell pepper, finely chopped (³/₄ cup)
1 garlic clove, finely chopped (1 teaspoon)
¹/₂ cup chopped lean ham
1 bay leaf
¹/₄ teaspoon salt (omit if using salted stock)
¹/₄ teaspoon ground white pepper
¹/₄ teaspoon cayenne
¹/₄ teaspoon freshly ground black pepper
¹/₂ cup tomato sauce
¹/₄ teaspoon Tabasco
1 cup uncooked long-grain brown rice
1¹/₂ cups defatted chicken stock (see page 22)
¹/₂ pound cooked chicken, chopped (2 cups)
2 cups Creole Sauce (page 57), heated
Parsley sprigs for garnish

Heat the water in a large skillet. Add the celery, onions, green peppers, garlic, and ham. Cook, stirring occasionally, over medium heat until the liquid is completely reduced and the vegetables become lightly browned and tender. Scrape the bottom of the pan often.

Add the seasonings, tomato sauce, and Tabasco. Continue to cook, stirring constantly, for 5 minutes more.

Stir in the rice, mixing well. Reduce the heat and simmer for about 15 minutes. Add the chicken stock and bring to a boil. Reduce the heat and simmer, covered, until the rice is tender but still firm, about 40 minutes. Add the chicken and mix well. Cover and continue to cook for 10 minutes more, or until the chicken is heated through. Remove the bay leaf.

To serve, spoon the Jambalaya into 6-ounce custard cups, packing tightly. Spoon ½ cup hot Creole Sauce onto a heated plate. Unmold the Jambalaya on top of the sauce. Garnish the top of each serving with a sprig of parsley.

Makes 4 servings

EACH SERVING CONTAINS APPROXIMATELY:
300 TOTAL CALORIES / 40 CALORIES IN FAT
10 MG CHOLESTEROL / 975 MG SODIUM
80 MG CALCIUM

CHICKEN LIVER PÂTÉ

I have a friend who calls this recipe fantasy pâté because it amuses her to have her favorite hors d'oeuvre for less than half the calories of regular pâté. It is wonderful for hors d'oeuvres and makes great sandwiches served open-faced on bagels or with sliced onions on rye bread.

> 1 medium potato
> ½ pound chicken livers
> 2 tablespoons cognac
> ¼ cup defatted chicken stock (see page 22)
> ¼ teaspoon salt (omit if using salted stock)
> ¼ teaspoon freshly ground black pepper
> ¼ teaspoon ground nutmeg
> 1 teaspoon powdered mustard
> 1 shallot, chopped (1 tablespoon)

Bake or boil the potato until tender. Peel and cut it into small pieces. Set aside.

Wash the chicken livers. Place them in a small saucepan with enough water to cover and cook over low heat until tender, about 10 minutes.

Blend the chicken livers to a paste in a food processor with a metal blade. Add the cooked potato and all the remaining ingredients and blend to a paste.

Pack into 2 or 3 small ramekins and serve as a spread with toast or as a filling for sandwiches.

Makes 2 cups

1 TABLESPOON CONTAINS APPROXIMATELY:
20 TOTAL CALORIES / 5 CALORIES IN FAT
45 MG CHOLESTEROL / 20 MG SODIUM
5 MG CALCIUM

ROCK CORNISH GAME HENS WITH CITRUS-SAGE SAUCE

At the Four Seasons Hotel and Resort in Dallas I serve these game hens with Rice Pilaf (page 119) and an assortment of colorful steamed vegetables. They are also good served with baked yams and green vegetables.

1 1/2 medium onions, finely chopped (2 1/4 cups)
2 Rock Cornish game hens, halved
Freshly ground black pepper to taste
1 cup freshly squeezed orange juice
1/2 cup sherry
1 teaspoon dried sage, crushed in a mortar and pestle
2 tablespoons orange zest
4 orange slices for garnish

Preheat the oven to 350°F. Spread the chopped onions on the bottom of a baking dish. Place the game hens in a single layer on top of the onions, cut side down. Sprinkle with black pepper. Bake for 15 minutes.

While the game hens are cooking, bring the orange juice to a boil and reduce it to ½ cup. Add the sherry, sage, and orange zest and set aside.

Remove the game hens from the oven and set aside until cool enough to handle. When cool, using a sharp knife or kitchen shears, cut the skin away from the meat and discard. Place the game hens back on the bed of onions, cut side down.

Pour the orange juice mixture over the game hens and return to the oven. Bake for 45 minutes more, basting often.

To serve, remove the game hens from the pan and place on individual serving plates, cut side down. Stir the onions thoroughly through the sauce and spoon the sauce over the servings. Garnish each with a twisted orange slice.

Makes 4 servings

EACH SERVING CONTAINS APPROXIMATELY:
335 TOTAL CALORIES / 110 CALORIES IN FAT
90 MG CHOLESTEROL / 55 MG SODIUM
60 MG CALCIUM

ROAST TURKEY WITH FENNEL

This is the recipe I used to roast my own turkey for Christmas last year. I served it with Italian Oyster Casserole (page 148) as the dressing and plated it on radicchio leaves. I served Italian green beans for a red and green Christmas dinner.

> *One 12- to 15-pound turkey*
> *3 onions, peeled and coarsely chopped*
> *2 tablespoons fennel seeds*
> *Salt to taste*

Wash the turkey and pat dry. Combine the onions and fennel seeds and stuff the turkey with the mixture.

Salt the outside of the turkey lightly and place it on its side on a rack in a roasting pan. Bake, uncovered, in a preheated 325°F oven for approximately 20 minutes per pound.

Halfway through the cooking, turn the turkey on its other side. If you wish to brown the turkey for a better appearance, place it on its back for the final 15 minutes.

Remove the turkey from the oven. Transfer it to a platter and allow it to rest for 20 minutes before carving.

Remove the turkey drippings from the pan to a bowl and place in the freezer. As soon as the fat has congealed on top of the drippings, remove from the freezer. Skim off the fat and make a light turkey gravy (see Light Gravy, page 49).

Remove the skin from the turkey after carving.

EACH 3½-OUNCE SERVING CONTAINS APPROXIMATELY:
210 TOTAL CALORIES / 90 CALORIES IN FAT
80 MG CHOLESTEROL / 70 MG SODIUM
25 MG CALCIUM

TURKEY TETRAZZINI

I have purposely made this recipe larger than most of the recipes in the book because it is such an ideal, easy, and inexpensive dinner to make for groups of all ages. Chicken, rabbit, or drained water-packed canned tuna substitute well for the turkey.

1 tablespoon corn-oil margarine
1 pound fresh mushrooms, sliced (4 cups)
1/2 green bell pepper, julienne cut (1/2 cup)
2 1/2 tablespoons flour
1/2 teaspoon salt
1/4 teaspoon freshly ground black pepper
3/4 cup nonfat dry milk powder
1 3/4 cups defatted chicken stock (see page 22)
3 cups julienne-cut cooked turkey
2 tablespoons sherry
1/2 cup sliced pimientos
Nonstick vegetable coating
4 cups cooked spaghetti (1/2 pound dry)
1/4 pound Parmesan cheese, freshly grated (1 cup)

Melt the margarine in a large skillet and sauté the mushrooms and green pepper over low heat until soft, about 5 minutes. Stir in the flour, salt, and pepper and cook until bubbly. Combine the dry milk powder and the chicken stock and add to the flour mixture. Cook, stirring constantly, over low heat until thickened, approximately 10 to 15 minutes.

Add the turkey, sherry, and pimientos and mix well. Remove from the heat and cool slightly.

Spray a casserole dish with nonstick vegetable coating. Place the spaghetti in the bottom, then pour the turkey mixture over the spaghetti and sprinkle with the Parmesan cheese. Bake in a preheated 350°F oven until the sauce bubbles and the cheese is melted and lightly browned, about 25 minutes.

Makes eight 1 1/4-cup servings

EACH SERVING CONTAINS APPROXIMATELY:
295 TOTAL CALORIES / 75 CALORIES IN FAT
50 MG CHOLESTEROL / 490 MG SODIUM
295 MG CALCIUM

GRILLED TURKEY BURGER WITH
CRANBERRY CATSUP

I designed this "holiday burger" for the Christmas season at the Four Seasons Hotel and Resort in Dallas, and to everyone's surprise it turned out to be their biggest-selling luncheon entrée. In fact it is so popular I plan to leave it on the menu as a permanent item.

> *1 pound ground lean turkey*
> *4 small buns, halved*
> *¹/₂ cup Cranberry Catsup (page 65)*
> *4 onion slices*
> *Lettuce leaves*

Form the ground turkey into four patties and grill (over mesquite if available) until done.

Spread 1 tablespoon Cranberry Catsup on each bun half. Place the patties on the buns and garnish with the onion slices and lettuce.

Makes 4 servings

EACH SERVING CONTAINS APPROXIMATELY:
370 TOTAL CALORIES / 145 CALORIES IN FAT
1 MG CHOLESTEROL / 350 MG SODIUM
65 MG CALCIUM

RABBIT FRICASSEE WITH DUMPLINGS

This recipe should probably be in the meat section, but, as I have said, rabbit actually substitutes better for chicken and turkey in a recipe than it does for any meat. For that reason I have included it in this section, so you may substitute chicken or turkey if rabbit is not available.

4 cups defatted chicken stock (see page 22)
1/2 cup chopped onion
1/2 cup sliced celery rib
1/2 cup sliced carrots
1/2 cup dry white wine
1/4 cup chopped parsley
1/4 cup finely chopped chives
1/4 teaspoon dried saffron
1 cup Magic Biscuit Mix (page 206)
1/2 cup skim milk
2 tablespoons cornstarch dissolved in 2 tablespoons water
1/2 cup canned evaporated skimmed milk
1/2 pound cooked rabbit, cut into thin strips (2 cups)
1/4 teaspoon freshly ground black pepper
1/2 teaspoon salt
Chopped parsley for garnish

Bring the stock to a boil in a large saucepan and reduce by one-third. Add the vegetables, wine, parsley, half of the chives, and the saffron. Reduce the heat, cover, and simmer until the vegetables are tender, about 15 minutes.

Meanwhile, combine the Magic Biscuit Mix, skim milk, and the remaining chives and mix thoroughly. Set aside.

Stir the dissolved cornstarch into the simmering broth. Add the evaporated skimmed milk and cook, stirring constantly, until slightly thickened.

Drop the batter into the broth by rounded tablespoonsful, making eight dumplings. Cover and cook for 12 minutes.

Transfer the dumplings to soup bowls, using a slotted spoon. Add the rabbit, salt (omit if using salted stock), and pepper to the broth and heat through.

Ladle the fricassee over the dumplings. Garnish with the parsley.

Makes 4 servings

EACH SERVING CONTAINS APPROXIMATELY:
340 TOTAL CALORIES / 100 CALORIES IN FAT
1 MG CHOLESTEROL / 635 MG SODIUM
265 MG CALCIUM

MEAT

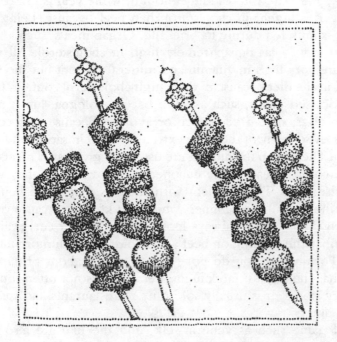

RED MEAT, while the least desirable animal protein source because of its fat content, is not all bad. Red meat is a complete protein and is abundant in minerals such as zinc that are often difficult to find in other foods. Meat is also packed with many of the B vitamins.

Red meat is actually very little higher in cholesterol than poultry and some fish. The problem lies in the fact that the fat content of meat is primarily in the saturated form and therefore adds to the buildup of the cholesterol it does contain. The biggest problem, however, is that the fat in meat runs through the red muscle of the meat and that even after you have removed all visible fat, it is impossible to get it all out the way you can by removing the skin and visible fat from poultry.

Currently beef is divided into three grades—select, choice, and prime—depending upon the amount of marbling it contains. The marbling consists of the streaks of fat running through the meat. Good contains the least amount of fat and prime the most. Efforts are being made to change the word *good* to *select* to encourage more people to buy it.

The leanest cuts of meat include flank and round steak, lean lamb or pork, and veal. Interestingly enough, while veal is lower in fat content, it is higher in cholesterol than beef because, being baby beef, it is milk fed during its brief life. Organ meats, such as liver, are also low in fat but extremely high in cholesterol. All organ meats are very high in vitamin and mineral content but should be limited in the diet because of their high cholesterol content. Cured and processed meats, such as ham, bacon, bologna, lunch meats, and hot dogs, should be limited or avoided because they contain nitrates. Also many of them are extremely high in saturated fat and sodium. The reason the nitrates are used is to give cured meats their pinkish color instead of the unappealing brown color they would otherwise have. The problem with them is that while being digested they form nitrosamines, which are known to cause cancer.

When buying meat, always look for the leanest cuts available. Remember the grading on beef and avoid cuts with more fat marbling. Fortunately you do not have to worry about prime beef, which has the highest fat content, because it is not often found in ordinary stores. It is usually sold only to restaurants and specialty meat markets.

Wild game such as venison, elk, and the like are also good choices but are not readily available. They are leaner because they have been allowed to run wild rather than being confined in small spaces to prevent them from losing weight.

If possible it is always better to grind your own meat for things like hamburgers and meat loaf because you can then better control the fat content.

When preparing meat, always carefully remove all visible fat. Use cooking methods that allow the fat to drain off the meat rather than being held in. For example, when you are baking or broiling meat, always put it on a rack above the pan so the fat is not served with it. When making stews or soups, try to always make them the day before you plan to serve them. Then remove all the visible fat that forms on the top before reheating to serve. This gives you not only a healthier dish but also a more appetizing-looking entrée because it will not have the fat globules floating around on the top. An interesting aside is that the pictures you see in magazines for recipes containing lots of fat are always taken of defatted versions in order to avoid the congealed fat that would show in the photographs.

The one thing about cooking meat that is much easier than cooking either fish or seafood is that cooking time is not so crucial. Even though there are many cuts of meat that are much better served very rare rather than well done, there are also many others that can be cooked for long periods of time and the time only improves both the taste and the texture.

The single most important tip in preparing and serving meat is to use less of it. I have been in restaurants where a steak weighing at least a pound was served to a person and arrived looking like a roast for the whole table. Remember that animal protein should never be more than one-fifth the volume of your meal. So think in terms of a small steak, a large baked potato, lots of vegetables, and a wonderful salad; or a stir-fry with a little beef, pork, or lamb to add flavor and texture. Treat all meat as a condiment rather than the focus or main part of the meal.

SZECHUAN BEEF AND VEGETABLE STIR-FRY

This is a delicious Oriental entrée that can also be made with poultry. If you want to make it as a vegetarian dish, you can substitute vegetable stock for the chicken stock called for in the recipe. You will note that I always suggest not only removing the strings from the pea pods but also notching the ends. By notching, I mean cutting a V-shaped wedge at each end of the pod. This removes the tough ends and also gives a finished, more decorative look to the vegetable. It's fun to serve this dish with chopsticks.

> *1 pound flank steak*
> *2 teaspoons dark sesame oil*
> *1 tablespoon reduced-sodium soy sauce*
> *1 tablespoon sherry*
> *1 teaspoon fructose or 1 1/2 teaspoons sugar*
> *2 teaspoons cornstarch*

2 teaspoons minced peeled ginger
2 garlic cloves, finely chopped (2 teaspoons)
1/4 cup defatted chicken stock (see page 22)
3 scallions, cut diagonally into 1-inch pieces
1/4 pound fresh mushrooms, sliced (1 cup)
1/4 pound Chinese pea pods, ends notched and strings removed
1 small red bell pepper, cut into 1/4-inch strips
1 medium yellow squash, cut in half lengthwise, then sliced crosswise into 1/4-inch slices
1/2 teaspoon crushed red pepper flakes

Remove all visible fat from the flank steak and cut it crosswise into 1/4-inch strips; then cut each strip in half.

Combine the sesame oil, soy sauce, sherry, fructose or sugar, cornstarch, half the ginger, and half the garlic in a medium bowl and mix well. Add the steak pieces and toss to combine. Set aside.

Heat half the chicken stock in a nonstick skillet over medium-high heat. Add the remaining garlic and ginger and the scallions and mushrooms. Stir-fry for 1 to 2 minutes. Transfer to a medium bowl.

Add the remaining chicken stock to the skillet and heat. Add the pea pods, bell pepper, and squash. Stir-fry until crisp-tender, about 3 to 4 minutes. Add this to the scallions and mushrooms.

Heat the skillet again. Add the steak and pepper flakes. Stir-fry until brown and tender, about 3 to 4 minutes. Return the vegetables to the skillet and heat through. Serve with brown rice.

Makes four 1-cup servings

EACH SERVING CONTAINS APPROXIMATELY:
255 TOTAL CALORIES / 80 CALORIES IN FAT
80 MG CHOLESTEROL / 310 MG SODIUM
35 MG CALCIUM

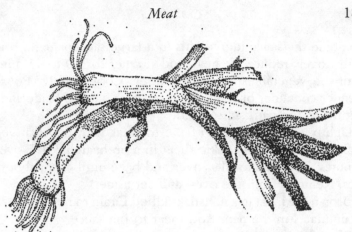

ENCHILADA TORTE

If you like enchiladas but don't like to take the time to make them, this Enchilada Torte is the perfect solution because you don't have to roll each individual enchilada. It also makes a very attractive plate presentation. I sometimes make this dish as a vegetarian entrée, omitting the beef and adding 4 cups of steamed sliced mushrooms in its place.

S A U C E :

> *One 28-ounce can crushed tomatoes (3½ cups)*
> *½ medium onion, chopped (¾ cup)*
> *1 medium carrot, sliced (½ cup)*
> *1 celery rib, without leaves, chopped (½ cup)*
> *1 garlic clove, chopped (1 teaspoon)*
> *¼ cup water*
> *1½ tablespoons chili powder*
> *1¼ teaspoons ground cumin*
> *¼ teaspoon salt*
> *¼ teaspoon freshly ground black pepper*
>
> *Nonstick vegetable coating*
> *12 corn tortillas*
> *1 pound lean ground beef*
> *9 scallions, thinly sliced*
> *6 ounces Cheddar cheese, grated (1½ cups)*
> *Cilantro or parsley sprigs for garnish*

Combine the sauce ingredients in a large saucepan and bring to a boil. Cover, reduce the heat, and simmer for 30 to 45 minutes or until the vegetables are very tender. Cool slightly. Pour into a blender container or food processor with a metal blade and puree. Return to the pan and set aside.

Lightly spray each side of the tortillas with nonstick vegetable spray and bake on a cookie sheet in a preheated 350°F oven for 7 minutes. Turn the tortillas over and bake until crisp, about 8 minutes. Remove from the oven and set aside.

Brown the meat in a nonstick skillet. Drain to remove any fat that accumulates in the pan. Add meat to the sauce.

Place one tortilla on an ungreased cookie sheet with sides. Top with 2 tablespoons scallions, 2 tablespoons cheese, and ¼ cup sauce. Repeat the layers three times (using four tortillas in all). Make two more stacks the same way on the cookie sheet. Divide the remaining sauce over the three enchilada tortes.

Bake in a preheated 350°F oven for 15 to 20 minutes or until hot.

To serve, cut each torte in half. Place a half torte on each plate and garnish with cilantro or parsley sprigs.

Makes 6 servings

EACH SERVING CONTAINS APPROXIMATELY:
420 TOTAL CALORIES / 145 CALORIES IN FAT
80 MG CHOLESTEROL / 670 MG SODIUM
370 MG CALCIUM

POT ROAST

Pot roast is a wonderful all-American entrée. It is also easy and economical. Leftovers are great for sandwiches and can also be frozen for another meal.

1 teaspoon corn-oil margarine
2 garlic cloves, finely chopped (2 teaspoons)

3 pounds boneless beef pot roast
1 medium onion, sliced (2 cups)
12 peppercorns
12 whole allspice
1 bay leaf, crumbled
2 tablespoons grated fresh horseradish
1/2 cup dry red wine
1/2 cup defatted beef stock (see page 23) or water
1/2 teaspoon salt

Early in the day on which you plan to serve the pot roast (or the day before): Preheat the oven to 325°F. Melt the margarine in a Dutch oven or roasting pan with a tight-fitting lid. Sauté the garlic in the margarine over low heat until lightly browned. Add the roast and brown well on all sides. Remove the roast from the pan.

Layer the onion slices in the bottom of the pan. Put the roast on top of the onions. Combine the remaining ingredients and pour over the roast. Cover tightly and simmer in the oven for 3 to 4 hours or until the roast is tender (or simmer, tightly covered, on top of the stove).

Remove from the pan, cool, cover, and refrigerate. Cool the cooking liquid to room temperature and refrigerate, uncovered, until the fat congeals on top.

When ready to serve, remove the fat from the cooking liquid. Slice the meat and return it to the pan along with the cooking liquid. Warm slowly. Serve with rice, noodles, or potatoes. Spoon the broth over the meat or serve it separately in a gravy boat.

Makes eight 3-ounce servings

EACH SERVING CONTAINS APPROXIMATELY:
325 TOTAL CALORIES / 215 CALORIES IN FAT
80 MG CHOLESTEROL / 190 MG SODIUM
30 MG CALCIUM

BURGUNDY-BRAISED BEEF

1 teaspoon corn-oil margarine
2 pounds lean beef, cut into 24 cubes
1/2 cup chopped leeks, white part only
1 small carrot, peeled and chopped (1/2 cup)
1/2 medium onion, chopped (3/4 cup)
1 tablespoon finely chopped parsley
1 tablespoon finely chopped chives
1 garlic clove, chopped (1 teaspoon)
2 whole cloves
3 1/4 cups Burgundy
1/4 teaspoon dried marjoram, crushed in a mortar and pestle
8 peppercorns, crushed
1/2 teaspoon salt

Preheat the oven to 350°F. Melt the margarine in a large nonstick skillet over medium heat. When the pan is hot, add the beef cubes and brown well on all sides.

Put the beef in a Dutch oven or large casserole with a tight-fitting lid. Add the leeks, carrots, onions, parsley, chives, garlic, and cloves to the skillet in which the beef was browned and brown lightly, stirring constantly. Add the vegetables to the beef in the casserole and mix well.

Deglaze the skillet by pouring 1/4 cup of the Burgundy over the drippings. Bring to a boil, stirring and scraping up the remaining bits of meat and vegetables in the pan. Pour over the meat and vegetables in the casserole.

Add the remaining Burgundy and the seasonings to the meat and vegetables and mix well. Bake, covered, for 3 hours.

Serve 4 squares of beef and 3 tablespoons of broth per person with rice or noodles.

Makes 6 servings

EACH SERVING CONTAINS APPROXIMATELY:
375 TOTAL CALORIES / 80 CALORIES IN FAT
120 MG CHOLESTEROL / 275 MG SODIUM
40 MG CALCIUM

CARROT-AND-MUSHROOM-STUFFED BRISKET

This stuffed brisket is a wonderful company entrée because it makes a pretty presentation on the plate. It can be plated either in individual servings or on a larger serving dish for buffet-style service. I like to serve it with new potatoes and a green vegetable such as broccoli, asparagus, or brussels sprouts.

> *1½ pounds brisket of beef*
> *2 tablespoons water or beef stock (see page 23)*
> *1 garlic clove, chopped (1 teaspoon)*
> *⅓ cup finely chopped onion*
> *¼ pound fresh mushrooms, finely chopped (1 cup)*
> *1 egg white, lightly beaten*
> *½ slice whole wheat bread, broken into crumbs (½ cup)*
> *¼ teaspoon salt*
> *¼ teaspoon freshly ground black pepper*
> *3 medium carrots, peeled*
> *1 medium onion, sliced (2 cups)*
> *½ cup beef stock (see page 23)*
> *½ cup dry red wine*
> *Herb leaves or parsley sprigs for garnish*

Preheat the oven to 325°F. Remove all visible fat from the brisket. Cut a pocket horizontally along one long side, leaving a ½-inch border around three sides.

In a large nonstick skillet, bring the 2 tablespoons water or beef stock to a boil. Add the garlic, onions, and mushrooms. Cook until soft, about 5 minutes, adding more liquid if necessary to prevent scorching. Transfer to a bowl and combine with the egg white, bread crumbs, salt, and pepper and mix thoroughly. Set aside.

Place about 4 yards of kitchen string in a small bowl of water to soak.

Coarsely grate one of the carrots. Slice the remaining carrots in ¼-inch rounds and set aside.

Place half the grated carrot in the bottom of the brisket pocket. Spread all the mushroom mixture evenly over the carrot layer. Place the remaining grated carrot over the mushrooms. Tie the string around the brisket in both directions at 1-inch intervals to contain the stuffing.

Reheat the skillet in which the mushrooms were cooked. Brown the brisket well on both sides, about 5 minutes per side.

Place the sliced carrots and onions in the bottom of a roasting pan or Dutch oven. Place the brisket on top. Combine the stock and wine and pour it over the brisket. Cover the pan with a lid or aluminum foil. Bake for 3½ to 4 hours or until fork-tender.

Remove the roast from the oven and let it stand for 20 minutes before slicing. Place the vegetables and broth in a blender and puree until smooth. Reheat in a small saucepan.

To serve, spoon ⅓ cup sauce on each of eight plates. Top with a slice of brisket. Garnish with an herb leaf or parsley sprig. Pass the remaining sauce.

Makes 4 servings

EACH SERVING CONTAINS APPROXIMATELY:
475 TOTAL CALORIES / 180 CALORIES IN FAT
130 MG CHOLESTEROL / 275 MG SODIUM
70 MG CALCIUM

LAMB SHISH KEBAB

I like to serve shish kebab on either a bed of Rice Pilaf (page 119) or a mixture of grains such as barley, millet, cracked wheat, or kasha.

MARINADE:

½ cup red wine or red wine vinegar
2 tablespoons extra-virgin olive oil
2 tablespoons reduced-sodium soy sauce
¼ teaspoon freshly ground black pepper
Dash cayenne
½ teaspoon salt
1 tablespoon dried oregano, crushed in a mortar and pestle
½ cup minced onion

1 1/2 pounds lean lamb, cut into 16 cubes or slices of 1 1/2 to 2
inches
8 small whole boiling onions, parboiled
1 medium green bell pepper, seeded and cut into 8 pieces
1 medium red bell pepper, seeded and cut into 8 pieces

Combine all the marinade ingredients and mix well.

Remove all the visible fat from the lamb. Place in a glass baking dish. Pour the marinade over the lamb, cover, and refrigerate overnight. Stir occasionally.

Remove the lamb from the marinade, reserving marinade to brush on the lamb while cooking.

Thread the kebab ingredients onto four skewers, alternating them to create a colorful presentation.

Cook over hot coals, 4 to 5 inches from the heat, for 15 to 20 minutes, brushing with the marinade and turning the skewers frequently to cook evenly and to prevent burning. The meat is done when it is nicely browned but still slightly pink in the center.

Makes 4 servings

EACH SERVING CONTAINS APPROXIMATELY:
470 TOTAL CALORIES / 305 CALORIES IN FAT
140 MG CHOLESTEROL / 635 MG SODIUM
55 MG CALCIUM

BALKAN LAMB AND APRICOT STEW

When I think of lamb stew, I always think of the traditional Irish lamb stew with vegetables and potatoes. This recipe was sent to me by one of my readers, and I found it not only delicious but delightfully different. I like to serve it with baked sweet potatoes and green peas.

1½ pounds lean lamb roast
1 quart water
1 teaspoon freshly ground black pepper
½ teaspoon salt
2 tablespoons white vinegar
2 tablespoons defatted chicken or beef stock (see page 22 or 23)
2 medium onions, coarsely chopped (3 cups)
2 tablespoons chopped fresh mint
One 16-ounce can whole peeled tomatoes, drained
¼ cup uncooked pearl barley
¾ cup dried apricots
2 teaspoons freshly squeezed lemon juice
Fresh chopped mint for garnish

Place the lamb, water, pepper, and salt in a large, heavy kettle and bring to a boil. Reduce the heat to low, cover, and simmer for 1½ hours.

Meanwhile heat the vinegar and stock in a medium skillet. Add the onions and mint and cook until the onions are soft and translucent, about 5 minutes, adding a little more stock if necessary to prevent them from scorching.

Add the onions, mint, tomatoes, barley, and apricots to the lamb. Cover and simmer for 1 hour more.

Remove the lamb from the mixture. Strain out the vegetables and transfer the stock to a bowl. Cool to room temperature; then refrigerate, uncovered, for several hours or overnight until all the fat has congealed on the surface. Remove the fat.

Remove the lamb from the bones and all visible fat from the meat. Cut into bite-size pieces and combine with the vegetable mixture. Cover and refrigerate.

When ready to serve, combine the meat/vegetable mixture with the defatted stock and the lemon juice. Reheat. Ladle into bowls and sprinkle each serving with chopped mint.

Makes four 1½-cup entrée servings

EACH SERVING CONTAINS APPROXIMATELY:
560 TOTAL CALORIES / 280 CALORIES IN FAT
140 MG CHOLESTEROL / 565 MG SODIUM
95 MG CALCIUM

CASSOULET

Cassoulet is a French country dish that was developed by French housewives to use up the week's leftovers in a hearty dish with white beans. It always amuses me that most American cooking schools teach Cassoulet making by also teaching the preparation of all the leftovers few American homemakers would ever have on hand. Consequently, rather than being an easy "clean the refrigerator" type of dish, it is a time-consuming ordeal that nonetheless results in an absolutely delicious casserole. I don't think you necessarily have to have all the ingredients called for in this recipe to make a good Cassoulet. Just combine your own leftovers with the white beans and suggested seasoning and develop your own Cassoulet.

> *1 pound lamb shoulder chops, with bones*
> *1 medium onion, chopped (1 1/2 cups)*
> *2 tomatoes, peeled and seeded*
> *1 teaspoon dried thyme, crushed in a mortar and pestle*
> *4 garlic cloves, peeled*
> *1 1/2 cups dry white wine*
> *Water*
> *2 tablespoons white vinegar*
> *1/2 teaspoon salt*
> *1/2 teaspoon freshly ground black pepper*
> *1 cup Great Northern beans, soaked overnight*
> *2 small carrots, peeled and diced (1 cup)*
> *1 celery rib, diced (1/2 cup)*
> *1 medium onion, finely chopped (1 1/2 cups)*
> *1 bay leaf*
> *2 tablespoons chopped parsley*
> *5 peppercorns*
> *1 Cornish game hen, quartered*
> *1 tablespoon dried thyme, crushed in a mortar and pestle*
> *1 cup whole wheat bread crumbs*
> *1 tablespoon corn-oil margarine, melted*

The day before serving, make the lamb-stew portion. Remove all the visible fat and cut the lamb into bite-size pieces, including the bones. Cook the lamb and onions in a heavy pot over medium heat for 10 minutes, adding a little water if necessary to prevent scorching. Add the tomatoes, thyme, and garlic. Cover with the wine, 1½ cups water, and the vinegar and season with the salt and pepper. Bring to a boil. Reduce the heat and simmer for 1 hour.

Strain the liquid and cool to room temperature. Refrigerate the liquid, uncovered. Transfer the lamb and vegetables to a bowl, cover, and refrigerate.

On the day you plan to serve the Cassoulet, remove the fat from the top of the reserved cooking stock and bring to a boil. Cook until reduced to 2 cups. Set aside.

Place the soaked beans in a large pot with the carrots, celery, onions, bay leaf, parsley, and peppercorns. Cover with water and simmer for 2 hours or until the beans are tender, adding more water as needed. Discard the bay leaf.

Sprinkle the quartered Cornish game hen with the thyme. Roast in a roasting pan in a preheated 325°F oven for 15 minutes. Remove from the oven and as soon as the hen is cool enough to handle, remove the skin.

To assemble, drain the bean mixture and reserve the cooking liquid. In a deep 3-quart casserole, layer half the beans, then the lamb and game hen. Top with the remaining beans. Add the stock reserved from cooking the lamb to 1 inch from the top, adding the reserved liquid from the beans if necessary.

Combine the bread crumbs and the melted margarine and mix thoroughly. Sprinkle over the top of the casserole. Bake, uncovered, in a preheated 250°F oven for 4 hours. Add more liquid if needed.

Makes 4 servings

EACH SERVING CONTAINS APPROXIMATELY:
620 TOTAL CALORIES / 280 CALORIES IN FAT
90 MG CHOLESTEROL / 460 MG SODIUM
130 MG CALCIUM

BREADS & CEREALS,
PANCAKES & SUCH

BREAD IS TRULY the staff of life, and the staff is stronger
when the breads are all made from whole grains. More than a third
of the world's population gets over half of its daily calories from
wheat alone.

We distinguish the different diets of various cultures around the
world more by the types of breads and grain products they eat than
by any other item in their diets. For example, we have Italian pasta,
Mexican tortillas, Indian chapatis, Middle Eastern pita, Chinese pao
ping, and a variety of French breads depending upon the region in
France.

Even in this country there are regional differences in breads and
grains. There are southern corn bread and grits and San Francisco
sourdough and Boston brown bread, to name a few.

In ancient times all breads were made from whole grains and
were completely unleavened and rather hard in texture. The

199

lighter-textured yeast breads we have today are thought to have been discovered in Egypt when someone, quite by accident, mixed sourdough with new dough and produced a lighter loaf. Hundreds of years elapsed before these same white or refined-grain breads were developed in England. In the nineteenth century the roller mill was invented, and the British were able to produce a pure white flour by removing the germ and the outside bran coating of the wheat kernel, leaving only the endosperm, or soft white center portion of the kernel. Of course by removing the germ or embryo of the berry, they were also taking out all the valuable vitamins and minerals, and by removing the bran, they were getting rid of the fiber. This new white bread was very expensive to produce and was in such limited supply that only royalty and the upper classes could afford it. Thus it was the peasants who were eating the dark, rough whole-grain breads and they were all much healthier than the upper classes who were eating the refined bread. To this day this rough bread is called peasant bread.

An interesting aside is that it took at least fifty years before scientists realized that all the important vitamins, minerals, and fiber were in the bran and the germ they were either discarding or feeding to animals. This discovery took place during World War II, when they stopped refining grains in order to stretch the supply available for bread. The general health of the population improved during this period; however, immediately following the war they went right back to refining as much of the grain as possible and the same health problems recurred primarily due to the lack of enough fiber in the diet.

Dietary fiber is the indigestible part of plant food; it is not absorbed by the body and does not supply calories. It absorbs moisture, adding bulk, and speeds up the transit time of all other foods through the body for proper bowel function. Because of this moisture absorption, it is essential to drink an adequate amount of water along with the necessary amount of fiber. Many people think they are unable to eat high-fiber foods simply because they don't drink enough liquid and therefore experience stomachaches. The solution is to drink water!

Increased dietary fiber is also encouraged for the prevention of heart disease and many types of cancer, as well as constipation.

Wheat, although it is the most popular and often-used grain, is certainly not the whole grain story. Many other grains are readily available that are excellent both for cereals and breads. Oats, in particular, have received a lot of publicity recently due to the fact that scientific studies have shown that oat bran can lower the LDL (low-density lipoprotein) cholesterol in the blood, which is the harmful type of cholesterol that causes hardening of the arteries. This, in turn, raises the ratio of the HDL (high-density lipoprotein) type of cholesterol, which is the beneficial form of blood lipids. Oats have also been shown to be helpful in the diabetic diet.

Rolled oats are certainly one of the most popular hot breakfast cereals; however, some people don't like oatmeal because of its "mushy" texture. For those people I have included an oatmeal-pancake recipe that is truly delicious and very popular on my spa menus. I have never cared much for hot cereals myself because I am partial to crunchy or chewy textures. I have included in this section my favorite hot cereal, which is made with rye berries and is called Danish Rye Cereal (page 220). The rye berries retain their texture in cooking, and therefore you have a hot cereal with lots of texture.

All whole grains and whole-grain flours should be stored in the refrigerator. Since all bugs are born nutrition-oriented, they will always attack the whole grains first.

TORTILLA WEDGES

Because it is impossible to buy fat-free tortilla chips, I always include baking instructions for making your own. Not only are they healthier and less expensive, I think they are tastier, and they certainly contain fewer calories.

10 corn tortillas

Cut the tortillas into eight wedges each. Place them on cookie sheets in a single layer and bake in a preheated 400°F oven for 10 minutes. Turn over and bake for 3 minutes more. Sprinkle with a salt-free seasoning mix of your choice if desired.

Makes 80 wedges

EIGHT WEDGES CONTAIN APPROXIMATELY:
70 TOTAL CALORIES / 10 CALORIES IN FAT
0 MG CHOLESTEROL / 55 MG SODIUM
40 MG CALCIUM

CROUTONS

As with Tortilla Wedges (preceding recipe), I always include baking instructions for croutons because they are healthier, less expensive, and better tasting than anything you can buy. Making your own croutons also allows you to have enormous variety in the type of crouton you use. You can make them with whole-grain bread, as suggested in the recipe, or with sourdough, rye, corn bread, or pumpernickel.

4 slices whole-grain bread

Allow the bread to dry out for several hours, turning occasionally to assist the process.

Cut the bread into ¼-inch squares and place on a cookie sheet in a preheated 300°F oven for 20 minutes or until brown. Turn occasionally so they will brown evenly.

Makes 2 cups

¼ CUP CONTAINS APPROXIMATELY:
30 TOTAL CALORIES / 5 CALORIES IN FAT
0 MG CHOLESTEROL / 60 MG SODIUM
10 MG CALCIUM

LIGHT CINNAMON POPOVERS

Serving these giant popovers will always get you at least one "wow" from an admiring guest impressed with your culinary talents. The really wonderful thing is that you can make them ahead of time and no one will know the difference.

> *Corn-oil margarine*
> *All-purpose flour*
> *4 egg whites, at room temperature*
> *1 cup low-fat milk, at room temperature*
> *1 cup calcium-fortified all-purpose flour*
> *1 teaspoon ground cinnamon*
> *2 tablespoons corn-oil margarine, melted*

Preheat the oven to 450°F. Grease six 3½-inch custard cups with corn-oil margarine, being careful to cover all inner surfaces. Lightly dust with flour.

Combine all the ingredients in a blender container for 15 seconds at medium speed. Do not overmix.

Divide the batter evenly among the custard cups and bake for 20 minutes at 450°. Reduce the oven temperature to 350° and bake for 25 minutes more. Pierce the side of each popover and bake for another 5 minutes.

Serve immediately with Apple Butter (page 61). If you wish to make them ahead, cool to room temperature, wrap tightly with plastic wrap or aluminum foil, and freeze. To serve, unwrap and place on a cookie sheet in a preheated 350° oven for about 15 minutes.

Makes 6 popovers

EACH POPOVER CONTAINS APPROXIMATELY:
130 TOTAL CALORIES / 35 CALORIES IN FAT
1 MG CHOLESTEROL / 55 MG SODIUM
60 MG CALCIUM

PIZZA CRUST

I have purposely made this recipe for two pizza crusts instead of one because it takes practically no more time to make two, and these pizza crusts freeze so successfully that even if you want only one, the next time you're making pizza, you don't have to take the time to make the crust.

> One *¼-ounce package active dry yeast (check the date on the package)*
> *1 cup lukewarm water (110° to 115°F)*
> *3 cups whole wheat flour*
> *1 tablespoon olive oil*
> *½ teaspoon salt*

Sprinkle the yeast over the water. Stir to dissolve and let stand in a warm place for a few minutes until bubbly.

Add 1½ cups of the flour and mix well. Add the olive oil and salt and stir until well mixed.

Add 1 more cup of flour and mix well. Turn out onto a floured board and knead until smooth and elastic, adding more flour as needed (knead for about 10 to 15 minutes).

Place in an oiled bowl and turn the dough so that the oiled side is up. Cover with wax paper or plastic wrap. Put in a warm place for 1½ to 2 hours or until the dough is doubled in bulk. Punch down. Refrigerate until cold.

Divide the dough into two balls and roll out on a lightly floured board. Place each crust in a 12-inch pizza pan (available in grocery stores). Wrap and freeze if you are not going to use it immediately. Thaw completely before placing sauce, toppings, and cheese on top (see recipe for Pizza, page 126).

Makes two 12-inch crusts

EACH CRUST CONTAINS APPROXIMATELY:
670 TOTAL CALORIES / 95 CALORIES IN FAT
0 MG CHOLESTEROL / 560 MG SODIUM
80 MG CALCIUM

VARIATION:

To make 4- or 6-inch crusts (for Fresh Fruit Pizza, page 229, or for smaller regular pizzas), divide the dough into smaller balls.

SOUTHWESTERN CORN BREAD

This robustly flavored corn bread is particularly good served with soups and salads and is hearty enough to turn them into full meals.

2 tablespoons canola or corn oil
½ cup finely chopped onions
½ cup canned chopped green California chilies
¼ cup finely chopped red bell pepper (optional)
1 cup yellow cornmeal
1 cup unbleached flour
1 tablespoon baking powder
½ teaspoon salt
½ teaspoon ground cumin
½ teaspoon chili powder
2 ounces sharp Cheddar cheese, shredded (½ cup)
1 cup skim milk
1 egg
1 cup cooked corn kernels
Nonstick vegetable coating

Preheat the oven to 400°F. Heat half the corn oil in a medium skillet. Add the onions, green chilies, and red bell pepper. Sauté until tender, about 5 minutes. DO NOT BROWN.

In a large bowl, combine the cornmeal, flour, baking powder, salt, cumin, and chili powder. Add the cheese and mix again.

In a separate medium bowl, combine the remaining corn oil, the milk, and the egg. Add the onion mixture and the corn. Add this to the dry ingredients and mix just until blended. Do not overmix.

Pour the batter into an 8-by-8-inch pan that has been sprayed with nonstick vegetable coating. Bake for 25 to 30 minutes or until lightly browned and a toothpick inserted in the center comes out clean. Cool for 5 to 10 minutes before cutting.

Makes 16 servings

EACH SERVING CONTAINS APPROXIMATELY:
115 TOTAL CALORIES / 30 CALORIES IN FAT
16 MG CHOLESTEROL / 165 MG SODIUM
100 MG CALCIUM

MAGIC BISCUIT MIX

I created this biscuit mix for a reader who wrote me requesting a recipe for an easy-to-make substitute for commercial mix that was lower in sodium and didn't contain preservatives. I am thrilled with the results and I think you will be too. You can use it in exactly the same way you would use any other biscuit mix—for pancakes, waffles, shortcake, and so on. Throughout the book I have recipes that use this Magic Biscuit Mix, including the following recipes for biscuits. In fact I called it magic because it will work in recipes in ways that literally seem impossible, if not magical. For convenience, you may wish to double this recipe. Most home food processors, however, will hold only a single recipe, so it is usually necessary to make a double recipe in two batches. Store in a tightly covered container either in a cool cupboard or in the refrigerator.

3 cups calcium-enriched all-purpose or unbleached flour
1/2 cup nonfat dry milk powder
2 tablespoons baking powder
3/4 teaspoon salt
1/3 cup canola or corn oil

Mix the dry ingredients in a food processor using a metal blade or with an electric mixer. Slowly pour in the oil as the machine is running. Scrape the sides of the bowl with a rubber spatula. Mix thoroughly again.

Store in a cool place in a tightly covered container.

Makes 5 loosely packed cups of mix

1 CUP CONTAINS APPROXIMATELY:
375 TOTAL CALORIES / 135 CALORIES IN FAT
1 MG CHOLESTEROL / 745 MG SODIUM
380 MG CALCIUM

BISCUITS

Once you have made the Magic Biscuit Mix, these biscuits are so easy to make that they will also seem like magic. Both this biscuit recipe and the Buttermilk Biscuit recipe that follows it can be made in much less time if you prefer to make drop biscuits, because you don't have to knead the dough or roll it out. After you have combined the ingredients, drop the dough by teaspoonsful onto an ungreased cookie sheet and bake for 8 to 10 minutes or until golden brown.

1½ cups Magic Biscuit Mix (page 206)
⅓ cup skim milk

Preheat the oven to 450°F. Combine the biscuit mix and milk and beat vigorously by hand. If the dough is sticky, gradually add a little more biscuit mix until the dough is easy to handle.

Turn onto a cloth-covered board that is lightly dusted with biscuit mix. Shape the dough into a ball, then knead about ten times.

Using a rolling pin or your hands, flatten to ½-inch thickness. Press a 2-inch biscuit cutter into biscuit mix and cut out eight biscuits. Place on an ungreased cookie sheet and bake until golden brown, 8 to 10 minutes.

Makes 8 biscuits

EACH BISCUIT CONTAINS APPROXIMATELY:
75 TOTAL CALORIES / 30 CALORIES IN FAT
0 MG CHOLESTEROL / 145 MG SODIUM
85 MG CALCIUM

BUTTERMILK BISCUITS

2 cups Magic Biscuit Mix (page 206)
⅔ cup buttermilk
¼ teaspoon baking soda

Preheat the oven to 450°F. Combine all the ingredients in a large bowl and beat vigorously by hand until a soft dough forms. If the dough is sticky, gradually add a little more biscuit mix until the dough is easy to handle.

Turn onto a cloth-covered board that is lightly dusted with biscuit mix. Shape the dough into a ball, then knead about ten times.

Using a rolling pin or your hands, flatten to ½-inch thickness. Press a 2-inch biscuit cutter into the biscuit mix and cut out twelve biscuits. Place on an ungreased cookie sheet and bake until golden brown, 8 to 10 minutes.

Makes 12 biscuits

EACH BISCUIT CONTAINS APPROXIMATELY:
70 TOTAL CALORIES / 25 CALORIES IN FAT
1 MG CHOLESTEROL / 155 MG SODIUM
80 MG CALCIUM

GINGERBREAD PANCAKES

These sugar-free gingerbread pancakes are one of the most popular breakfast items I have ever created for any menu. When you make the pancake batter for this recipe, if you think it is too thick, add a little water. Each time I make it, I find the consistency is slightly different; also after the batter has been sitting for any length of time it will start to thicken and need to be thinned a little before making the pancakes. Just be careful not to overmix it or the pancakes will not be as light in texture. If you have any pancakes left over, make Gingerbread Pancake Pinwheels for after-school snacks or tea-party finger sandwiches. Spread each pancake with Light Cheese (page 52) and roll the pancake like a jelly roll. To serve, trim off the ends of each pancake roll and then cut it into pinwheels. If you really want to get fancy, using a pastry tube, pipe a little rosette of pastry cream on the top of each pinwheel.

1 cup whole wheat flour
3/4 teaspoon baking soda
1/2 teaspoon ground ginger
1/2 teaspoon ground cinnamon
1/4 teaspoon ground cloves
1/4 teaspoon salt
2 teaspoons instant decaffeinated coffee powder
1/4 cup hot water
1 egg, beaten
One 6-ounce can frozen unsweetened apple juice concentrate
2 tablespoons corn-oil margarine, melted
Nonstick vegetable coating

Combine the flour, baking soda, ginger, cinnamon, cloves, and salt in a large mixing bowl.

In another, smaller bowl, dissolve the instant coffee in the hot water. Add the egg, apple juice concentrate, and melted margarine and mix well.

Add the liquid ingredients to the dry ingredients and mix just enough to moisten the dry ingredients. The mixture will be lumpy.

Pour the batter, 1/4 cup at a time, onto a hot skillet or griddle that has been sprayed lightly with nonstick vegetable coating. Cook until the top of each pancake is covered with tiny bubbles and the bottom is brown. Turn and brown the other side.

Serve with Apple Butter (page 61) and Light Cheese (page 52).

Makes 12 pancakes

EACH PANCAKE CONTAINS APPROXIMATELY:
85 TOTAL CALORIES / 23 CALORIES IN FAT
18 MG CHOLESTEROL / 180 MG SODIUM
13 MG CALCIUM

OATMEAL-RAISIN PANCAKES

For people who don't particularly like cooked oatmeal as a break-fast cereal, this is a wonderful way to get this healthful grain into their breakfast menus. I like to serve them with Apple Butter (page 61). A delicious variation of this recipe is to use banana slices instead of raisins. Spoon the pancake batter on the grill and arrange the banana slices on each pancake before turning it over. I serve Spiced Bananas (page 228) with Oatmeal-Banana Pancakes.

> *¼ cup raisins*
> *1½ cups uncooked old-fashioned oatmeal*
> *¼ teaspoon salt*
> *¼ teaspoon baking powder*
> *¼ teaspoon baking soda*
> *1 egg, lightly beaten, or ¼ cup liquid egg substitute*
> *1 cup plain nonfat yogurt*
> *1 tablespoon corn-oil margarine*

Cover the raisins with warm water and allow to soak for 15 minutes. Drain thoroughly.

Put the oatmeal in a blender or food processor with a metal blade and blend for approximately 1 minute or until the consistency of flour is attained. Combine the oat flour, salt, baking powder, and baking soda in a large mixing bowl and mix well.

Combine all the remaining ingredients except for the margarine in another bowl and mix well. Combine the liquid and dry ingredients and mix until just moist. Allow to rest for 5 minutes.

Heat a cast-iron skillet or nonstick pan and melt the margarine. When the pan is hot, wipe out the margarine with a paper towel. Spoon 3 tablespoons of batter into the pan for each pancake. Cook over medium heat until bubbles form on the surface and the underside is lightly browned. Turn over and cook until the other side is lightly browned.

Makes eight 4-inch pancakes

EACH PANCAKE CONTAINS APPROXIMATELY:
105 TOTAL CALORIES / 20 CALORIES IN FAT
27 MG CHOLESTEROL / 135 MG SODIUM
80 MG CALCIUM

CINNAMON-APPLE-PASTA PANCAKES

The first comment I received after putting these pancakes on a spa menu was, "Pasta—for breakfast!" My answer was, "Why not?" Pasta is a grain product, just like breakfast cereals, breads, and muffins. If variety is the spice of life, then why not literally spice up your breakfast menus with pasta?

> 2 tablespoons chopped walnuts
> 1 egg plus 1 egg white, lightly beaten
> 1 tablespoon skim milk
> 1 tablespoon fructose or 4 teaspoons sugar
> 1/2 teaspoon ground cinnamon
> 1 1/2 teaspoons vanilla extract
> 2 green apples, cored and thinly sliced (1 1/2 cups)
> 1/4 cup raisins
> 2 cups cooked spaghetti (about 1/4 pound dry)
> 1 tablespoon corn-oil margarine

Place the walnuts in a preheated 350°F oven for 8 to 10 minutes. Watch them carefully, as they burn easily.

Combine the eggs, milk, fructose or sugar, cinnamon, vanilla, apples, raisins, and walnuts in a large bowl. Add the spaghetti and mix well.

For each pancake, heat ½ teaspoon of the margarine in a small skillet. Spread ¾ cup of the pasta mixture in the pan, packing it evenly. Cover and cook over medium heat until it is golden brown on the bottom, about 10 minutes. Turn over and brown the other side, about 3 to 5 minutes.

Makes 6 pancakes

EACH PANCAKE CONTAINS APPROXIMATELY:
150 TOTAL CALORIES / 45 CALORIES IN FAT
35 MG CHOLESTEROL / 25 MG SODIUM
20 MG CALCIUM

WHOLE WHEAT CREPES

1 cup skim milk
¾ cup whole wheat flour
¼ teaspoon salt
1 egg, lightly beaten
Corn oil for coating pan

Combine the milk, flour, and salt in a medium bowl and beat with an egg beater until well mixed. Beat in the egg and mix well.

Wipe the inside of a crepe pan with corn oil after the pan is hot. Spoon 2 tablespoons of the crepe batter into the pan and tilt from side to side to spread evenly. When the edges start to curl, turn the crepe with a spatula and brown the other side. Place the crepes in a covered container as you make them in order to keep them pliable.

To freeze the crepes, seperate them with pieces of aluminum foil or wax paper. Wrap tightly and place in the freezer. To use, bring the crepes to room temperature. Put them in a preheated 300°F oven for 20 minutes or until they are soft and pliable. This will preclude their breaking when folded.

Makes 12 crepes

EACH CREPE CONTAINS APPROXIMATELY:
40 TOTAL CALORIES / 10 CALORIES IN FAT
20 MG CHOLESTEROL / 60 MG SODIUM
30 MG CALCIUM

FOUR-GRAIN WAFFLES

These waffles have a wonderful crunchy texture that I love. I like to serve them with Light Cheese (page 52) and Apple Butter (page 61). Or sometimes I make blueberry waffles by adding 1½ cups unthawed frozen blueberries just before folding the egg whites into the batter. If you are making the waffle batter to use later, don't add the frozen blueberries until you're ready to make the waffles. The cooking time in the waffle iron is adequate to thaw the blueberries and plump them up so they look and taste like fresh blueberries. Four-grain cereal is made from wheat, rye, barley, and oats and is available in health food stores.

> ½ cup uncooked four-grain cereal
> 2 eggs, separated
> 4 teaspoons canola or corn oil
> 2 tablespoons fructose or 3 tablespoons sugar
> 1⅓ cups skim milk
> 1¾ cups whole wheat flour
> 2 teaspoons baking powder
> ½ teaspoon salt

Soak the cereal in enough water to cover. Set aside.

Combine the egg yolks, oil, fructose or sugar, and milk and mix thoroughly.

Combine the flour, baking powder, and salt and mix well. Drain the cereal and add to the flour mixture. Add the milk mixture to the flour mixture and stir lightly. Add additional milk if necessary to thin sufficiently to ladle.

Beat the egg whites until stiff but not dry and fold into the waffle mixture before baking.

Preheat a waffle iron and pour ½ cup of the mixture at a time onto the hot iron; bake for approximately 6 minutes.

Makes 6 waffles

EACH WAFFLE CONTAINS APPROXIMATELY:
350 TOTAL CALORIES / 55 CALORIES IN FAT
50 MG CHOLESTEROL / 340 MG SODIUM / 180 MG CALCIUM

WAFFLES

These waffles are another in the "magic" series of truly quick-and-easy recipes. If you do not have buttermilk, you can make them with skim milk as well, but reduce the amount of milk to 1 cup and omit the baking soda.

> *Nonstick vegetable coating or 1 teaspoon corn oil*
> *2 cups Magic Biscuit Mix (page 206)*
> *1 egg*
> *1½ cups buttermilk*
> *½ teaspoon baking soda*

Spray a round waffle iron with nonstick vegetable coating or add the corn oil to the waffle batter. Preheat the waffle iron.

Combine the Magic Biscuit Mix, egg, buttermilk, and baking soda (or 1 cup skim milk without the soda). Beat with a rotary beater until smooth.

Pour ½ cup of the mixture into the center of the hot waffle iron. Bake until the steaming stops.

Makes 6 waffles

EACH WAFFLE CONTAINS APPROXIMATELY:
245 TOTAL CALORIES / 90 CALORIES IN FAT
65 MG CHOLESTEROL / 590 MG SODIUM
305 MG CALCIUM

OUR FAMOUS SUGAR-FREE BRAN MUFFINS

Of all of the recipes I have created, this one has become the most popular with all of the spa, hotel, and restaurant guests. We always have trouble making enough of them to meet the demand. Since Apple Butter is an ingredient, it is impossible to make the muffins before making Apple Butter; and since we also serve Apple Butter with these muffins, several chefs have told me they feel like they have gone into the apple butter business. To make Carrot-Bran Muffins, add 1 cup grated carrot to the mixture at the same time the raisins are added.

> *2 ounces dried unsulfured apples, diced (1 cup)*
> *1 cup unsweetened apple juice*
> *1½ cups uncooked four-grain cereal*
> *¾ cup unprocessed wheat bran*
> *¾ cup raisins*
> *1 cup buttermilk*
> *1 cup Apple Butter (page 61)*
> *1½ cups whole wheat flour*
> *2 teaspoons baking powder*
> *2 teaspoons baking soda*
> *½ teaspoon salt*
> *½ teaspoon ground cinnamon*
> *2 eggs*
> *1 teaspoon vanilla extract*
> *½ cup canola or corn oil*
> *Nonstick vegetable coating*

Preheat the oven to 375°F. Combine the diced apples and apple juice in a small bowl. Set aside.

In a large mixing bowl, combine the four-grain cereal, bran, raisins, and buttermilk. Stir in the Apple Butter. Mix the apple mixture and the bran mixture and set aside.

In a third, smaller bowl, combine the flour, baking powder, baking soda, salt, and cinnamon. Set aside.

In a fourth, small bowl, combine the eggs, vanilla, and corn oil and beat lightly. Stir this into the apple/bran mixture. Add the flour mixture and stir until just blended. Do not overmix.

Spray a muffin pan (including the top of the pan) with nonstick vegetable coating. Divide the batter among twelve muffin cups. Heap the batter above the edge of the cups. Bake for 35 minutes or until a toothpick inserted in the center of a muffin comes out clean. Cool for 10 minutes. Remove the muffins from the pan, cutting apart where necessary. Cool on a wire rack.

Makes 12 muffins

EACH MUFFIN CONTAINS APPROXIMATELY:
345 TOTAL CALORIES / 105 CALORIES IN FAT
35 MG CHOLESTEROL / 325 MG SODIUM
90 MG CALCIUM

CRUNCHY WHEAT BERRY BREAD

When making this bread, don't forget to soak the wheat berries for at least 24 hours. You want the bread to have the crunchiness its name implies, but unsoaked wheat berries can be dangerous to your teeth!

Two ¼-ounce packages active dry yeast (check the date on the package)
3 tablespoons fructose or ¼ cup sugar
¼ cup lukewarm water (110° to 115°F)

¹/₂ cup low-fat milk
2 tablespoons corn-oil margarine
¹/₂ teaspoon salt
1 egg, lightly beaten
¹/₄ cup wheat berries, soaked in water to cover for at least 24
  hours and drained
3 cups whole wheat pastry flour
Corn-oil margarine

Combine the yeast, 1 tablespoon of the fructose or the sugar, and water. Set aside in a warm place and allow to double in bulk. This takes a very short time.

While the yeast is rising, combine milk and margarine in a small saucepan and heat slowly until the margarine melts. Add the remaining fructose or sugar and salt and mix well. Combine the beaten egg with the milk mixture and again mix well.

Combine the milk mixture with the yeast mixture in a large bowl. Add the soaked wheat berries. Add the flour 1 cup at a time, mixing well. The last ¹/₂ cup will have to be kneaded in with your hands. Cover and allow to double in bulk in a warm place, about 1¹/₂ hours.

Punch the dough down until it is reduced to its original size. Form into a loaf and place in an oiled loaf pan. Cover and again allow to rise until doubled in size, about 30 minutes. Bake in a preheated 325°F oven for 35 to 40 minutes or until the loaf is golden brown and sounds hollow when tapped. Rub the top with a little margarine and put back in the oven for about 3 minutes.

Allow the bread to cool to room temperature on a rack before slicing. To reheat, wrap in foil and place briefly in the oven.

Makes 20 slices

1 SLICE CONTAINS APPROXIMATELY:
90 TOTAL CALORIES / 20 CALORIES IN FAT
12 MG CHOLESTEROL / 65 MG SODIUM
15 MG CALCIUM

HERB BREAD

I love to make this bread because it's so easy and so tasty. Two important tips for the success of this bread include checking the date on the package of yeast to make certain it is still effective and having the egg at room temperature. If the egg is not at room temperature, simply put it in a bowl of lukewarm water long enough to bring it to room temperature before proceeding with the recipe. This bread is especially good served warm.

One ¼-ounce package active dry yeast (check the date on the package)
¼ cup lukewarm water (110° to 115°F)
1 cup low-fat cottage cheese
1 tablespoon fructose or 4 teaspoons sugar
¼ cup finely chopped parsley
¼ cup finely chopped scallion tops
1 egg, lightly beaten
1 teaspoon dried basil, crushed in a mortar and pestle
1 teaspoon dried oregano, crushed in a mortar and pestle
1 teaspoon dried tarragon, crushed in a mortar and pestle
1 teaspoon salt
1 cup whole wheat flour
1 cup unbleached white flour
Vegetable oil for coating pan

Sprinkle the yeast over the water. Stir to dissolve and let stand until bubbly.

Warm the cottage cheese in a small saucepan. Transfer to a large mixing bowl and stir in the yeast. Add the fructose or sugar, the parsley, scallion tops, egg, and seasonings and mix well.

Sift the flours together and add to the cottage cheese/herb mixture, a little at a time, to form a dough. Knead until smooth. Cover with a tea towel and let stand in a warm place for several hours, or until doubled in bulk.

Punch the dough down until it is reduced to its original size. Form into a loaf and place in an oiled loaf pan. Cover with a tea towel and let stand in a warm place until again doubled in bulk.

Preheat the oven to 350°F. Bake for 40 minutes or until the bread has a hollow sound when rapped with the knuckles.

Serve warm or place on a rack to cool. When cool, wrap in foil and store in the refrigerator until ready to use. It slices better when it is cold.

Makes 20 slices

1 SLICE CONTAINS APPROXIMATELY:
60 TOTAL CALORIES / 10 CALORIES IN FAT
12 MG CHOLESTEROL / 160 MG SODIUM
20 MG CALCIUM

CRANBERRY BREAD

I developed this recipe for a holiday menu, but now I use it all during the year because it is so pretty and goes so well with luncheon salads of many types. During the holidays it is fun to make it in tiny loaves and wrap them up for gifts.

Nonstick vegetable coating
2 cups whole wheat flour
1½ teaspoons baking powder
½ teaspoon baking soda
½ teaspoon salt
½ teaspoon ground cinnamon
One 6-ounce can frozen unsweetened apple juice concentrate,
* undiluted, thawed*
1 egg, lightly beaten
2 tablespoons canola or corn oil
2 teaspoons vanilla extract
1½ cups cranberries, blanched and coarsely chopped (1 cup
* chopped)*

Preheat the oven to 350°F. Spray a standard loaf pan with nonstick vegetable coating.

In a large bowl, combine the flour, baking powder, baking soda, salt, and cinnamon. Mix thoroughly.

In another bowl, combine the apple juice concentrate, egg, corn oil, and vanilla and mix well.

Pour the liquid ingredients into the dry ingredients. Add the cranberries and mix well. Pour into the loaf pan and bake for 45 to 50 minutes.

Makes 24 slices

1 SLICE CONTAINS APPROXIMATELY:
65 TOTAL CALORIES / 15 CALORIES IN FAT
8 MG CHOLESTEROL / 120 MG SODIUM
25 MG CALCIUM

DANISH RYE CEREAL

This is my own favorite cooked hot cereal. I named it Danish Rye Cereal because I think it tastes like a Danish sweet roll, which is also good for you. I cook it in large amounts and store it in the freezer, then reheat it in the microwave for breakfast. I like it best hot, topped with Light Cheese (page 52), but I sometimes use it as a cold ingredient in fruit salads.

> 1 cup unprocessed rye berries
> 2 teaspoons ground cinnamon
> 1 teaspoon caraway seeds
> 1 tablespoon vanilla extract
> 3 cups water
> 1/4 cup raisins

Combine all the ingredients except the raisins in a saucepan. Mix well and bring to a boil. Reduce the heat and cook, covered, for 1 hour, stirring occasionally and adding more water if necessary to prevent scorching.

During the last 15 minutes of cooking time, add the raisins and mix well.

Makes 2¹/₂ cups

¹/₂ CUP CONTAINS APPROXIMATELY:
125 TOTAL CALORIES / 5 CALORIES IN FAT
0 MG CHOLESTEROL / 1 MG SODIUM
20 MG CALCIUM

DESSERTS

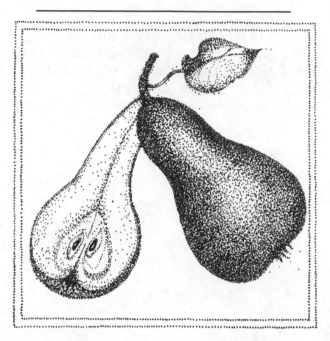

FRUIT IS THE ideal dessert because it is naturally sweet and doesn't contain the fat found in most man-made sweets. It contains no cholesterol, is very low in sodium, and is packed with vitamins and fiber.

Even though everyone's favorite fruits may not be the same, I don't know of anyone who just plain doesn't like fruit. Due to both popular demand and modern refrigerated transportation, there is an incredible variety of fresh fruit available all over the country during most of the year. Vine- and tree-ripened fruits are always both sweeter and more flavorful, but they are not always available.

When you buy fruit that is not quite ripe, allow it to ripen at room temperature before refrigerating it. Refrigerate ripe fruit to prevent spoilage. Don't peel or slice fresh fruits until you are ready to serve them or they will lose some of their vitamin content, dry out, and some, such as apples, will turn brown. To prevent apples from discoloring, brush them with citrus juice immediately after slicing them.

Fresh fruit provides the optimum amount of vitamins, and there are many ways to add variety in serving them. You can combine several types of fruit; puree fruits to serve on other fruits as sauces; marinate in fruit juices, wines, or liqueurs; or combine fresh fruits with cooked or canned and dried fruits to create what the French call a composed compote. Fresh fruits also make wonderful accompaniments and sauces for all other types of desserts, such as custards, puddings, cakes, and pies.

Without destroying too many of the vitamins in fruit and still creating very healthy desserts, it is possible to steam, poach, bake, or broil fruit. You can also freeze fruit for sorbets, sherbets, and ice cream.

When poaching peaches, plums, apricots, or cherries, remove the pits before cooking. An interesting aside about these fruits is that the nutlike kernel in the center of the pits is potentially poisonous. I was horrified to learn this because as a child I used to open peach pits and eat the almond flavored "nut" in the center. Fortunately I never had too many of them at one time because supposedly eight to ten of them, if chewed, can release enough hydrogen cyanide to kill you!

When fresh fruits are not available, there is a wide selection of canned fruits packed in water or in natural juices without sugar added. Not only are they better for you, they also taste better than the insipidly sweet fruit packed in heavy syrup.

Dried fruits make wonderful sweet snacks, which can be eaten like cookies or candy. They also make delicious compotes and sauces when cooked. Their high caloric content can be understood easily when you realize that it takes almost 6 pounds of a fresh fruit to yield 1 pound of dried fruit. Raisins or currants have more moisture and flavor if you plump them up first by presoaking them for 15 minutes before adding them to a mixture. When adding them to baked goods, either soak them in water and drain them, or soak them in one of the liquids you are using in the recipe.

I usually don't have very large dessert sections in my books; however, I have received so many letters from my readers requesting revisions of their dessert recipes that I decided to share some of those revised recipes with you. I have also included some of my own favorite spa creations for you to try on your family and friends. When you have a craving for a really rich dessert, eat only half of it. On my menu at the restaurant at Neiman-Marcus in Newport

Beach, California, I offer rich desserts in full portions for "sinners" and half portions for "saints." You would be surprised how few "sinner" portions we serve!

FANTASY IN FRUIT

This dessert has literally become my signature on many menus. It is more colorful if you use two fruit purees as suggested; however, it is easier and also beautiful using just one. When using raspberries, strain the puree to remove the seeds or it will be gritty. This is an incredibly beautiful and very healthy dessert. It is also a practical approach to using up all of the varied types of fresh fruit you may have on hand. I used the Honey Cream variation (see page 250) of the Pastry Cream recipe with Fantasy in Fruit for a Rosh Hashanah dessert in a magazine article and received hundreds of letters from people telling me how much they liked it.

½ cup fresh fruit puree (two colors: ¼ cup of each—mango or papaya and raspberry are most colorful)
1½ cups assorted seasonal fresh fruit, sliced in different shapes (melon balls, wedges of citrus, slivers of peach, whole grapes, etc.)
¼ cup Pastry Cream (page 250)

Place 2 tablespoons of each color puree on each of two large round plates, preferably white. Spread the puree out in an interesting pattern with the back of a spoon.

Arrange ¾ cup of the various fruits in an interesting pattern on the puree, creating a work of art on each plate.

Decorate the fruit with the Pastry Cream. For a truly exciting treat, use a pastry bag and pipe squiggles, swirls, and rosettes onto the fruit.

Makes 2 servings

EACH SERVING CONTAINS APPROXIMATELY (VARIES WITH
FRUIT USED): 140 TOTAL CALORIES / 25 CALORIES IN FAT
10 MG CHOLESTEROL / 45 MG SODIUM
125 MG CALCIUM

VANILLA ICE MILK CREPE WITH PAPAYA - RUM SAUCE

This is both a delicious and an impressive dessert, and it can be made ahead of time. You can make the sauce in the morning and store it in the refrigerator. The crepes may be filled with ice milk and frozen in a single layer in a covered pan or dish. (Be sure to cover it tightly or the ice milk will pick up the flavors of other foods in the freezer.) Ten minutes before serving, remove the crepes from the freezer and allow them to soften slightly. I particularly like this dessert after curried dishes.

PAPAYA-RUM SAUCE:

> *1 pound papaya*
> *1½ teaspoons dark rum*
> *½ teaspoon vanilla extract*
>
> *1 cup vanilla ice milk*
> *4 Whole Wheat Crepes (page 212)*
> *Ground cinnamon for garnish*
> *Mint sprigs for garnish*

Peel the papaya and remove the seeds. Cube the papaya, place it in a blender container or food processor with a metal blade, and puree. Add the rum and vanilla and blend thoroughly. Refrigerate in a covered container. You should have 1 cup.

When ready to serve, spoon 2 tablespoons of the sauce on each plate, turning the plate to distribute the sauce evenly over the bottom.

Spoon ¼ cup of the ice milk down the center of each crepe. Wrap the crepe around it, placing it in the center of the sauce on the plate, fold side down. Spoon 2 tablespoons Papaya-Rum Sauce over the top. Garnish with a sprinkle of ground cinnamon and a mint sprig.

Makes 4 servings

EACH SERVING CONTAINS APPROXIMATELY:
105 TOTAL CALORIES / 20 CALORIES IN FAT
25 MG CHOLESTEROL / 90 MG SODIUM
85 MG CALCIUM

STRAWBERRIES ROMANOFF

This is the easiest version I have come up with to date of this Russian dessert. It is classically made with whipped cream, but for far less fat and calories this provides a healthier version for a Russian menu—or any other menu!

SAUCE:

> 1½ cups skim milk
> 3 tablespoons uncooked Cream of Rice
> 1 tablespoon fructose or 4 teaspoons sugar
> 1½ teaspoons vanilla extract
> ¼ teaspoon rum extract
> 2 tablespoons Grand Marnier
> 2 egg whites, at room temperature
>
> 4 cups sliced fresh strawberries
> 8 whole strawberries
> 8 sprigs mint

Bring the milk to a boil in a small saucepan. Add the Cream of Rice and stir for 30 seconds. Remove from the heat and allow to stand for 5 minutes.

Mix well and pour into a blender container. Add the fructose or sugar, the vanilla and rum extracts, and the Grand Marnier and blend until smooth.

Beat the egg whites until stiff but not dry in a small mixing bowl. Pour the milk mixture into another small mixing bowl and fold in the egg whites until smooth.

To serve, spoon ½ cup sliced strawberries into each of eight sherbet glasses. Spoon ¼ cup sauce over the top. Place 1 whole strawberry, with a mint sprig in the center, on top of each serving.

Makes 8 servings

EACH SERVING CONTAINS APPROXIMATELY:
80 TOTAL CALORIES / 5 CALORIES IN FAT
1 MG CHOLESTEROL / 40 MG SODIUM
70 MG CALCIUM

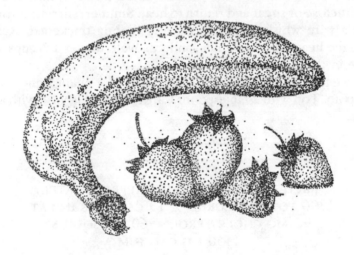

CAROB - YOGURT SUNDAE

This sundae is one of the most popular desserts at the Canyon Ranch Spa in Tucson, Arizona, where it is served appropriately after a "burger and fries." To make a Strawberry-Yogurt Parfait, use the Easy Strawberry Jam (page 60) in place of this Carob Sauce.

CAROB SAUCE:

> 2 tablespoons corn-oil margarine
> 2 tablespoons unbleached flour
> 1 1/2 cups boiling water
> 1/2 cup roasted carob powder
> 1 1/2 teaspoons instant coffee powder
> 1/4 cup fructose or 1/3 cup sugar
> 1 tablespoon vanilla extract
>
> 1 1/3 cups plain nonfat yogurt
> Mint sprigs for garnish

Melt the margarine in a medium saucepan over low heat. Add the flour and cook, stirring constantly, for at least 3 minutes.

Remove from the heat and add the boiling water all at once, stirring with a wire whisk. Add the carob powder, instant coffee, and fructose or sugar and return to heat. Simmer, stirring constantly with a wire whisk, until the sauce is slightly thickened. Remove from the heat, add the vanilla, and mix well. Makes 1 3/4 cups sauce. Store in the refrigerator.

For each serving, place 1/3 cup yogurt in a champagne glass or compote. Top with 2 tablespoons Carob Sauce. Garnish with a mint sprig.

Makes 4 servings

EACH SERVING CONTAINS APPROXIMATELY:
90 TOTAL CALORIES / 15 CALORIES IN FAT
1 MG CHOLESTEROL / 60 MG SODIUM
150 MG CALCIUM

SPICED BANANAS

Remember when the most famous fruit slogan was "An apple a day keeps the doctor away"? Now researchers tell us that a banana a day is a good idea, too, because of its high potassium content. Spiced Bananas are a quick, easy, and tasty dessert. To turn this recipe into a wonderful topping for other fruit, pancakes, waffles, yogurt, and ice milk, chop the bananas into small pieces rather than quartering them. When adding the ground cloves, be very careful not to add more than a dash. A dash is defined as less than ⅛ teaspoon. A little clove is a wonderful spicy accent; too much can quickly make anything taste like toothpaste!

¼ cup frozen unsweetened apple juice concentrate, undiluted
2 bananas, peeled and quartered lengthwise
¼ teaspoon ground cinnamon
¼ teaspoon ground allspice
⅛ teaspoon ground nutmeg
Dash ground cloves
Mint sprigs for garnish

Heat the apple juice concentrate in a medium skillet. Add the banana quarters and cook until heated through, about 5 minutes.

Combine the spices and sprinkle over the top of the bananas.

For each serving, place two banana quarters on a plate and spoon 2 teaspoons sauce over the top. Garnish with a mint sprig.

Makes 4 servings

EACH SERVING CONTAINS APPROXIMATELY:
100 TOTAL CALORIES / 5 CALORIES IN FAT
0 MG CHOLESTEROL / 75 MG SODIUM
10 MG CALCIUM

FRESH FRUIT PIZZA

If you want to make Fresh Fruit Pizza in a hurry and you don't have the Pizza Crusts waiting for you in the freezer, you can use either four whole wheat flour tortillas or two pita breads for the crust.

When using pita bread, place it under the broiler just long enough for it to puff up slightly and then separate into two round flat halves. Toast each half lightly before spreading it with the cheese and fruit and proceeding with the recipe. When using tortillas, I also like to toast them lightly before proceeding.

1 cup assorted fresh fruit
Apple juice to cover
Four 4-inch Pizza Crusts (see page 204)
1/2 cup Pastry Cream (page 250)

Prepare the fruit for poaching. Some fruits are better peeled before poaching, such as peaches, apples, pears, and melons of all types; however, plums, nectarines, and cherries should not be peeled. Slice the fruit and place it in a saucepan with apple juice to cover. Bring to a boil. Reduce the heat and simmer until the fruit can be pierced with a fork. Drain well.

For each serving, spread 2 tablespoons Pastry Cream on a Pizza Crust. Arrange 1/4 cup of poached fruit on top. Place under a broiler until hot.

Makes 4 servings

EACH SERVING CONTAINS APPROXIMATELY:
230 TOTAL CALORIES / 45 CALORIES IN FAT
10 MG CHOLESTEROL / 185 MG SODIUM
115 MG CALCIUM

GINGERED FRUIT COMPOTE

This uniquely different dessert keeps well for days in the refrigerator. It is also good served on hot cereal for breakfast. I even like it instead of jam on whole wheat toast.

3 tablespoons pine nuts
1 cup water

½ cup dried apricots, sliced
½ cup dried unsulfured apples, sliced
¼ cup dried currants
¼ cup golden raisins
1½ teaspoons finely chopped peeled ginger
¾ cup Cinnamon-Apple Yogurt Sauce (page 54)
Mint sprigs for garnish
Ground cinnamon for garnish

Place the pine nuts in a preheated 350°F oven for 8 to 10 minutes. Watch carefully, as they burn easily. Set aside.

Combine the water, apricots, and apples in a medium saucepan and bring to a boil. Turn down the heat, cover, and simmer for 20 to 30 minutes or until tender. Remove from the heat and add the currants, raisins, and ginger.

Cool to room temperature, cover, and refrigerate overnight (or at least 12 hours).

To serve, spoon 2 tablespoons of the Cinnamon-Apple Yogurt Sauce into each of six wine goblets. Spoon ¼ cup compote on top of the sauce. Then top with 1½ teaspoons toasted nuts and a sprig of mint. Sprinkle with a light dusting of cinnamon.

Makes six ¼-cup servings

EACH SERVING CONTAINS APPROXIMATELY:
130 TOTAL CALORIES / 15 CALORIES IN FAT
0 MG CHOLESTEROL / 50 MG SODIUM
65 MG CALCIUM

BAKED APPLESAUCE

This applesauce is a good accompaniment to a variety of meats and poultry. It is also a good breakfast as well as a light dessert. For dessert, I like to serve it either with Pastry Cream (page 250) or Cinnamon-Apple Yogurt Sauce (page 54).

1½ pounds cooking apples (4½ cups cubed)
¾ cup water
¾ cup unsweetened apple juice, undiluted
¼ teaspoon ground nutmeg
¼ teaspoon ground cinnamon
½ teaspoon vanilla extract

Wash, peel, and core the apples. Cut into 1-inch cubes.

Combine the remaining ingredients. Place the diced apples in a glass loaf pan or baking dish (the apples stay more moist in the loaf pan) and pour the juice mixture over the top.

Bake, uncovered, in a preheated 325°F oven for 45 minutes. Remove from the oven and allow to cool to room temperature. Store tightly covered in the refrigerator.

Makes 2 cups

¼ CUP CONTAINS APPROXIMATELY:
90 TOTAL CALORIES / 4 CALORIES IN FAT
0 MG CHOLESTEROL / 110 MG SODIUM
15 MG CALCIUM

SUGAR-FREE APPLE OR PEAR CRISP

As well as being a good dessert after the meal, these fruit crisps make excellent snacks. You can serve them in place of cookies, with coffee or tea or with milk for after-school treats.

1½ pounds apples or pears, peeled, cored, and thinly sliced
3 tablespoons all-purpose flour
¼ cup frozen unsweetened apple juice concentrate
½ teaspoon ground cinnamon
Dash freshly ground nutmeg
3 tablespoons corn-oil margarine, softened
10 graham cracker squares, crushed (¾ cup)

Preheat the oven to 375°F. In an 8-inch-square baking dish, toss the apples or pears with 1 tablespoon of the flour. Add the concentrated apple juice. Coat well.

In a small bowl, combine the remaining 2 tablespoons flour and the spices with the margarine and mix until well blended.

Gradually stir in the graham cracker crumbs until the mixture resembles coarse crumbs. Sprinkle evenly over the fruit.

Bake for 30 minutes or until the topping is lightly browned and the fruit is tender.

Makes sixteen 2-inch-square servings

EACH SERVING CONTAINS APPROXIMATELY:
75 TOTAL CALORIES / 25 CALORIES IN FAT
0 MG CHOLESTEROL / 40 MG SODIUM
10 MG CALCIUM

INDIAN APPLE PUDDING

For a uniquely different sweet after your next Southwestern-style dinner, try this Indian pudding. Because it is sugar-free and full of healthy ingredients, I have even served it for breakfast on spa menus with Light Cheese (page 52) instead of Pastry Cream.

> *2 cups canned evaporated skimmed milk*
> *1½ teaspoons Minute Tapioca*
> *1 tablespoon yellow cornmeal*
> *1 egg, beaten*
> *⅓ cup frozen unsweetened concentrated apple juice, undiluted*
> *¼ teaspoon salt*
> *¼ teaspoon ground ginger*
> *¼ teaspoon ground cinnamon*
> *½ cup Pastry Cream (page 250)*

Preheat the oven to 300°F. Scald the milk in the top of a double boiler over simmering hot water. Stir in the tapioca and cornmeal.

Continue to cook for 10 minutes, stirring occasionally with a wire whisk.

In a medium bowl, beat the egg. Add the apple juice concentrate, salt, ginger, and cinnamon.

Combine the milk mixture and the egg mixture and mix well. Divide the mixture evenly into eight 3-inch ramekins or eight 6-ounce custard cups or pour it into a 1½-quart baking dish. Place small baking dishes on a cookie sheet for easier handling.

Bake the individual puddings for 25 to 30 minutes, the large pudding for 1½ hours. Serve warm with 2 tablespoons Pastry Cream per serving.

Makes four ½-cup servings

EACH SERVING CONTAINS APPROXIMATELY:
220 TOTAL CALORIES / 40 CALORIES IN FAT
70 MG CHOLESTEROL / 440 MG SODIUM
480 MG CALCIUM

APPLE FLUFF

This is a recipe I modified for a reader who wanted a healthier, very easy-to-make recipe for her Cub Scout troop. It is a great recipe for a group of children to make because they can take turns beating the mixture for the 15-minute period it requires.

1½ cups frozen unsweetened apple juice concentrate, undiluted
2 cups water
½ cup uncooked farina or Cream of Wheat
Freshly grated nutmeg for garnish (optional)

Combine the apple juice concentrate, water, and farina or Cream of Wheat in a large saucepan and bring to a boil over medium heat, stirring constantly.

Reduce the heat to low and cook, stirring occasionally, for about 10 minutes or until thickened.

Pour into a large bowl and beat for 15 minutes with an electric mixer or until the mixture is very light in color and about twice its original volume.

Spoon ½ cup of the mixture into each dessert dish or goblet and refrigerate for up to 2 hours. Garnish with a sprinkle of freshly grated nutmeg.

Makes 10 servings

EACH SERVING CONTAINS APPROXIMATELY:
130 TOTAL CALORIES / N CALORIES IN FAT
0 MG CHOLESTEROL / 180 MG SODIUM
10 MG CALCIUM

RAISIN - RICE PUDDING

This is a nutritious and easy-to-make version of an old favorite. The major difference between this recipe and most of the "old favorites" is that it calls for brown rice and skim milk rather than white rice and cream.

> *1 cup cooked brown rice*
> *1 cup skim milk*
> *2 eggs*
> *2 tablespoons fructose or 3 tablespoons sugar*
> *1½ teaspoons ground cinnamon*
> *1 teaspoon vanilla extract*
> *½ cup raisins*
> *Freshly ground nutmeg for garnish*
> *Mint sprigs for garnish*

Combine all the ingredients except for the garnish and mix well. Pour into a casserole and set the casserole in a larger deep pan. Add boiling water to a depth of ¾ inch.

Bake in a preheated 350°F oven for 1¼ hours.

Spoon ¼ cup of warm pudding into individual dishes and sprinkle lightly with freshly ground nutmeg. Garnish with a sprig of mint.

Makes 2 cups

¼ CUP CONTAINS APPROXIMATELY:
100 TOTAL CALORIES / 15 CALORIES IN FAT
55 MG CHOLESTEROL / 100 MG SODIUM
60 MG CALCIUM

PERNOD SORBET

This is a good dessert after a heavy meal because it is light and not too sweet. It is particularly nice served between courses to clear the palate, as is the custom at most formal wine and food dinners. Many of the sorbets served for this purpose are too sweet and tend to diminish the appetite rather than clearing the palate.

> *6 ripe pears, peeled, cored, and halved*
> *1 cup water*
> *2 tablespoons Pernod*

Combine the pears and water in a large saucepan and bring to a boil. Reduce the heat, cover, and simmer for 20 minutes or until the pears are soft. At this point the liquid should be reduced by half. If not, remove the pears and continue to simmer the liquid until it is reduced by half.

Place the cooked mixture in a blender container and blend until completely smooth. Add the Pernod and mix again. Pour into a sorbet machine and process according to the manufacturer's directions.

Makes 2 cups

2 TABLESPOONS CONTAIN APPROXIMATELY:
40 TOTAL CALORIES / N CALORIES IN FAT
0 MG CHOLESTEROL / 0 MG SODIUM
10 MG CALCIUM

PINEAPPLE PIE

Talk about a tropical treat! If you like piña coladas, you'll love this pie.

>*1 tablepoon corn-oil margarine, melted*
>*16 graham cracker squares, crushed (1 cup)*
>*1/4 cup water*
>*1 envelope unflavored gelatin*
>*2 tablespoons cool water*
>*1/4 cup boiling water*
>*3/4 cup low-fat cottage cheese*
>*1/4 cup skim milk*
>*1 teaspoon vanilla extract*
>*1 teaspoon coconut extract*
>*2 tablespoons fructose or 3 tablespoons sugar*
>*One 20-ounce can crushed pineapple, packed in natural juice, undrained*
>*Ground cinnamon for garnish*

Preheat the oven to 350°F. Combine the melted margarine and graham cracker crumbs, mixing thoroughly. Add the 1/4 cup water a little at a time until the crumbs are moist enough to hold together (too much water makes the mixture mushy).

Place the crumb mixture in a 9-inch pie pan and press to cover the bottom and sides. Bake for 8 to 10 minutes or until browned. Set aside to cool.

In a small bowl, soften the gelatin in the 2 tablespoons cool water. Add the 1/4 cup boiling water and stir until the gelatin is completely dissolved. Combine the gelatin mixture and all the other ingredients except for the pineapple and cinnamon in a blender container and blend until smooth.

Pour the mixture into a large bowl. Add the crushed pineapple and mix well. Pour the mixture into the cooled graham cracker piecrust and sprinkle with cinnamon. Refrigerate until firm before serving.

Makes 12 servings

EACH SERVING CONTAINS APPROXIMATELY:
95 TOTAL CALORIES / 20 CALORIES IN FAT
1 MG CHOLESTEROL / 125 MG SODIUM
25 MG CALCIUM

CHERRY TRIFLE

This recipe is a revision of a very rich dessert a reader wanted to serve for a Valentine's Day party. It was loaded with eggs and cream, and her husband had just been put on a low-cholesterol diet. This is a delicious compromise and contains practically no cholesterol at all. For an Italian Cherry Trifle substitute sweet marsala for the sherry.

> 2 tablespoons fructose or 3 tablespoons sugar
> 1 tablespoon cornstarch
> 1/4 cup liquid egg substitute
> 1 cup skim milk
> 2 teaspoons vanilla extract
> 1/4 pound angel food cake, torn into bite-size pieces (2 cups)
> 3 tablespoons sherry
> 1 cup frozen unsweetened dark sweet cherries, thawed and thoroughly drained

To make the custard, mix the fructose or sugar and the cornstarch in a small saucepan. Add the liquid egg substitute and the milk and mix well. Heat to boiling over medium heat, stirring constantly, until thickened. Remove from the heat; add the vanilla. Cool to room temperature.

Place one-third of the cake pieces in the bottom of a 1-quart glass bowl or soufflé dish. Sprinkle with 1 tablespoon of the sherry. Pour one-third of the custard over the cake. Spoon ⅓ cup of the cherries over the custard. Repeat the process twice. Cover and refrigerate.

Makes 4 servings

EACH SERVING CONTAINS APPROXIMATELY:
190 TOTAL CALORIES / 10 CALORIES IN FAT
1 MG CHOLESTEROL / 140 MG SODIUM
90 MG CALCIUM

CARROT CAKE

In order to keep the calories low enough to serve this carrot cake as a dessert in spas, it does not have the usual cream cheese frosting. If you prefer carrot cake frosted, spread 1 cup of Pastry Cream (page 250) over the top.

½ cup chopped walnuts
2 cups all-purpose flour
2 teaspoons baking soda
2 teaspoons cinnamon
½ teaspoon salt
3 eggs
¾ cup canola or corn oil
¾ cup buttermilk
1½ cups fructose or 2 cups sugar
2 teaspoons vanilla extract
¾ cup canned crushed pineapple, packed in natural juice, drained
4 small carrots, peeled and grated (2 cups)
Nonstick vegetable coating

GLAZE:

> ⅔ *cup fructose or 1 cup sugar*
> ½ *teaspoon baking soda*
> ½ *cup buttermilk*
> ½ *cup corn-oil margarine*
> *1 tablespoon light corn syrup*
> *1 teaspoon vanilla extract*

Place the walnuts in a preheated 350°F oven for 8 to 10 minutes. Watch carefully, as they burn easily. Set aside, leaving oven at 350°.

Sift the flour, baking soda, cinnamon, and salt together and set aside. Beat the eggs in a large bowl. Add the oil, buttermilk, fructose or sugar, and vanilla and mix well. Add the flour mixture, pineapple, carrots, and walnuts and stir well. Pour into a 9-by-13-by-2-inch baking pan that has been sprayed with a nonstick vegetable coating and bake for 45 to 50 minutes or until a toothpick inserted in the center comes out clean.

While the cake is baking, make the glaze. Combine all the ingredients except the vanilla in a small saucepan and bring to a boil. Cook for 5 minutes, stirring occasionally. Remove from the heat and stir in the vanilla.

Remove the cake from the oven, poke holes in the top with a fork, and slowly pour the glaze over the hot cake so the glaze will enter the cake through the holes. Cool completely.

Makes 15 pieces (for fewer calories, cut in smaller pieces)

EACH PIECE CONTAINS APPROXIMATELY:
380 TOTAL CALORIES / 185 CALORIES IN FAT
48 MG CHOLESTEROL / 250 MG SODIUM
50 MG CALCIUM

LEMON-CREAM CAKE

> *Finely grated rind of 2 lemons*
> *3 tablespoons freshly squeezed lemon juice*
> *2 cups sifted all-purpose or unbleached flour*

1/2 teaspoon baking soda
2 1/2 teaspoons baking powder
1/2 teaspoon salt
1 cup fructose or 1 1/2 cups sugar
1/2 cup canola or corn oil
2 egg yolks
3/4 cup buttermilk
8 egg whites (1 cup)
1/2 teaspoon cream of tartar
2 3/4 cups Lemon Pastry Cream (page 250)

Preheat the oven to 325°F. Mix the lemon rind and lemon juice and set aside.

Sift the flour before measuring. Then sift together the flour, baking soda, baking powder, salt, and fructose or sugar into a large bowl. Add the oil, egg yolks, buttermilk, and lemon juice mixture in that order. Mix with an electric mixer at medium speed until satin smooth.

In another large mixing bowl, combine the egg whites and cream of tartar and beat at high speed with the electric mixer until the whites are very, very stiff (be sure the beaters are free of oil).

Fold the batter very gradually into the beaten egg whites. Fold with a wide spatula in a continuous motion until the batter is completely mixed into the egg whites.

Pour the batter into an ungreased 10-inch tube cake pan. Rotate the pan briskly back and forth to level the batter. Run a knife through the batter to eliminate holes in the cake. Bake for 1 hour and 10 minutes. Turn the cake upside down over a funnel or bottle and cool completely.

Loosen the cake with a spatula. Turn it upside down and hit the pan sharply on the edge of a table. Transfer the cake to a serving plate. Frost the top and sides with the Lemon Pastry Cream.

Makes 16 servings

EACH SERVING CONTAINS APPROXIMATELY:
250 TOTAL CALORIES / 100 CALORIES IN FAT
43 MG CHOLESTEROL / 240 MG SODIUM
190 MG CALCIUM

LEMON FROST

This is an easy, fast, and inexpensive dessert. It is surprisingly good and very refreshing.

>   1 egg white
>   ¹/₂ cup water
>   ¹/₂ cup nonfat dry milk powder
>   1 egg yolk, slightly beaten
>   ¹/₄ cup fructose or ¹/₃ cup sugar
>   ¹/₄ teaspoon grated lemon peel
>   3 tablespoons freshly squeezed lemon juice
>   Dash salt
>   3 graham cracker squares, crushed (3 tablespoons)

Combine the egg white, water, and milk powder and beat until stiff peaks form.

Combine the egg yolk, fructose or sugar, lemon peel, lemon juice, and salt and mix well. Beat gradually into the whipped egg-white-and-milk mixture.

Sprinkle 2 tablespoons of the graham cracker crumbs in a refrigerator tray and spoon in the lemon mixture. Top with the remaining crumbs. Freeze.

Makes 6 servings

EACH SERVING CONTAINS APPROXIMATELY:
80 TOTAL CALORIES / 10 CALORIES IN FAT
35 MG CHOLESTEROL / 55 MG SODIUM
75 MG CALCIUM

SLIM LEMON PIE

1 tablespoon corn-oil margarine, melted
16 graham cracker squares, crushed (1 cup)
1 envelope unflavored gelatin
¼ cup cold water
½ cup liquid egg substitute
⅔ cup fructose or 1 cup sugar
3 tablespoons freshly squeezed lemon juice
Grated rind of 1 lemon
4 egg whites
Lemon wheels for garnish
Mint sprigs for garnish

Preheat oven to 350°F. Combine the melted margarine and graham cracker crumbs, mixing thoroughly. Add the ¼ cup water a little at a time until the crumbs are moist enough to hold together (too much water makes the mixture mushy). Place the crumb mixture in a 9-inch pie pan and press to cover bottom and sides. Bake for 8 to 10 minutes or until lightly browned. Set aside to cool.

Soften the gelatin in the cold water for 5 minutes. In the top of a double boiler, over simmering water, cook the liquid egg substitute, half the fructose or sugar, the lemon juice, and the lemon rind until thick, stirring constantly. Add the softened gelatin and stir until dissolved. Do not boil. Set aside to cool to room temperature.

In a small bowl, beat the egg whites until foamy. Gradually add the remaining fructose or sugar and continue beating until the egg whites are stiff but not dry. Fold into the cooled lemon mixture and pour into the baked shell. Refrigerate for 4 hours or overnight.

To serve, slice into 8 wedges. Garnish each slice with a twisted lemon wheel and a sprig of mint.

Makes 8 servings

EACH SERVING CONTAINS APPROXIMATELY:
155 TOTAL CALORIES / 130 CALORIES IN FAT
0 MG CHOLESTEROL / 150 MG SODIUM
15 MG CALCIUM

PEANUT BUTTER DELIGHT

I love peanut butter so much that I am always trying to figure out a way to make a very little bit of it go a long way by combining it with other ingredients that don't interfere with its basic taste. When blending the ingredients in this recipe, make certain that you blend them long enough to get a really creamy satin-smooth consistency. I serve this in sherbet glasses using an ice-cream scoop to fill them, and garnish with a whole peanut in the shell and a sprig of mint.

1 cup part-skim ricotta cheese
1/4 cup unhomogenized smooth peanut butter
2 tablespoons skim milk
2 1/4 teaspoons vanilla extract
1/2 teaspoon ground cinnamon
4 1/2 teaspoons fructose or 2 tablespoons sugar

Combine all the ingredients in a food processor with a metal blade and blend until satin smooth. Refrigerate in a tightly covered container.

Makes 1 1/4 cups

1/4 CUP CONTAINS APPROXIMATELY:
165 TOTAL CALORIES / 95 CALORIES IN FAT
15 MG CHOLESTEROL / 125 MG SODIUM
150 MG CALCIUM

FLAN

Classic flan is always made with cream. While trying to lower the fat content I found that skim milk makes a flan that is much too watery. I was still able to lighten it enormously over the original version by using a combination of low-fat milk and evaporated skimmed milk. If your flan tends to be a little watery, don't worry about it—just pour off the water and rejoice in the fact that you're not getting all that extra fat in the flan.

> *2 eggs*
> *1 cup low-fat milk*
> *1 cup canned evaporated skimmed milk*
> *1/8 teaspoon salt*
> *2 tablespoons fructose or 2 1/2 tablespoons sugar*
> *1/2 teaspoon ground coriander*
> *1 teaspoon vanilla extract*
> *1/2 teaspoon maple extract*
> *Ground cinnamon for garnish*
> *Mint sprigs for garnish*

Preheat the oven to 225°F. Put all the ingredients except the garnishes in a blender container and blend well.

Pour the mixture into six custard cups and sprinkle the tops generously with cinnamon. Place on a cookie sheet in the center of the oven and bake for 2 hours and 30 minutes or until the flan is set and a knife inserted in the center comes out clean.

Serve warm or cold. Sprinkle each serving with additional cinnamon and garnish with a mint sprig.

Makes 6 servings

EACH SERVING CONTAINS APPROXIMATELY:
120 TOTAL CALORIES / 25 CALORIES IN FAT
120 MG CHOLESTEROL / 180 MG SODIUM
200 MG CALCIUM

PUMPKIN PIE

To make this traditional light pumpkin pie still lower in calories, you can omit the crust.

FILLING:

3 egg whites
1 tablespoon canola or corn oil
1 cup part-skim ricotta
One 16-ounce can solid-pack pumpkin (2 cups)
1/3 cup fructose or 1/2 cup sugar
1/4 teaspoon salt
1 1/2 teaspoons ground cinnamon
1/2 teaspoon ground nutmeg
1/4 teaspoon ground ginger
1/8 teaspoon ground cloves
1 teaspoon vanilla extract
2/3 cup canned evaporated skimmed milk

CRUST:

1 cup whole wheat pastry flour
1/4 teaspoon salt
1/4 cup canola or corn oil
3 tablespoons ice water
1 cup Pastry Cream (page 250)

Combine all the ingredients for the filling in a large bowl. Mix thoroughly with an electric mixer or in a food processor with a metal blade. Set aside to rest while you make the crust.

Combine the flour and salt in a 9-inch glass pie dish and mix well. Measure the oil in a large cup. Add the ice water to the oil and mix well, using a fork. Slowly add the liquid to the flour mixture, mixing with the same fork. Continue mixing until all the ingredients are well blended. Press onto the bottom and sides of the dish with your fingertips. Make sure the crust covers the entire inner surface of the dish evenly. Flute the edges if desired.

Mix the filling ingredients again until very smooth. Pour into the prepared pie shell and bake in a preheated 350°F oven for 40 to 45 minutes. Cool and chill.

To serve, cut into eight wedges and top each wedge with 2 tablespoons Pastry Cream.

Makes 8 servings

EACH SERVING CONTAINS APPROXIMATELY:
300 TOTAL CALORIES / 125 CALORIES IN FAT
20 MG CHOLESTEROL / 265 MG SODIUM
265 MG CALCIUM

ROCKY ROAD CAKE

I created this chocolatelike cake for spa menus where I do not use chocolate. It serves as a wonderful placebo for chocoholics who are trying to alter their habits.

¼ cup chopped almonds
1 cup flour
1 teaspoon baking soda
1 teaspoon baking powder
1 cup frozen unsweetened apple juice concentrate, undiluted, thawed
¼ cup corn-oil margarine
½ cup roasted carob powder
2 tablespoons plain nonfat yogurt
Nonstick vegetable coating
¼ cup Pastry Cream (page 250)
2 tablespoons unsweetened carob chips

Place the chopped almonds in a preheated 350°F oven for 8 to 10 minutes. Watch them carefully, as they burn easily. Set aside.

Raise the oven temperature to 375°.

Sift the flour, baking soda, and baking powder together. In a medium saucepan, mix the apple juice concentrate, margarine, and carob powder. Heat and stir until the margarine is melted and the carob powder is dissolved. Add the flour mixture to the carob mixture and blend.

In a separate small bowl, mix the yogurt with a wire whisk until all the lumps disappear and the yogurt is smooth and creamy. Add to the cake batter and mix gently. Add the almonds and again mix gently.

Pour into an 8-inch round cake pan that has been sprayed with nonstick vegetable coating. Bake at 375° for 20 minutes or until a toothpick inserted in the center comes out clean. Cool completely. Spread the Pastry Cream over the top and sprinkle with the carob chips.

Makes 12 servings

EACH SERVING CONTAINS APPROXIMATELY:
160 TOTAL CALORIES / 55 CALORIES IN FAT
1 MG CHOLESTEROL / 205 MG SODIUM
60 MG CALCIUM

BAKLAVA

Baklava is a classic Middle Eastern dessert that is loaded with butter, honey, and nuts. It is traditionally made in sheets and cut diagonally into diamond-shaped pieces and is almost impossible to portion exactly. I finally figured out a way to lower the calories and control the serving size—by rolling the filo dough like a jelly roll, then slicing it diagonally into the traditionally shaped pieces.

6 tablespoons walnuts
1/2 cup honey
1/4 cup corn-oil margarine
1 teaspoon ground cinnamon

Dash ground cloves
1/2 teaspoon vanilla extract
Vegetable oil
1/2 pound filo dough

Using a food processor with a metal blade, grind the walnuts to the consistency of fine gravel. Set aside.

Combine 1/4 cup of the honey and the margarine in a small saucepan and cook over low heat until the margarine is melted. Add the cinnamon, cloves, and vanilla and mix well.

Oil a 10-by-14-inch cookie sheet.

Place one layer of filo dough on a slightly damp towel. Brush the entire surface lightly with the honey/margarine mixture, using a pastry brush. Add another layer of filo dough and repeat. Sprinkle the top layer with 2 tablespoons of the ground walnuts, leaving a bare edge along one end.

Using the towel to help, roll the filo dough as you would a jelly roll, toward the bare edge and close neatly. Place on the prepared cookie sheet. Brush with another light layer of the honey mixture and slice diagonally into eight even portions, allowing for two half slices at the ends. Make two more rolls in the same manner.

Bake the three rolls in a preheated 250°F oven until brown, about 40 minutes. Watch closely after 30 minutes because the rolls will brown suddenly. Cool. When cool, warm the remaining 1/4 cup honey and paint honey on each roll with a pastry brush.

Makes 24 slices

EACH SLICE CONTAINS APPROXIMATELY:
80 TOTAL CALORIES / 55 CALORIES IN FAT
0 MG CHOLESTEROL / 45 MG SODIUM
5 MG CALCIUM

PASTRY CREAM

This Pastry Cream is really a variation on my Light Cheese (page 52); however, I decided to include it as a separate recipe, with variations for lemon, honey, and maple flavors, in the Dessert section because it is most frequently used here. Pastry Cream can be used to replace a classic French Crème Pâtissière, which would be used to garnish fruits, pies, and cakes but which also adds enormously to their fat and calorie content.

> *1 cup part-skim ricotta cheese*
> *3 tablespoons plain nonfat yogurt*
> *2 tablespoons fructose or 3 tablespoons sugar*
> *1 teaspoon vanilla extract*

Blend all the ingredients in a food processor with a metal blade until satin smooth. Refrigerate in a tightly covered container.

Makes 1 cup

2 TABLESPOONS CONTAIN APPROXIMATELY:
50 TOTAL CALORIES / 20 CALORIES IN FAT
10 MG CHOLESTEROL / 40 MG SODIUM
95 MG CALCIUM

VARIATIONS:

Lemon Pastry Cream: Add 2 tablespoons freshly squeezed lemon juice and 1 teaspoon grated lemon rind, and omit the vanilla extract.

Honey Cream: Substitute 2 tablespoons honey for the fructose or sugar.

Maple Cream: Substitute 2 tablespoons maple syrup for the fructose or sugar.

BEVERAGES

WATER IS BY FAR the healthiest beverage in the world, and it has finally come into its own as a status drink. You can now buy bottled water from almost everyplace in the world, plain or sparkling, flavored or natural, and with price tags ranging from nominal to outrageous. For anyone on a low-sodium diet, there are now many low-sodium soda waters available, as well as bottled distilled water, which is completely sodium-free.

There was a time when your guests would have been rather surprised, if not shocked, to have been offered water at a cocktail party. Now that it is the beverage of choice among many fitness-oriented young urban professionals, it is considered chic in many circles to serve a variety of waters for parties.

Water is also the basic ingredient for the two most popular beverages, coffee and tea. Here we are seeing decaffeinated coffee and caffeine-free herb tea becoming much more popular and available. In fact, even the chemically processed decaffeinated coffees, which some researchers believe contain carcinogens, are being replaced in many places with water-washed (often called the Swiss process) decaffeinated coffees.

Even the makers of many popular cola-type soft drinks that contain caffeine are now changing their formulas and touting the fact that they no longer contain even a trace of caffeine.

Caffeine is a drug that stimulates the adrenal glands to produce more adrenaline, which then acts as a stimulant, giving a false sense of energy.

Healthy alternatives to chocolate milk for children can be either carob milk or milk blended with old-fashioned unhomogenized peanut butter. Carob tastes a lot like chocolate, but it does not contain caffeine or saturated fat as chocolate does. Also it is naturally sweet so it doesn't need a lot of sugar and, being a plant, it contains fiber. It also has about four times the calcium found in chocolate or cocoa and none of the oxalic acid, which binds calcium and prevents its absorption. Carob milk is perfect for teenagers who have allergy problems affecting their complexions because of chocolate.

Also try "fruity" milk. Blend milk and fresh fruit such as peaches, strawberries, and bananas for after-school treats.

With alcohol consumption on the decline, many hotels and restaurants have asked me to create nonalcoholic alternative drinks they can serve for "happy hour." The general decline in the consumption of alcoholic beverages has come about because of the growing interest in fitness and the efforts of dedicated and powerful groups such as MADD (Mothers Against Drunk Driving), who have been instrumental in getting legislation passed for much stricter enforcement of the laws against drunk driving.

In this section I have included a few of these "mocktails," both hot and cold, as well as some of the drinks I have on spa menus.

This section is short because so many recipes in this book can actually be turned into beverages simply by blending the ingredients with enough added liquid to make them easily drinkable. Many of the soups make good hot or cold beverages without any alteration.

It always amazes me when people tell me they are trying to lose weight by going on a liquid diet. *Liquid* certainly cannot be interpreted as low-calorie. There can be just as much nutrition in a liquid diet as in solid food. If you or anyone in your family is ever put on a liquid diet, simply blend up all of your favorite dishes and serve them in mugs!

SUGAR-FREE LEMONADE

This delightfully refreshing summer cooler is delicious just as the recipe is given; however, I often combine it with cold sparkling water and serve it in wineglasses with the meal.

1/2 cup very hot water
Grated zest of 1 lemon
One 6-ounce can frozen unsweetened apple juice concentrate
3/4 cup freshly squeezed lemon juice
3 cups cold water

Combine hot water and the lemon zest and let cool.

Add the apple juice concentrate, mixing well. Add the lemon juice and cold water and mix well again. Refrigerate until ready to serve.

To serve, strain to remove the zest. Pour over ice in tall glasses.

Makes 5 cups

1 CUP CONTAINS APPROXIMATELY:
75 TOTAL CALORIES / N CALORIES IN FAT
0 MG CHOLESTEROL / 180 MG SODIUM
15 MG CALCIUM

STRAWBERRY COOLER

1/2 cup sparkling water
1 cup fresh strawberries
2 teaspoons fructose or 1 tablespoon sugar
1/4 cup ice cubes
1 whole strawberry for garnish

Place all the ingredients in a blender container and blend until frothy.

Serve in a chilled glass and garnish with a whole strawberry on the rim of the glass.

Makes 1 serving

EACH SERVING CONTAINS APPROXIMATELY:
75 TOTAL CALORIES / 5 CALORIES IN FAT
0 MG CHOLESTEROL / 30 MG SODIUM
30 MG CALCIUM

PEACH DAIQUIRI

This recipe is a satisfying and delicious "mocktail" that can easily be turned into a cocktail by substituting a jigger of real rum for the rum extract.

1 large peach, chopped (1 cup)
1 tablespoon freshly squeezed orange juice
1/2 teaspoon freshly squeezed lemon juice
1/2 teaspoon rum extract
1 teaspoon fructose or 1 1/2 teaspoons sugar
1/3 cup crushed ice

Combine all the ingredients in a blender container and blend until smooth and frothy.

Makes 1 cup

1 CUP CONTAINS APPROXIMATELY:
85 TOTAL CALORIES / N CALORIES IN FAT
0 MG CHOLESTEROL / 0 MG SODIUM
10 MG CALCIUM

HOT SPICED CIDER

This hot, soothing beverage is also good served cold.

> *1 quart apple cider*
> *12 whole cloves*
> *2 cinnamon sticks, broken into pieces*
> *8 whole allspice*
> *4 cinnamon sticks for stirrers (optional)*

Combine the first four ingredients in a 2-quart saucepan and bring to a boil. Reduce the heat and simmer for 5 minutes. Pour into 8-ounce mugs, with a cinnamon stick for stirring in each one if desired.

Makes four 8-ounce servings

EACH SERVING CONTAINS APPROXIMATELY:
65 TOTAL CALORIES / 5 CALORIES IN FAT
0 MG CHOLESTEROL / 5 MG SODIUM
25 MG CALCIUM

WASSAIL

I have purposely made this recipe large enough to be served in a punch bowl. It is a festive drink for fall and winter parties and goes well with popcorn, which is a very healthy snack.

> *2 quarts apple cider*
> *1 quart orange juice*
> *One 6-ounce can frozen unsweetened apple juice concentrate*
> *3 cinnamon sticks, broken*
> *8 whole cloves*

Combine all the ingredients in a large pot and bring to a boil. Reduce the heat and simmer, uncovered, for 2 hours. Strain and serve hot.

Makes eighteen ¹/₂-cup servings

EACH SERVING CONTAINS APPROXIMATELY:
100 TOTAL CALORIES / 5 CALORIES IN FAT
0 MG CHOLESTEROL / 55 MG SODIUM
30 MG CALCIUM

SUGAR-FREE WHITE EGGNOG

Traditional holiday drinks don't get any healthier than this. Amazingly enough, it is still delicious!

> 1 egg
> ³/₄ cup skim milk
> 1 tablespoon frozen unsweetened apple juice concentrate,
>   undiluted
> 1 teaspoon vanilla extract
> ¹/₄ teaspoon rum extract
> 2 ice cubes, crushed
> Ground nutmeg or cinnamon for garnish

Dip the whole egg, in its shell, in boiling water for 30 seconds. Break the egg and put the white *only* in a blender container.

Add the milk, apple juice concentrate, vanilla and rum extracts, and ice cubes and blend until smooth and frothy. Pour into a large glass and sprinkle with nutmeg or cinnamon.

Makes 1 serving

EACH SERVING CONTAINS APPROXIMATELY:
125 TOTAL CALORIES / 5 CALORIES IN FAT
3 MG CHOLESTEROL / 220 MG SODIUM
235 MG CALCIUM

BANANA SMOOTHIE

This smoothie is not only a sensational beverage, it is also a satisfying snack drink and my favorite topping for dry breakfast cereals.

> *1 small banana, sliced and frozen*
> *3/4 cup skim milk*
> *1 slice of banana for garnish*
> *Mint sprig for garnish*

Combine the frozen banana and milk in a blender container and blend until frothy. Serve in a chilled glass. Garnish with the slice of banana and mint sprig.

Makes 1 serving

EACH SERVING CONTAINS APPROXIMATELY:
170 TOTAL CALORIES / 10 CALORIES IN FAT
3 MG CHOLESTEROL / 95 MG SODIUM
235 MG CALCIUM

MAKE-BELIEVE MARGARITA

If you want to have a real Mexican fiesta but want to forgo the tequila, this Make-believe Margarita is just what el doctor ordered for your party.

> *1 egg*
> *1 1/2 cups soda water or Perrier water*
> *2 tablespoons freshly squeezed lime juice*
> *1 tablespoon fructose or 4 teaspoons sugar*
> *1/2 cup crushed ice*
> *1/2 lime*
> *Ice cubes*
> *Lime slices for garnish*

Dip the whole egg, in the shell, in boiling water for 30 seconds. Break the egg and put the white *only* in a blender container.

Add the soda water or Perrier water, lime juice, fructose or sugar, and crushed ice. Blend until frothy.

Rub the lime around the rims of four chilled glasses. Fill each glass with ice cubes and pour the Margaritas over them. Garnish with lime slices.

Makes 4 servings

EACH SERVING CONTAINS APPROXIMATELY:
20 TOTAL CALORIES / 0 CALORIES IN FAT
0 MG CHOLESTEROL / 35 MG SODIUM
5 MG CALCIUM

PEANUT BUTTER SHAKE

This shake recipe was published in my column a while ago. I recently received a letter from one of my readers telling me that if I ever ran it again, I should add the warning that it can become habit-forming.

> 2 cups vanilla ice milk
> 1/4 cup unhomogenized peanut butter
> 1/2 cup skim milk
> 1/2 teaspoon vanilla extract

Combine all the ingredients in a blender container and blend until well mixed.

Makes 2 cups

1 CUP CONTAINS APPROXIMATELY:
220 TOTAL CALORIES / 60 CALORIES IN FAT
20 MG CHOLESTEROL / 145 MG SODIUM
250 MG CALCIUM

GLOSSARY OF TERMS
USED IN LIGHT COOKING

AL DENTE: An Italian term meaning literally "to the tooth." Usually used with reference to pasta, which should be cooked only to the point where it is still resistant to the bite. When used to describe vegetables, it means crisp-tender.

BAKE: To cook in a heated oven.

BARBECUE: To cook over hot coals.

BASTE: To spoon liquid over food while it is cooking, or use a baster for this purpose.

BEAT: To beat with an egg beater or electric mixer in order to add air and increase volume.

BLANCH: To plunge quickly into boiling water. Usually refers to fruits and vegetables. To blanch nuts, cover shelled nuts with cold water and bring to a boil. Remove from the heat and drain, then slip the skins from the nuts.

BLEND: To combine two or more ingredients well, often using a blender or food processor.

BLEND UNTIL FROTHY: To blend until foamy and the volume is almost doubled.

BOIL: To cook food in liquid in which bubbles rise to the surface and break. Water boils at 212°F at sea level.

BONE: To remove all bones. Usually refers to roasts and poultry.

BRAISE: To brown meat well on all sides, then add a small amount of water, stock, juice, or wine. The food is then covered and simmered over low heat or placed in a moderate oven and cooked until tender or as the recipe directs.

BROIL: To cook under the broiler at a designated distance from the heat.

BROWN: To brown in the oven, under a broiler, or in a heavy skillet to the desired color.

BUTTERFLY: To bone and open flat. When using this term with half chicken breasts, it means to cut horizontally and lay open so that they again look like whole breasts.

CHILL: To refrigerate until cold.

CHOP: Using a large chopping knife, to hold the point end down with one hand and use the other hand to chop. Check your hardware or appliance store for other chopping devices.

COARSELY CHOP: To chop in pieces approximately ½ inch square.

COAT: To shake in a paper bag containing coating material (cornmeal, flour, etc.) until coated. You may also use a sifter to sprinkle coating material.

CODDLE: Usually used when referring to eggs. When a raw egg is called for in a recipe, put the egg in boiling water for 30 seconds before using it. Avidin, a component of raw egg whites, is believed to block the absorption of biotin, one of the water-soluble vitamins, but it is extremely sensitive to heat and is inactivated when the egg is coddled.

COOL: To allow to stand at room temperature until no longer warm to the touch.

CORE: To remove the core from fruits such as pears and apples.

COVER TIGHTLY: To seal so that steam cannot escape.

CREAM: With a spoon, to rub against the sides of a bowl until creamy. Food can also be creamed with the use of a pastry blender or food processor.

CRUMBLE: To crush with your hands or a fork into crumblings.

CRUSH: To crush dry herbs with a mortar and pestle before using.

CUBE: To cut into approximately 1-inch cube-shaped pieces or into a specified size.

DEGLAZE: To pour excess fat from the pan in which poultry or meat has been sautéed or roasted and add liquid such as water, stock, wine, or juice, scraping the remaining cooking juices and other accumulated material into the liquid as it simmers in order to obtain a tasty base for poultry or meat sauces.

DICE: To cut into ¼-inch cubes or smaller.

DISSOLVE: To mix dry ingredients with liquid until they are no longer visible in the solution.

DOT: To scatter in small bits over the surface of the food; usually refers to corn-oil margarine.

DREDGE: To sprinkle lightly with flour or coat with flour.

FILLET: To remove all the bones; usually refers to fish.

FINELY CHOP: To chop into pieces smaller than ¼ inch.

FOLD IN: Using a rubber spatula or spoon in a circular motion coming across the bottom, to fold the bottom of a mixture over the top. The motion is slowly repeated until the mixture is folded in as indicated in the recipe.

FORK-TENDER: When food can be pierced easily with a fork.

GRATE: To rub a surface on a grater for desired-size particles. Finely grated and coarsely grated foods require two different size graters.

GREASE: To rub lightly with corn-oil margarine, corn oil, or other oil specified in the recipe.

GRIND: To use a food processor or other food-chopping device or grinder.

JULIENNE-CUT: To cut in strips about ¼ inch by 2 inches.

KNEAD: To place a ball of dough on a floured surface, flatten it down with floured hands, and then fold it toward you, and, with the heels of your hands, press down and flatten again. This motion is continued until the dough is smooth and satiny, or as the recipe directs. Usually refers to bread dough.

MARINATE: To allow a mixture to stand in a marinade for the length of time indicated in the recipe.

MASH: To reduce to a soft pulpy state by beating with a food processor or using pressure with a potato masher. Refers most often to potatoes and other vegetables.

MINCE: To chop as fine as gravel.

PANBROIL: To cook in an ungreased or nonstick skillet, pouring off the fat as it accumulates.

PARBOIL: To boil in water or other liquid until partially cooked. This usually precedes another step in the cooking process.

PARE: To remove the outer covering of foods such as fruits and vegetables with a knife.

PEEL: To remove the outer covering of foods such as oranges, lemons, and bananas.

PIT: To remove the seed or pit from fruits such as peaches and plums.

PLATING: Refers to presentation on plate; "plating a sauce" means putting it on the plate first and placing food on top of it.

POACH: To cook for a short time in simmering liquid.

PREHEAT: To set the oven to a desired temperature and wait until that temperature is reached before putting food in to bake.

PRESS: Usually refers to garlic when using a garlic press.

PUREE: To reduce to a liquid state using a food processor or blender.

REDUCE: To boil a liquid until it has reduced the desired amount in volume.

ROAST: To bake meat or poultry in the oven.

SAUTÉ: To cook in a small amount of water, stock, juice, or wine (and occasionally a little oil) in a skillet.

SCALD: To heat to just under the boiling point, when tiny bubbles begin to form around the sides of a pan. Also called "bring to the boiling point."

SCORE: To make shallow cuts or slits on the surface of a food with a knife.

SCRAPE: To remove the outer skin of foods such as carrots and parsnips with a knife. Also to rub the surface of a food, such as an onion, with a knife in order to produce juice.

SEAR: To brown the surface of a food rapidly over high heat in a hot skillet.

SEED: To remove the small seeds completely from such foods as tomatoes, cucumbers, and bell peppers.

SHRED: To slice thinly or use a food processor, grater, or other shredding device.

SIFT: To put flour, sugar, and so on through a flour sifter or sieve.

SIMMER: To cook just below the boiling point (about 185°F at sea level).

SINGE: To hold over a flame in order to burn off all the feathers or hairs. Usually refers to poultry.

SKEWER: To hold together with metal or wooden skewers or to spear chunks of meat and/or vegetables on wooden skewers as for shish kebab.

SKIN: To remove the skin from such foods as chicken and turkey; sometimes used when referring to onions.

SLICE: To slice through food evenly to a specified thickness with a sharp knife or slicing machine.

SNIP: To cut into small pieces using scissors or kitchen shears.

SPRINKLE: To use your fingers or a spoon to spread garnish over a finished dish or to add ingredients to a recipe as directed.

STEAM: To cook food over boiling water, using either a steamer or a large kettle with a rack placed in the bottom of it to hold the pan or dish of food above the boiling water for the specified time. Collapsible steamer baskets are available in hardware and cookware shops.

STEEP: To allow to stand in hot liquid.

STIFF BUT NOT DRY: This term is often used for egg whites and means they should form soft, well-defined peaks but not be beaten to the point where the peaks look as though they will break.

STIFFLY BEATEN: To beat until the mixture stands in stiff peaks.

STIR: To mix with a spoon in a circular motion until all the ingredients are well blended. If more vigorous stirring is necessary, use a food processor.

SWEAT: To cook, covered, over low heat until the natural moisture of what you are cooking is released; usually used in reference to onions, garlic, or leeks.

THICKEN: To mix a thickening agent such as arrowroot, cornstarch, flour, or cream of rice with a small amount of liquid to be thickened, then add slowly to the hot liquid, stirring constantly. The mixture is then cooked until slightly thickened or until it coats a metal spoon.

THINLY SLICE: To slice vegetables such as cucumbers and onions using the slicing side of a four-sided grater. A food processor or other slicing device may also be used.

TOAST: To brown in a toaster, oven, or under a broiler. Nuts and seeds may be toasted at 350°F until the desired color is attained. They may also be placed in the broiler but must be watched carefully, as they burn easily.

TOSS: To mix from both sides in an under-and-over motion toward the center, using two spoons or a fork and spoon. Usually refers to salads.

WHIP: To beat rapidly with a fork, whisk, egg beater, electric mixer, or food processor and thereby increase the volume of a mixture.

WHISK: To stir, beat, or fold using a wire whisk.

FOOD MEASUREMENTS
& EQUIVALENTS

VEGETABLES (FRESH)

Arugula, ½ pound = 2 cups bite-size pieces

Beans, green, 1 pound = 5 cups 1-inch pieces raw

Beets, 1 pound (2½-inch diameter) = 6 cups sliced raw; 2½ cups sliced cooked

Bell pepper, 1 pound (3 medium) = 2 cups finely chopped raw; 4 cups sliced raw

Broccoli, 1 pound (2 stalks) = 6 cups chopped cooked

Cabbage, 2½ pounds (average head) = 10 cups shredded raw; 6¼ cups chopped cooked

Carrots, 1 pound (8 small; 6 medium) = 4 cups grated raw; 3 cups sliced raw

Cauliflower, 1½ pounds (1 average head) = 6 cups chopped cooked

Celery, ½ pound = 1½ cups chopped raw; 1 rib = ½ cup finely chopped raw

Celery root, 1¾ pounds (1 average) = 4 cups grated raw; 2 cups cooked and mashed

Chilies, jalapeño, ½ pound (16 chilies) = 2 cups chopped raw

Corn, 6 ears = 2½ cups cut raw

Cucumber, ½ pound (1 medium) = 1½ cups sliced raw; 1 cup diced raw

Eggplant, 1 pound (1 medium) = twelve ¼-inch slices raw; 6 cups cubed raw

Garlic, 1 clove = 1 teaspoon finely chopped raw

Leeks, white part only, ½ pound (1 pound before trimming) = 2 cups chopped raw; 1 cup chopped cooked

Lettuce, 1½ pounds (1 average head) = 6 cups bite-size pieces

Mushrooms, fresh, ½ pound = 2 cups sliced raw

Onion, ½ pound (1 medium) = 1½ cups finely chopped raw; 2 cups sliced raw

   Boiling onions, 1 pound = 32 (½ ounce each)

   Pearl onions, 10 ounces = 2 cups whole raw

   Scallions, ¼-pound bunch (6 average) = 1 cup chopped raw

Parsley, 1 pound = 8 cups tightly packed raw; 8 cups finely chopped raw

   2 ounces = 1 cup tightly packed raw; 1 cup finely chopped raw

Peppers, see bell peppers

Pimiento, one 4-ounce jar = ½ cup chopped

Potatoes, 1 pound (2 medium all purpose or 6 to 8 new) = 2½ cups diced cooked; 3 cups coarsely chopped or thinly sliced

Pumpkin, 3 pounds (1 average) = 4 cups cooked and mashed

Radicchio, 10 ounces (1 average head) = 2½ cups bite-size pieces

Shallots, ¼ pound = ¼ cup chopped raw

Spinach, 1 pound = 4 cups bite-size pieces raw; 1½ cups cooked

Squash, acorn, 1½ pounds (1 average) = 2 cups cooked mashed

   Banana, 3 pounds (1 average) = 4 cups cooked mashed

   Chayote, 1–1½ pounds (1 average) = ½ cup diced; ¾ cup sliced cooked

   Spaghetti, 5 pounds (1 medium) = 8 cups cooked

   Summer, 1 pound (4 average) = 1 cup chopped cooked

   Zucchini, 1 pound (2 average) = 1¼ cups chopped cooked; 3 cups diced raw; 4 cups thinly sliced raw

Tomatillos, ¼ pound (4 small; 2 large) = 1 cup chopped raw

Tomatoes, 1 pound (3 medium) = 2 cups chopped raw; 1¼ cups chopped cooked

Turnips, 1 pound = 2 cups grated raw; 4 cups bite-size pieces raw; 1¼ cups cooked mashed

Watercress, ¼ pound (1 bunch) = 1 cup loosely packed raw

VEGETABLES (DRIED)

Brown rice, 1 pound = 2½ cups uncooked; 7½ cups cooked

Garbanzo beans (chick-peas), 1 pound = 2 cups dry; 6 cups cooked

Kidney beans, 1 pound = 1½ cups dry; 4 cups cooked

Lentils, ½ pound = 1 cup dry; 2 cups cooked

Lima or navy beans, 1 pound = 2½ cups dry; 6 cups cooked

White rice, 1 pound = 2½ cups uncooked; 5 cups cooked

PASTA

Linguine noodles, 1 pound = 5 cups cooked

Macaroni, 1 pound = 3 cups dry; 12 cups cooked

Oriental noodles, ¾ pound dry = 5 cups cooked

Rotelle pasta, 1 pound = 4 cups dry; 6 cups cooked

Spaghetti, 1 pound = 8 cups cooked

FRUITS (FRESH)

Apples, 1½ pounds (6 small) = 4 cups sliced; 4½ cups chopped

Apricots, 1 pound (6 to 8 average) = 2 cups chopped

Bananas, 1 pound (4 small) = 2 cups mashed

Cantaloupe, 2 pounds (1 average) = 3 cups diced

Cherries, 2 cups = 1 cup pitted

Cranberries, 1 pound = 4½ cups raw

Figs, 1 pound (4 small) = 2 cups chopped

Grapefruit, 1 pound (1 small) = 1 cup sectioned

Grapes, Thompson seedless, ¼ pound = 40 grapes; 1 cup

Lemon, ¼ pound (1 medium) = 3 tablespoons juice; 2 teaspoons grated zest

Limes, ½ pound (5 average) = 4 tablespoons juice; 4 to 5 teaspoons grated zest

Orange, 1 pound (3 average) = 3 cups sectioned

Papaya, 1 pound = 2 cups cubed; 1 cup pureed

Peaches, 1 pound (3 average) = 2 cups chopped
Pears, 1 pound (3 average) = 2 cups chopped
Pineapple, 3 pounds (1 medium) = 2½ cups chopped
Rhubarb, 1 pound (4 stalks) = 2 cups chopped cooked
Tangerines, 1 pound (4 average) = 2 cups sectioned

FRUITS (DRIED)

Apples, 1 pound = 8 cups diced
Apricots, 1 pound = 8 cups diced
Figs, 1 pound (2½ cups) = 4½ cups whole cooked; 2 cups chopped
raw
Pears, 1 pound (3 cups) = 5½ cups cooked
Prunes, pitted, 1 pound (2½ cups) = 3¾ cups cooked
Raisins, seedless, 1 pound (2¾ cups) = 3¾ cups cooked; 2 cups
chopped raw

FISH

Crab, ½ pound = 1 cup cooked, canned, fresh, or frozen
Lobster, ½ pound = 1 cup fresh, frozen, or cooked
Oysters, ½ pound = 1 cup raw
Scallops, ½ pound = 1 cup shucked, fresh or frozen
Shrimp, 1 pound = 3 cups shelled cooked
Tuna, 6½- to 7-ounce can = ¾ cup drained

POULTRY

Chicken or turkey, 1 pound = 4 cups chopped cooked

HERBS AND SPICES

Garlic powder, ¼ teaspoon = 2 small garlic cloves
Ginger, ground, ½ teaspoon = 1 teaspoon fresh
Herbs, dried, ½ teaspoon = 1 tablespoon fresh

CHEESE

Cottage cheese, ½ pound = 1 cup
Cheese, ¼ pound = 1 cup grated

EGGS

Eggs, 6 medium = 1 cup whole raw
Egg whites, 8 medium = 1 cup raw

MILK

Dry, instant nonfat powdered, ⅓ cup plus ⅔ cup water = 1 cup
liquid milk
Dry, noninstant powdered, 3 tablespoons plus 1 cup water = 1 cup
liquid milk

NUTS

Almonds, 32 chopped = ¼ cup; 8 chopped = 1 tablespoon
Peanuts, 44 chopped = ¼ cup; 11 chopped = 1 tablespoon
Pecans, 20 halves chopped = ¼ cup; 5 halves chopped = 1 table-
spoon
Walnuts, 12 halves chopped = ¼ cup; 3 halves chopped = 1
tablespoon

BIBLIOGRAPHY

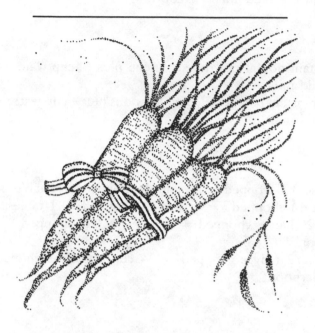

We have used Practorcare, Inc., software for the nutritional analysis throughout this book. Whenever an ingredient was not on this database, we referred to other publications in this bibliography to complete the nutritional information.

Church, Helen Nichols, and Jean A. T. Pennington. *Bowes and Church's Food Values of Portions Commonly Used.* 14th rev. ed. New York: Harper and Row, 1985.

Jones, Jeanne. *The Calculating Cook.* 2d ed. rev. San Francisco: 101 Productions, 1977.

———. *Diet for a Happy Heart.* 2d ed. rev. San Francisco: 101 Productions, 1981.

———. *The Fabulous High-Fiber Diet.* San Francisco: 101 Productions, 1985.

———. *The High-Calcium Diet* (cassette). Chicago: Nightingale-Conant Corporation, 1986.

————. *Jeanne Jones' Food Lover's Diet.* San Francisco: 101 Productions, 1982.

————. *Jet Fuel: The New Food Strategy for the High-Performance Person.* New York: Villard Books, 1984.

————. *More Calculated Cooking.* San Francisco: 101 Productions, 1981.

————. *Secrets of Salt-Free Cooking.* San Francisco: 101 Productions, 1979.

Jones, Jeanne, and Karma Kientzler. *Fitness First: A 14-Day Diet and Exercise Program.* San Francisco: 101 Productions, 1980.

Notelovitz, Morris, M.D., Ph.D., and Marsha Ware. *Stand Tall! Every Woman's Guide to Osteoporosis.* Bantam, 1985.

Practorcare, Inc. *Menu Planner 2000, Practorcare* (software). San Diego: Practorcare, 1986.

U.S. Department of Agriculture. *Nutritive Value of Foods.* USDA Home and Garden Bulletin 72, 1986.

INDEX

273